PRAXIS I MATH: My Private Tutor

by

Daniel Eiblum, M.S.Ed., Editor-in-Chief
Nicholas Frederick Bennett, Editor
Philip Chang
Dave Darling, M.A., Editor
Sarah Hand, M.S.
Timothy Sean Kelly, J.D.
Michael Lapidus, J.D.
Colleen McVearry
Ali Mushtaq, M.S.
Andrew Newens, M.A., Editor
Ben Swartz, M.A.
Sheri Weathers, M.S.Ed.
Daniel Zielaski, M.S.

Copyright © 2011 Dan Eiblum
All rights reserved
ISBN: 978-1-4610-9314-5
Library of Congress Control Number: 2011905974

CONTENTS

4

Introduction

Praxis I Math: My Private Tutor contains nearly 600 Praxis I math problems suited for students who need to review the mathematics covered in the Praxis I exam. This book will be particularly useful for those who have forgotten math from elementary school and need to brush up on key high school math principles. The chapters in this book will provide students with ample opportunity to practice math in 21 areas that the Praxis exam covers. Students may study only sections in which they are particularly challenged, or benefit from reviewing the book cover-to-cover. Whether the student's goal is to merely pass the exam or maximize his or her potential score, our goal is to provide students with enough practice to enter the exam and tackle problems with confidence. As of this books publication in 2011, Praxis I Math: My Private Tutor, is the only Praxis I book available that covers solely the math section of the Praxis I exam.

How to Use this Book

Before you begin, we strongly recommend that you take the practice Praxis I math test in chapter 1. After you have completed most or all of the problems throughout this book, take the second test at the end of the book. With discipline, focus, and practice, you will be amazed at how many more problems you will be able to answer correctly. Note: we assume that you have a strong knowledge of arithmetic. If you need to review arithmetic, we recommend purchasing an arithmetic book first before using this book.

About the Authors

Daniel Eiblum, M.S.Ed., Editor-in-Chief holds a B.A. in Geophysical Sciences from the University of Chicago, and then earned his Master of Education degree from Johns Hopkins University. He has over ten years of tutoring experience in mathematics ranging from Algebra I through Calculus, in addition to Math SAT preparation. He is the Editor-in-Chief of Math SAT 800: How to Master the Toughest Problems. He founded a tutoring agency in 2000, called TutorPro, based in Bethesda, MD and serving the Washington DC Metropolitan area. He resides in Bethesda, MD.

Nicholas Frederick Bennett, Editor holds a B.S. in Mathematics and Psychology from Grand Valley State University; and has a grade 6-8 certification in VA and grade 7-12 with a secondary license in Michigan and Washington DC. He has been teaching math for six years, and is currently teaching discrete math and precalculus at the School Without Walls in the District of Columbia. He resides in Fairfax, VA.

Andrew Newens, M.A. Editor holds a B.S. in Mechanical and Aerospace Engineering from Princeton University (1995) and a Master of Arts in Christian Counseling from Capital Bible Seminary (2006). He has over ten years of experience teaching and tutoring 7-12th grade math, science, and SAT preparation. His recent tutoring experience includes: TutorPro and C2 Education Centers. He is also a contributing author to Math SAT 800: How to Master the Toughest Problems. He currently works as an engineer for the U.S. Department of Energy. He resides in Washington, D.C.

Dave Darling, Editor, M.A. holds a B.S. in mathematics from State University of NY at New Paltz and a M.A. in mathematics from Wesleyan University. He has eight years of tutoring experience, and three years of teaching under his belt at Community Colleges and at Chance Academy. He resides in Severn, MD .

Phillip Chang graduated in 2003 from the University of North Carolina at Chapel Hill with a B.S. in Computer Science. He has worked with students of all ages, tutoring subjects ranging from 6th grade math to calculus, and standardized tests such as the SAT, ACT, and GMAT. He worked for TutorPro as a math tutor. He resides in Arlington, Virginia.

Sarah Hand, M.S. holds a B.S. in Electrical Engineering from the University of Maryland and a M.S. in Engineering from Johns Hopkins University. Since 2006, she has operated her own business providing private and small group math tutoring services to students from elementary school through college. Ms. Hand is also an adjunct professor of mathematics at the College of Southern Maryland. She resides in Huntingtown, Maryland.

Timothy Sean Kelly, J.D. holds a BS in Physics and Political Science from Lewis & Clark College in Portland, Oregon. He joined the Teach for America program in 2006 and significantly raised student test scores and academic awareness as a Math and Science Teacher in inner city Oakland, CA. He has been a successful tutor for years in numerous cities across the country, and recently completed a law degree in patent law from George Washington University School of Law. He has also worked as a tutor at TutorPro. He resides in Cazadero, CA.

Michael Lapidus, J.D. earned his B.A. in Mathematics, cum laude, from Columbia University, his J.D. from American University, and an L.L.M. in taxation from Georgetown. He is a former high school math teacher and is currently a tax lawyer. He resides in Washington, DC.

Ali Mushtaq, M.S. holds his masters degree in Electrical Engineering from the University of Illinois in Urbana-Champaign. He has been working as an independent statistical consultant in Washington, DC since 2003. He has been teaching and tutoring since 2000 (TutorPro), including test preparation strategies for various standardized tests. He is a contributing author to Math SAT 800: How to Master the Toughest Problems. He resides in Falls Church, VA.

Ben Swartz, M.A. received an M.A. in Education from Marymount University and a B.A. in Biology from the University of Virginia. He has been tutoring SAT preparation and other standardized tests since 2009, and he also teaches English as a Second Language to adult learners. He attended Marymount University, where he is pursuing a Master of Education. He resides in Falls Church, VA

Sheri Weathers, M.S.Ed. earned her B.S. in Mathematics and M.S.Ed. from the University of Florida. She taught high school math in Fairfax County, Virginia for three years. She is currently tutoring as she finishes her degree in School Counseling at George Mason University. She resides in Arlington, Virginia

Daniel Zielaski, M.S. earned his B.S. from Catholic University of America in Environmental Chemistry and his M.S. from The George Washington University in Secondary Science Education. He is currently employed by District of Columbia Public Schools as a chemistry instructor. He has developed, authored, and co-authored teacher training materials and SAT/ACT/PRAXIS/ASVAB test preparation materials aimed at both content and strategy. He resides in Washington DC.

Thanks to Colleen McVearry of Baltimore, Maryland who edited the book for grammar.

To MARTHA BRAMHALL

Section I: Assessment Test

Chapter 1

Assessment Test

1. Evaluate the expression, $4 + 6(2^2 + 2) - 3 =$

   A. 35
   B. 36
   C. 37
   D. 43
   E. 55

2. Which of the following is <u>false</u>?

   I. $-7 > 3 + -4$
   II. $0 < -10$
   III. $(-2 + -18) = (-2 - 18)$

   A. I only   B. II only   C. III only   D. I and II   E. I and III

3. Which of the following is <u>greatest</u>?

   A. -7×7
   B. $(-6)^2$
   C. $35 \div -7$
   D. $(17 + -19)^3$
   E. $-100 \div -20$

4. Evaluate the expression, $10 + 3(2 + 6) =$

    A. 22
    B. 28
    C. 34
    D. 240
    E. 320

5. Evaluate the expression, $50 - 10(4 - 2) + 6 =$

    A. 12
    B. 36
    C. 144
    D. 246
    E. 324

6. Evaluate the expression, $\dfrac{(8 + 24)}{(4 \times 2)} =$

    A. 2
    B. 4
    C. 16
    D. 32
    E. 44

7. Which of the following is <u>false</u>?
       I. $-12 > -4$
      II. $0 < -8$
     III. $-3 \times -4 = -12$

    A. I only   B. II only   C. III only   D. I and II   E. I,II, and III

8. Compute $(-6 - [-5]) \times 4$.

9. Which of the following is the <u>greatest</u>?

    A. $\sqrt{144} - \sqrt{121}$
    B. 8^{-2}
    C. $(-9)^2$
    D. -9^2
    E. $\frac{1}{\sqrt{4}}$

10. If $x \leq 5$ and $x \geq -3$, which of the following must be true?

   A. $5 \leq x \geq -3$
   B. $-3 \leq x \leq 5$
   C. $-3 \geq x \leq 5$
   D. $5 \geq x \leq -3$
   E. $x \leq 5$ or $x \geq -3$

11. If $x = 3$ and $y = 12$, which of the following must be true?

   A. $x = y$
   B. $x < y$
   C. $x \geq y$
   D. $x > y$
   E. None of the above

12. Which of the following numbers falls between 35% and 45% of 437?

   A. 125
   B. 150
   C. 175
   D 200
   E. 225

13. If A is 25% of 60, and B is 50% of 40. What is the value of $B - A$?

   A. 5
   B. 10
   C. 15
   D. 20
   E. 25

14. $\frac{7}{8}$ of 4,924 is equal to what percent of 4,924?

   A. 37.5%
   B. 43%
   C. 62.5%
   D. 86%
   E. 87.5%

15. In triangle ABC, $\angle A = 90°$, $\angle B = 60°$. What is the measure of $\angle C$?

    A. 15°
    B. 30°
    C. 45°
    D. 60°
    E. Cannot be determined from the information above

16. Circumference is analogous to which of the following measurements?

    A. Perimeter
    B. Density
    C. Area
    D. Volume
    E. Mass

Questions 17, 18, and 19 refer to the chart below.

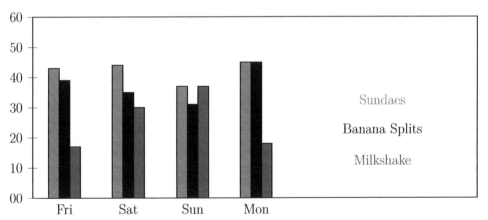

17. On what day were more milkshakes sold than Sundaes?

    A. Friday
    B. Saturday
    C. Sunday
    D. Monday
    E. None of the Above

18. How many days out of the four day weekend did the Divine Chocolate shop sell at least twice as many sundaes as milkshakes?

    A. 0
    B. 1
    C. 2
    D. 3
    E. 4

19. If only these three items were sold, approximately what percentage of the milkshake sales were on Friday?

    A. 12%
    B. 16%
    C. 17%
    D. 23%
    E. 28%

20. A jar contains 4 blue marbles, 3 red marbles, 2 green marbles and 3 white marbles. What is the probability of picking a blue marble, then a red marble, then a white marble, if none of the marbles that are taken out are replaced?

    A. $\dfrac{2}{45}$

    B. $\dfrac{3}{67}$

    C. $\dfrac{4}{67}$

    D. $\dfrac{3}{110}$

    E. $\dfrac{2}{55}$

21. Given the following data set, find the sum of the mean, median, and mode:

$$\{3.5, 4.5, 6.5, 6.5, 9.5, 11.5, 14\}$$

    A. 21
    B. 22
    C. 23.5
    D. 24
    E. 25.5

22. 500×1000 is equal to:

    A. 5×10^5
    B. 10×5^5
    C. 50×10^6
    D. 50,000
    E. None of the above

23. If 1 red chip equals 100 blue chips, then 62 red chips equal how many blue chips?

    A. 0.62
    B. 6.2×10^{-1}
    C. 6.2×10^2
    D. 6.2×10^3
    E. 620

24. A standard cell phone has a mass of 0.100 kg. How many grams is the cell phone?

    A. 100 grams
    B. 120 grams
    C. 134 grams
    D. 156 grams
    E. 170 grams

25. Phillip can lift 30.0lbs. How many ounces can Philip lift?

    A. 240 ounces
    B. 300 ounces
    C. 420 ounces
    D. 480 ounces
    E. 660 ounces

26. Stephen wants to buy an extension cord that is 10 meters long. How many centimeters is the extension cord?

    A. .1 cm
    B. 100 cm
    C. 360 cm
    D.1,000 cm
    E. 3,600 cm

27. Given that $y = 55 - 6(4 + x)$, what is the value of y when $x = -7$?

28. Given that $m = 44 + 3 \times 2^n$, what is the value of m when $n = 4$?

29. Find the next number in the sequence:

$$12, -2, -10, -12, -8...$$

30. It takes Blake 2 hours to mow a lawn. It takes Jake 3 hours to mow the same lawn. How much time, in hours and minutes, would it take Blake and Jake to mow the same lawn if they worked together?

    A. 50 minutes
    B. 1 hour 12 minutes
    C. 1 hour 36 minutes
    D. 1 hour 56 minutes
    E. 5 hours

31. In a room there are a large group of people who always lie, always tell the truth, or sometimes lie and sometimes tell the truth. Of these, 60 sometimes lie and sometimes tell the truth, 100 tell the truth some or all of the time, and 80 lie some or all of the time. How many people are there in the room?

    A. 100
    B. 110
    C. 115
    D. 120
    E. Cannot be determined from the information given

32. Which of the following is <u>false</u>?

  I. $\sqrt{3^2} = 9$
  II. $\sqrt{3^{-4}} = \frac{1}{81}$
  III. $\frac{1}{3^4} = 3^4$

  A. I only
  B. II only
  C. III only
  D. I and II
  E. I, II, and III

33. Three facts: All Toopees are Bootees. All Groopees are Bootees, and all Toopees are Groopees. If only some Groopees are Toopees, which of the following must also be true?

  A. Groopees that are Toopees are not Bootees.
  B. Not all Bootees are Toopees.
  C. Bootees that are Toopees are not Groopees.
  D. There are no Toopees that are both Groopees and Bootees.
  E. Some Bootees that are Toopees aren't Groopees.

34. Bob buys one milk and a loaf of bread for $6.55. With the same prices for bread and milk, he could buy 3 milks and 4 loaves of bread for $23.65. How much would 1 milk and 2 loaves of breads cost?

  A. $8.65
  B. $9.75
  C. $10.05
  D. $10.15
  E. $10.55

35. Translate segment $\overline{AB}$ (shown in Figure 1.1) three units right and two units down.

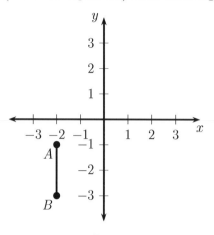

Figure 1.1

36. In Figure 1.2 below, the circles have a common center, O. If the smaller circle has a radius of 2cm, and the larger circle a radius of 4cm, what is the area of the shaded region?

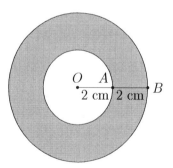

Figure 1.2

A. 4π cm^2
B. 8π cm^2
C. 12π cm^2
D. 16π cm^2
E. 20π cm^2

37. Which point has the coordinates $(4, 1)$ in Figure 1.3?

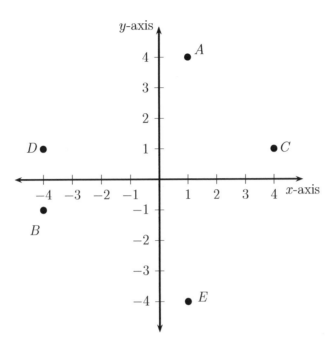

Figure 1.3

38. The following two triangles are congruent (Figure 1.4): This can be determined because:

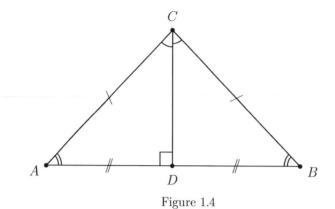

Figure 1.4

I. All angles are equal

II. All sides are equal

III. Two angles and a side in between them are equal.

A. I only

B. II only

C. I and II only

D. II and III only

E. I, II, and III

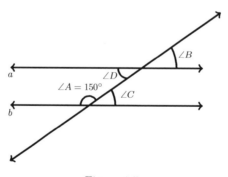

Figure 1.5

39. In Figure 1.5, what is the measure of $\angle B$? (Assume that $\overleftrightarrow{a} \parallel \overleftrightarrow{b}$).

A. 15°   B. 22°   C. 30°   D. 40°   E. 50°

40. The graph below shows the temperature reading in Fahrenheit outdoors in Manhattan during a night in the winter. Based on the graph, which of the following is the least likely event that took place at 11pm?

    A. Black ice formed on the roads
    B. Snow began to fall
    C. Snow began to melt on top of the Empire State Building
    D. A weatherman lowered his forecast for the overnight low temperature
    E. The skies began to clear

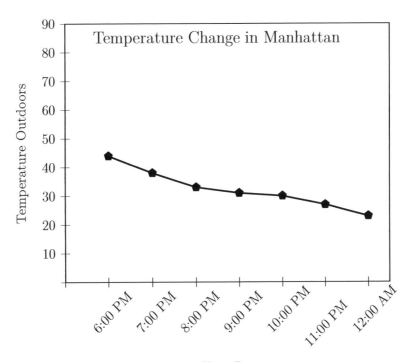

Solutions to Assessment Test

1. **C.**

   First, simplify the exponents inside the parentheses. $\quad 4 + 6(4 + 2) - 3 =$

   Now, add the numbers inside the parentheses. $\qquad\qquad 4 + 6(6) - 3 =$

   Next, multiply. $\qquad\qquad\qquad\qquad\qquad\qquad 4 + 36 - 3 =$

   Finally, add from left to right. $\qquad\qquad\qquad\qquad\qquad 37$

2. **C.** I. False. -7 is not greater than but less than $3 + -4 = -1$. -7 is more negative than -1 and therefore less than -1.
   II. False. Zero is greater than any negative numbers. Therefore 0 is greater than and not less than -10.
   III. True. $(-2 + -18) = -(2 + 18) = -20, (-2 - 18) = -2 + -18 = -(2 + 18) = -20$.

3. **B.** Only B and E are positive. $(-6)^2 = (-6)(-6) = 36$ and $-100 \div -20$ is 5. Therefore, B is the solution.

4. **C.** First, add the numbers inside of the parentheses to get, $10 + 3(8)$. Now, multiply, and arrive at $10 + 24$. Finally, add, for an answer of 34.

5. **B.** First, subtract the numbers inside of the parentheses, $50 - 10(2) + 6$. Now, multiply, $50 - 20 + 6$. Finally, add and subtract from left to right, to arrive at 36.

6. **B.** First, perform all operations inside parentheses, $\dfrac{(32)}{(8)}$. Now, divide 32 by 8, to arrive at 4.

7. **E.**

   I. False. This is because -12 is more negative than -4 and is therefore less than and not greater than -4.

   II. False. This is because zero is greater than all negative numbers.

   III. False. This is because multiplying an even number of negative numbers together results in a positive number. $-3 \times -4 = 12$.

8. **-4.** $(-6 - [-5]) \times 4 = (-6 + 5) \times 4 = -1 \times 4 = -4$. Subtracting a negative number is the same as adding a positive number. $-6 - -5 = -6 + 5 = -1$. Multiplying a negative number by a positive number equals a negative number. $-1 \times 4 = -4$.

9. **C.**

   A. $\sqrt{144} - \sqrt{121} = 12 - 11 = 1$
   B. $8^{-2} = \frac{1}{8^2} = \frac{1}{64}$
   C. $(-9)^2 = -9 \times -9 = 81$
   D. $-9^2 = -(9)^2 = -(9 \times 9) = -(81) = -81$
   E. $\frac{1}{\sqrt{4}} = \frac{1}{2}$

10. **B.** The second inequality $x \geq -3$ can be rewritten as $-3 \leq x$, making sure to switch both sides of the equation the terms are on as well as the comparison symbol. So $-3 \leq x$ and $x \leq 5$, or $-3 \leq x \leq 5$. Also you cannot have $\geq$ and $\leq$ in the same expression. They must go in the same directions; either $< \ldots < $ or $> \ldots >$.

11. **B.** If $x = 3$ and $y = 12$, then we are comparing 3 (x) with 12 (y). The statement $x < y$ means $3 < 12$ which is the only true statement.

12. **C.** The simplest way to approach this problem is to calculate both percentage values and find a number between the two.

$$\frac{35}{100} \times 437 = \frac{7 \times 437}{20} \approx 153 \qquad \frac{45}{100} \times 437 = \frac{9 \times 437}{20} \approx 197$$

The only answer choice that falls between 153 and 197 is C: 175.

13. **A.** Calculate the two values first:

$$A = \frac{25}{100} \times 60 = \frac{1}{4} \times 60 = 15 \qquad B = \frac{50}{100} \times 40 = \frac{1}{2} \times 40 = 20$$

The difference is 5.

14. **E.** In this problem, the number 4,924 itself is irrelevant to the problem. Here, we are only looking for the percent equivalent of the fraction $\frac{7}{8}$. Divide 7 into 8 and multiply by 100 to obtain 87.5%.

15. **B.** The sum of the angles in a triangle is 180°. So we have:

$$\angle A + \angle B + \angle C = 180°$$
$$\angle C = 180° - \angle B - \angle A$$
$$= 180° - 90° - 60°$$
$$= 30°$$

16. **A.** The circumference is the measure around a circle like perimeter is the measure around any other plane figure.

17. **E.** The correct answer is none of the above. The chart shows that on 3 days, there were more sundaes sold than milkshakes. Additionally, there was one day (Sunday) when the amount of both those items sold was the same.

18. **C.** On 2 Days (Friday and Monday) the number of Sundaes sold was over 40 and the number of milkshakes was below 20.

19. **C.** This requires us to calculate the total number of milkshakes that were sold on Friday and compare it to the total number of milkshakes sold on all four days. On Friday there were 18 milkshakes sold. On Saturday there were 30 milkshakes sold, Sunday 38, and Monday 20. Together we have $18 + 30 + 38 + 20 = 106$. So 18 out of 106 milkshakes were sold on Friday or approximately 17%.

20. **D.** All together there are 12 marbles. The probability of picking a blue marble is $\frac{4}{12}$. After the blue marble is removed, there are 11 marbles left. The probability of picking a red marble is $\frac{3}{11}$. Now there are 10 marbles left. The probability of picking a white marble is $\frac{3}{10}$. Together the probability of the three events taking place is $\frac{4}{12} \times \frac{3}{11} \times \frac{3}{10} = \frac{36}{1320} = \frac{3}{110}$.

21. **A.** The mean is: $\frac{3.5+4.5+6.5+6.5+9.5+11.5+14}{7} = 8$. The mode is the most frequent number, or 6.5, and the median is the middle number, or 6.5. The sum is $8 + 6.5 + 6.5 = 21$.

22. **A.** $500 \times 1000 = 500,000.$ Then change each answer to decimal form to compare. Choice A equals 500,000.

23. **D.** Set up a proportion of blue to red chips: $\frac{100}{1} = \frac{x}{62}$. Solve for x to get $x = 100 \times 62 = 6200$. Move the decimal 3 places to the left to get 6.2×10^3, which is in scientific notation.

24. **A.** This problem requires a knowledge of the Metric System of Measurement. To solve this problem you must convert between kilograms and grams. The following represents this calculation:

$$0.100 \text{ kg} \times \frac{1,000 \text{ g}}{1 \text{ kg}} = 100 \text{ grams}$$

25. **D.** This problem requires a knowledge of the Standard System of Measurement. To solve this problem you must convert between pounds and ounces. The following represents this calculation:

$$30.0 \text{ lbs} \times \frac{16 \text{ oz}}{1 \text{ lb}} = 480 \text{ ounces}$$

26. **D.** This problem requires a knowledge of the Metric System of Measurement. To solve this problem you must convert between meters and centimeters. The following represents this calculation:

$$10 \text{ m} \times \frac{100 \text{ cm}}{1 \text{ m}} = 1,000 \text{ cm}$$

27. **73.** $y = 55 - 6(4 + -7) = 55 - 6(-3) = 55 + 18 = 73$.

28. **92.** $m = 44 + 3(2^4) = 44 + 3(16) = 92$.

29. **2.** Using the common difference method described above to look at the difference between each of the terms provides us with a secondary sequence of: -14, -8, -2, 4... This secondary sequence is increasing by 6 each time. The next term in the secondary sequence will be 10. Therefore, it makes sense that the difference between the last term in the first sequence and the subsequent term is 10. $-8 + 10 = 2$.

30. **B.** If it takes Blake 2 hours to mow the lawn, he can mow $\frac{1}{2}$ of the lawn in one hour. If it take Jake 3 hours to mow the lawn, Jake can mow $\frac{1}{3}$ of the lawn in one hour. Together in one hour, Blake and Jake can mow $\frac{1}{2} + \frac{1}{3} = \frac{5}{6}$ of the lawn. If they can mow $\frac{5}{6}$ of the lawn in one hour, then they can mow the lawn in $\frac{1}{\frac{5}{6}} = \frac{6}{5} = 1.2$ hours. In minutes, 1.2 hours is 72 minutes, or 1 hour and 12 minutes.

31. **D.** If 100 tell the truth and 60 sometimes lie and sometimes tell the truth, then $100 - 60 = 40$ only tell the truth. Similarly if 80 people lie and 60 people sometimes lie and sometimes tell the truth, then $80 - 60 = 20$ only lie. Together, we have 20 people who always lie, 60 people who sometimes lie and sometimes tell the truth, and 40 people who only tell the truth. Adding, we obtain: $20 + 60 + 40 = 120$.

32. **E.** I. False. $\sqrt{3^2} = 3 \neq 9$.
    II. False. $\sqrt{3^{-4}} = \sqrt{\frac{1}{3^4}} = \sqrt{\frac{1}{81}} = \frac{\sqrt{1}}{\sqrt{81}} = \frac{1}{9} \neq \frac{1}{81}$. When 3 is raised to a negative exponent, -4, the result is 1 divided by 3^4 applying the rule that any non-zero number when raised to a negative exponent equals one divided by that number raised to the positive exponent. We then arrive at $\sqrt{\frac{1}{3^4}} = \sqrt{\frac{1}{81}} = \frac{\sqrt{1}}{\sqrt{81}}$. Here, we apply the rule that the square root of a fraction equals the square root of the numerator over the square root of the denominator.
    III. False. $3^{-4} = \frac{1}{3^4} = \frac{1}{3 \times 3 \times 3 \times 3} = \frac{1}{81} \neq 3^4$ since $3^4 = 3 \times 3 \times 3 \times 3 = 81$.

33. **B.** Draw three concentric circles, as in the figure shown below. The innermost circle represents Toopees. The middle circle represent Groopees, and the outer circle represents Bootees. The innermost circle, implies that all Toopees are also Groopees and Bootees, as the problem states. According to the middle circle, only some Groopees are Toopees, as the problem also states. Let's exam each answer choice. Choice A is false since Groopees that are also Toopees are represented in the innermost circle. They are also Bootees since the innermost circle is contained in the outermost circle. Choice B is true. Some Bootees are contained outside the middle circle. Those Bootees are only Bootees. Choice C is false, since Bootees that are Toopees are also Groopees. Choice D is incorrect because all Toopees are both Groopees and Bootees. Choice E is incorrect because all Toopees are Groopees.

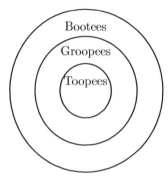

34. **E.** We let M equal milk and B equal bread. We can then write two equations with two unknowns:

$$M + B = 6.55$$
$$3M + 4B = 23.65$$

Using the first equation, we can subtract B from both sides of the equal sign to obtain:

$$M = 6.55 - B$$

Plugging in $6.55 - B$ into M in the second equation we obtain:

$$3(6.55 - B) + 4B = 23.65$$
$$19.65 - 3B + 4B = 23.65$$
$$19.65 + B = 23.65$$
$$B = 23.65 - 19.65$$
$$B = 4.00$$

Going back to the first equation, if one milk is M and $M + 4 = 6.55$, then $M = 2.55$. So milk costs \$2.55 and bread costs \$4. The question asks for the price of 1 milk and 2 loaves of bread, which is $\$2.55 + 2 \times \$4 = \$10.55$.

35. Each x-value moves 3 units right while each y-value moves 2 units down. The result is shown below.

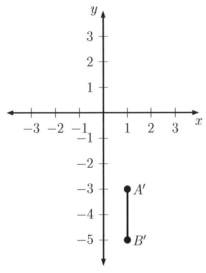

36. **C.** The shaded region is the difference between the larger and the smaller circles, like the area of the scrap of paper if we were to cut the smaller circle out of the larger one. Area of a circle is pi times the radius squared. For the larger circle it is $\pi(4 \text{ cm})^2 = 16\pi \text{ cm}^2$. From this area we are cutting out an area of $\pi(2 \text{ cm})^2 = 4\pi \text{ cm}^2$. The difference is $12\pi \text{ cm}^2$.

37. **C.** If we look at the ordered pair $(4, 1)$ we see that we must move right 4 units along the x-axis and move up 1 unit along the y-axis where point C is located.

38. **D.** I is not true. Just because all angles are the same, does not necessarily imply that the triangles are congruent (they are similar, however). As in the following case (Figure 1.6):

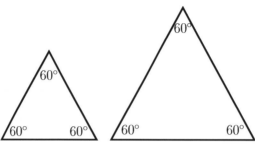

Figure 1.6

39. **C.** Since $\angle C$ and $\angle A$ are supplementary angles, $\angle C = 30°$. $(180° - 150°)$. So $\angle$ D is 30°. (alternate interior). Therefore $\angle B = 30°$. (vertical angles).

40. **C.** Since the temperature fell below freezing, it was improbable for snow to begin to melt. All other answers are conceivable, although not necessarily true.

How to interpret your score

The better you perform on the assessment test, the better your chances of performing well on the real PRAXIS I Math portion. However, this does not mean that you do not have strong promise to do well on future exams if you score low. Practice is the name of the game.

If you answered few questions correctly, don't worry, you still have the ability to learn the material and score high. A score of twenty out of forty demonstrates considerable promise. If you scored higher than twenty out of forty, congratulations. With practice, you can easily ace the test.

Right now, you should pay attention to what kinds of problems stump you. Are they mostly pre-algebra problems? (in which case you should spend more time on the pre-algebra chapters), or are they geometry problems (in which case the geometry problem chapters are especially important that you work on).

Working through the entire book will greatly increase the change that you will attain a higher score on the real PRAXIS I Math.

Section II: Pre-Algebra

Chapter 2

Fractions

A general fraction has the form $\frac{a}{b}$, where $b \neq 0$. The variable a is the numerator and b is the denominator. This fraction can also be considered "a parts out of b parts", or "a divided by b". The denominator specifies the number of parts in a whole, while the numerator tells how many parts you have out of the whole. An example of a fraction would be $\frac{3}{4}$. Here $a = 3$ and $b = 4$. This tells you, "3 parts out of 4." An *improper fraction* such as $\frac{7}{3}$ is one in which the numerator is greater than the denominator, and indicates a fraction value greater than 1. A *mixed number* contains both a whole number and a fraction, such as $3\frac{2}{3}$: three wholes, and 2 of three parts.

Simplifying Fractions

When simplifying fractions we want to make sure that the fraction is **always** in its lowest terms. To write a fraction in lowest terms, we have to find the common factors. Take a look at Example 1 below. To simplify $\frac{12}{27}$, we must find the common factors of 12 and 27 and cancel that factor out (a number divided by itself equals 1). Continue to do this until you cannot cancel/reduce anymore; you have found the simplest form. It is important to try to find the largest factor of both numerator and denominator. We see that the largest common factor of 12 and 27 is 3.

Example 1   Simplify $\dfrac{12}{27}$.

$$\frac{12}{27} = \frac{4 \cdot 3}{9 \cdot 3} = \frac{4 \cdot \cancel{3}}{9 \cdot \cancel{3}} = \frac{4}{9}$$

Example 2   Simplify $\dfrac{11}{121}$.

In Example 2, 11 and 121 share a common factor of 11, since both 121 and 11 are divisible by 11. Rewrite 121 and 11 as factors of 11, and *cancel* the common factor to find the simplified fraction.

$$\frac{11}{121} = \frac{1 \cdot 11}{11 \cdot 11} = \frac{1 \cdot \cancel{11}}{11 \cdot \cancel{11}} = \frac{1}{11}$$

Mixed Number to an Improper Fraction

Example 3   Convert $3\frac{2}{5}$ to an improper fraction.

To convert a mixed number to an improper fraction, multiply the whole number by the denominator, and add the result (product) to the numerator. This is your new numerator. For this example, multiply 3 (the whole number) by 5 (the denominator) to find the product of 15. Add 15 to the numerator of the fraction to find the numerator of the improper fraction ($15 + 2 = 17$). The denominator does not change. The reason the denominator stays the same can be explained by the breakdown of $3\frac{2}{5}$. $3\frac{2}{5} = \frac{5}{5} + \frac{5}{5} + \frac{5}{5} + \frac{2}{5}$. Notice, that denominator is all fifths, we are just simplifying the mixed number to make an improper fraction.

$$3\frac{2}{5} = \frac{(3 \cdot 5 + 2)}{5}$$
$$= \frac{17}{5}$$

Example 4   Convert $2\frac{6}{7}$ to an improper fraction.

In Example 4, the product of 2 and 7 (14) is added to 6 ($14 + 6 = 20$) to find the numerator of the improper fraction.

$$2\frac{6}{7} = \frac{(2 \cdot 7) + 6}{7}$$
$$= \frac{20}{7}$$

Improper Fraction to a Mixed Number

In the examples above, we started with a mixed number and converted to an improper fraction. In this case, we start with an improper fraction and convert to a mixed number. To simplify, we see how many times the denominator goes into the numerator evenly. Then what is left becomes the fraction. The denominator will stay the same.

Example 5 Write $\dfrac{23}{7}$ as a mixed number.

To convert an improper fraction to a mixed number, divide the numerator by the denominator. We see that 7 does not go into 23 evenly, but 7 goes into 21 three times with 2 left over. Put the remainder of the division operation over the original denominator to find the fraction portion of the mixed number. So, 3 is our whole number (out front) the remainder is 2 (new numerator) and the denominator (7) stays the same.

$$
\begin{array}{r}
3 \\
7 \overline{) 23} \\
21 \\
\hline
2
\end{array}
$$
$$
= 3\dfrac{2}{7}
$$

Example 6 Write $\dfrac{18}{11}$ as a mixed number.

Example 6 is done the same way. 11 goes into 18 one time, $(18 \div 11 = 1)$, with 7 left over (remainder). Therefore 1 is the whole number (out front) with 7 becoming the new numerator and 11 remaining as the denominator.

$$
\begin{array}{r}
1 \\
11 \overline{) 18} \\
11 \\
\hline
7
\end{array}
$$
$$
= 1\dfrac{7}{11}
$$

Adding Fractions when the Denominators Are the Same

When adding fractions, we must pay attention to one important detail: the denominators of the fractions we are adding. This will tell us if the addition will be simple or more difficult.

To find the sum of two fractions with the same denominator, add the numerators and keep the denominator unchanged in the answer. In Example 7, the numerators can be added to find the numerator of the answer since the denominators for the two fractions in the question are equivalent. The numerator of the sum will be $3+2 = 5$, and the denominator of the sum will be unchanged.

When adding fractions, think of it as a puzzle: Mary has 3 pieces of a 7 piece puzzle, and Sandra has 2 pieces of that same 7 piece puzzle. They have 5 pieces total of the 7 piece puzzle.

Example 7 Simplify $\dfrac{3}{7} + \dfrac{2}{7}$.

$$\frac{3}{7} + \frac{2}{7} = \frac{3+2}{7}$$
$$= \frac{5}{7}$$

Example 8 (below) is solved in same manner, with the numerator of the answer equal to the sum of the original numerators. Since the answer is an improper fraction, *it may be necessary to convert to a mixed number, as shown previously.*

Example 8 Simplify $\dfrac{5}{9} + \dfrac{6}{9}$.

$$\frac{5}{9} + \frac{6}{9} = \frac{5+6}{9}$$
$$= \frac{11}{9}$$
$$= 1\frac{2}{11}$$

Adding Fractions with different denominators

To find the sum of two fractions that have different denominators, find a common multiple of the denominators. A **common multiple** is a specific number that is a multiple of two or more numbers. For instance, 24 is a common multiple of the numbers 4 and 8 because $4 \cdot 6$ is 24 and $8 \cdot 3$ is also 24.

Another way to find a common denominator is by multiplying the two denominators together. This product will be a common multiple of the two (or more) individual denominators, as shown in Step 1 of the general example below. If you choose this method, you will probably have to simplify your fraction to lowest terms as shown in Example 1 and Example 2.

$$\frac{a}{b} + \frac{c}{d} = \frac{?}{b \cdot d} + \frac{?}{d \cdot b} \qquad \text{Step 1}$$
$$= \frac{a \cdot d}{b \cdot d} + \frac{c \cdot b}{d \cdot b} \qquad \text{Step 2}$$
$$= \frac{(a \cdot d) + (c \cdot b)}{b \cdot d} \qquad \text{Step 3}$$

After step one, return to the fraction addition problem and multiply each denominator by the appropriate value to obtain a common denominator (the common multiple of the denominators), and also multiply the respective numerators by the same values (that the denominator was multiplied by) to obtain the fractions to be added, as shown is Step 2 above. Then, follow the steps to add fractions with the same denominator, seen above in Step 3.

In Example 9 below, the denominators (6 and 9) are multiplied together to find the common denominator to be used, which is $6 \cdot 9 = 54$. The numerator 1 will also be multiplied by 9 to maintain equality, resulting in the fraction $\frac{9}{54}$. The numerator 2 of the second fraction will also be multiplied by 6, resulting in the fraction $\frac{12}{54}$. These two fractions, with common denominators, can be added according to the method described for Examples 7 and 8 from above. Notice that the answer $\left(\frac{21}{54}\right)$ will need to be simplified using a common factor of 3.

Example 9   What is $\dfrac{1}{6} + \dfrac{2}{9} =$

$$
\begin{aligned}
\frac{1}{6} + \frac{2}{9} &= \frac{1 \cdot 9}{6 \cdot 9} + \frac{2 \cdot 6}{9 \cdot 6} \\
&= \frac{9}{54} + \frac{12}{54} \\
&= \frac{9 + 12}{54} \\
&= \frac{21}{54} \\
&= \frac{7 \cdot 3}{18 \cdot 3} \\
&= \frac{7}{18}
\end{aligned}
$$

Example 10 demonstrates a method of finding the sum of mixed numbers.

Example 10   Find the sum of $2\dfrac{3}{4} + 1\dfrac{3}{7}$. We have:

$$
\begin{aligned}
2\frac{3}{4} + 1\frac{3}{7} &= \frac{11}{4} + \frac{10}{7} \\
&= \left(\frac{11 \cdot 7}{4 \cdot 7} + \frac{10 \cdot 4}{7 \cdot 4}\right) \\
&= \frac{117}{28} \\
&= 4\frac{5}{28}
\end{aligned}
$$

Finding the Least Common Denominator (LCD)

Example 11   Find the least common denominator of $\dfrac{3}{14}$ and $\dfrac{5}{32}$.

Step 1: Find the prime factorization of each denominator in the (addition or subtraction problem). Prime numbers are those numbers that only have factors of 1 and the number itself, such as 2,3,5,7 and 11 (not 9). Factor each denominator into primes as in the example below, first considering the smallest prime number (2) and trying larger primes if the smaller are not factors of the given denominator. So, let's find the prime factors of 14 and 32.

$$14 = 2 \cdot 7$$
$$32 = 2 \cdot 2 \cdot 2 \cdot 2 \cdot 2$$

Once the prime factorization of each denominator is complete, find the instances that each prime factor appears in the factorization of each denominator, as shown in Step 2 (below). Note the greatest number of times that each prime number appears for individual denominators.

Step 2:

for 14 →"2" appears once and "7" appears once

for 32 → "2" appears five times

Listing each prime number in the greatest number of appearances and finding the product of these prime numbers will produce the least common denominator, as shown in Step 3.

Step 3 Since "2" appears only once in the factorization of "14" and appears five times in the factorization of "32", "2" will be listed five times; "7" appears once for "14". So, we have 2,2,2,2,2 and 7, all of which will be multiplied together to find the least common denominator. Therefore $2 \cdot 2 \cdot 2 \cdot 2 \cdot 2 \cdot 7 = 224$ is the least common denominator of 14 and 32.

Multiplying Fractions

To find the product of fractions, multiply straight across the numerators to obtain the numerator of the answer, and multiply straight across the denominators to find the new denominator, as in Examples 1 and 2 below.

Example 12 Simplify $\dfrac{3}{7} \cdot \dfrac{2}{5}$.

$$\frac{3}{7} \cdot \frac{2}{5} = \frac{3 \cdot 2}{7 \cdot 5}$$
$$= \frac{6}{35}$$

Example 13 Simplify $\dfrac{2}{5} \cdot \dfrac{-2}{9}$.

$$\frac{2}{5} \cdot \frac{-2}{9} = \frac{2 \cdot (-2)}{5 \cdot 9}$$
$$= \frac{-4}{45}$$
$$= -\frac{4}{45}$$

If there is a mixed number in the question, convert it to an improper fraction before finding the product, as in Example 14.

Example 14 Find the product of $2\dfrac{3}{4}$ and $\dfrac{4}{7}$.

$$2\frac{3}{4} \cdot \frac{4}{7} = \frac{11}{\cancel{4}} \cdot \frac{\cancel{4}}{7}$$
$$= \frac{11}{7}$$
$$= 1\frac{4}{7}$$

Dividing Fractions

To find the quotient of two fractions, take the reciprocal (flip the fraction) of the divisor (the second fraction) and multiply the two fractions, as shown in Examples 15 and 16 below.

Example 15 $\dfrac{3}{7} \div \dfrac{2}{5}$.

To divide these fractions, we must change the operation to multiplication. To do this, we take the reciprocal of the second fraction $\frac{5}{2}$ which is $\frac{2}{5}$. Then we can change the operation to multiplication. We can now follow our rules of multiplication to simplify the problem.

$$
\begin{aligned}
\frac{3}{7} \div \frac{2}{5} &= \frac{3}{7} \cdot \frac{5}{2} \\
&= \frac{15}{14} \\
&= 1\frac{1}{14}
\end{aligned}
$$

Example 16 $\dfrac{2}{5} \div \dfrac{1}{9}$.

$$
\begin{aligned}
\frac{2}{5} \div \frac{1}{9} &= \frac{2}{5} \cdot \frac{9}{1} \\
&= \frac{18}{5} \\
&= 3\frac{3}{5}
\end{aligned}
$$

Comparing Fractions

To find the fraction with greatest value, cross-multiply, as shown below. The larger fraction will correspond to the larger product obtained from the cross-multiplication.

Example 17 Which fraction is larger $\dfrac{5}{8}$ or $\dfrac{4}{7}$?

First, we cross multiply the numerator of the left fraction with the denominator of the right fraction. The product is $5 \cdot 7 = 35$. Write this value above the left fraction. Next, multiply the numerator of the right fraction by the denominator of the left which gives us $4 \cdot 8 = 32$. Write this value above the right fraction. The number above the fraction on the left is larger, therefore, $\frac{5}{8}$ is larger.

$$
\overset{5\cdot7=35}{\frac{5}{8}} \quad > \quad \overset{4\cdot8=32}{\frac{4}{7}}
$$

Practice Problems

1. Find the least common denominator of each pair of fractions.

    (a) $\dfrac{7}{9}$ and $\dfrac{1}{6}$ (b) $\dfrac{3}{11}$ and $\dfrac{5}{8}$

2. Add the fractions and write the answer in simplest form (no improper fractions).

    (a) $\dfrac{7}{9} + \dfrac{1}{6}$ (b) $2\dfrac{1}{9} + 3\dfrac{4}{5}$

3. Subtract the fractions and write the answer in simplest form (no improper fractions).

    (a) $\dfrac{4}{9} - \dfrac{1}{3}$ (b) $3\dfrac{2}{7} - 2\dfrac{1}{13}$

4. Multiply the fractions and write the answer in simplest form (no improper fractions).

    (a) $\dfrac{5}{4} \cdot \dfrac{8}{25}$ (b) $2\dfrac{1}{3} \cdot 1\dfrac{2}{5}$

5. Divide the fractions and write the answer in simplest form (no improper fractions).

    (a) $\dfrac{1}{4} \div \dfrac{1}{5}$ (b) $2\dfrac{3}{8} \div \dfrac{3}{5}$

Solutions to Practice Problems

1(a). **18**. We take the factors of each denominator to get the LCD (least common denominator). If any factors repeat, we take the factor that appears most often. We know that $9 = 1 \cdot 3 \cdot 3 = 3^2$ and $6 = 1 \cdot 2 \cdot 3$. Notice how both denominators (6 and 9) have factors of 3, however, 9 has two factors of 3 $(3 \cdot 3)$, so we use this factor for our LCD. We also see that 2 is a factor of 6, but not of 9, so 2 also belongs in the LCD. Therefore the LCD=$3 \cdot 3 \cdot 2 = 18$.

1(b.) **88**. Re-writing each denominators in terms of their factors gives us: $11 = 1 \cdot 11$ and $8 = 1 \cdot 2 \cdot 4$. We take the factors that appear in each denominator. These numbers don't share any factors other than 1. (We call this relatively prime). Therefore, the LCD=$11 \cdot 2 \cdot 4 = 88$.

2(a). $\frac{17}{18}$. We must first find a common denominator which is 18. Then, we multiply the first fraction $\frac{7}{9}$ by $\frac{2}{2}$, and the second fraction, $\frac{1}{6}$ by $\frac{3}{3}$. Thus,

$$
\begin{aligned}
\frac{7}{9} + \frac{1}{6} &= \frac{7 \cdot 2}{9 \cdot 2} + \frac{1 \cdot 3}{6 \cdot 3} \\
&= \frac{14}{18} + \frac{3}{18} \\
&= \frac{14 + 3}{18} \\
&= \frac{17}{18}
\end{aligned}
$$

2(b). $\mathbf{5\frac{41}{45}}$. We are adding two mixed numbers, therefore add the whole parts $3 + 2 = 5$. Add the fractions separately. The denominators are both factors of 45. This is the smallest number that 5 and 9 go into. Therefore 45 is the LCD. Simplifying we get:

$$
\begin{aligned}
2\frac{1}{9} + 3\frac{4}{5} &= 2\frac{1 \cdot 5}{9 \cdot 5} + 3\frac{4 \cdot 9}{5 \cdot 9} \\
&= 2\frac{5}{45} + 3\frac{36}{45} \\
&= 2 + 3 + \frac{5 + 36}{45} \\
&= 5\frac{41}{45}
\end{aligned}
$$

3(a). $\frac{1}{9}$. We see that 3 is a factor of 9; therefore, the LCD is 9. We only have to multiply the second fraction by $\frac{3}{3}$ since the first fraction already has a denominator of 9.

$$\frac{4}{9} - \frac{1}{3} = \frac{4}{9} - \frac{1 \cdot 3}{3 \cdot 3}$$
$$= \frac{4}{9} - \frac{3}{9}$$
$$= \frac{1}{9}$$

3(b). $\mathbf{1\frac{19}{91}}$. First change each mixed number to an improper fraction. This yields $\frac{23}{7}$ and $\frac{27}{13}$. Seven and 13 are both prime numbers therefore, the LCD is $7 \cdot 13 = 91$. Thus, the first fraction will be multiplied by $\frac{13}{13}$, and the second fraction by $\frac{7}{7}$. This yields,

$$\frac{23}{7} - \frac{27}{13} = \frac{23 \cdot 13}{7 \cdot 13} - \frac{27 \cdot 7}{13 \cdot 7}$$
$$= \frac{299}{91} - \frac{189}{91}$$
$$= \frac{110}{91}$$
$$= 1\frac{19}{91}$$

4(a). $\frac{2}{5}$. We can divide 4 into 8 and 5 into 25 to obtain,

$$\frac{5}{25} \cdot \frac{8}{4} = \frac{1}{5} \cdot \frac{2}{1}$$
$$= \frac{2}{5}$$

4(b). $3\frac{4}{15}$. First we will change the mixed numbers to improper fractions. We will then multiply the fractions straight across and simplify if necessary.

$$
\begin{aligned}
2\frac{1}{3} \cdot 1\frac{2}{5} &= \frac{7}{3} \cdot \frac{7}{5} \\
&= \frac{7 \cdot 7}{3 \cdot 5} \\
&= \frac{49}{15} \\
&= 3\frac{4}{15}
\end{aligned}
$$

5(a). $1\frac{1}{4}$. To divide these fractions, take the reciprocal (flip) of the second fraction and take the product of the two fractions.

$$
\begin{aligned}
\frac{1}{4} \div \frac{1}{5} &= \frac{1}{4} \cdot \frac{5}{1} \\
&= \frac{1 \cdot 5}{4 \cdot 1} \\
&= \frac{5}{4} \\
&= 1\frac{1}{4}
\end{aligned}
$$

5(b). $3\frac{23}{24}$. First change our mixed number into an improper fraction. Take the reciprocal of the second fraction and multiply the fractions together.

$$
\begin{aligned}
2\frac{3}{8} \div \frac{3}{5} &= \frac{19}{8} \cdot \frac{5}{3} \\
&= \frac{19 \cdot 5}{8 \cdot 3} \\
&= \frac{95}{24} \\
&= 3\frac{23}{24}
\end{aligned}
$$

Chapter 3

Order of Operations

The phrase **Order of Operations** refers to a set method for solving arithmetic expressions. This universal method helps to ensure that everyone goes about solving arithmetic expressions in the same order, thus arriving at the same solution. The following table represents the **Order of Operations** necessary for solving any arithmetic expression:

Order of Operations	
1. Parentheses	First complete all operations within parentheses (or brackets). Try to find the inner most, or smallest, grouping and begin there. For example, if a set of parentheses are located within a set of brackets, begin with the operations within the parentheses.
2. Exponents and Roots	Simplify all exponents and roots beginning with those inside of parentheses.
3. Multiplication and Division	Complete all multiplication and division operations from left to right beginning with those inside of parentheses.
4. Addition and Subtraction	Complete all addition and subtraction operations from left to right beginning with those inside grouping symbols.

The **Order of Operations**, while seemingly complicated, is remarkably easy to remember. Mathematicians have created a mnemonic device for students to quickly and easily recall the intended order. That mnemonic device is Please Excuse My Dear Aunt Sally, or PEMDAS, where the **P** represents parentheses, the **E** represents exponents and roots, the **MD** represents multiplication and division, and the **AS** represents addition and subtraction. Using this simple mnemonic device, you should be able to quickly and easily arrive at the correct solution for any mathematical expression!

Example 1 Evaluate the expression, $12 \times 10 - 40 + 200 \div 10$.

   A. 10
   B. 15
   C. 100
   D. 150
   E. 200

ANSWER: C. Following the order of operation, multiplication is done first in this problem, $12 \times 10 = 120$. Secondly, we will use division to simplify $200 \div 10$ which is 20. These operations are performed before the addition/subtraction according to PEMDAS. Now after performing multiplication and division we have $120 - 40 + 20$. Next, perform the addition and subtraction from left to right to arrive at an answer of 100.

Example 2 Evaluate the expression, $5 \times [(10 - 40) + 200] \div 10$.

   A. 85
   B. 95
   C. 105
   D. 110
   E. 125

ANSWER: A. First, perform operations inside of the inner most grouping symbols to result in the following, $5 \times [-30 + 200] \div 10$. Next, perform the operation inside of the brackets to get, $5 \times 170 \div 10$. Finally, multiply and divide from left to right, to arrive at 85.

Example 3 Evaluate the expression, $\dfrac{12}{4} \times \dfrac{10}{5} - \dfrac{40}{10} + \dfrac{200}{20}$.

   A. 11
   B. 12
   C. 13
   D. 14
   E. 15

ANSWER: B. Begin by simplifying all fractions (fractions can act as grouping symbols) as follows, $3 \times 2 - 4 + 10$. Next, multiply from left to right, $6 - 4 + 10$. Finally, add and subtract from left to right, to get the correct answer of 12.

Example 4   Evaluate the expression, $\dfrac{(4+1)^2}{5} + 5 \times 0$.

   A. 4
   B. 5
   C. 7
   D. 9
   E. 13

ANSWER: B. Begin by performing the addition within the parentheses, $\dfrac{(5)^2}{5} + 5 \times 0$. Next, raise 5 to exponent 2, or $\dfrac{25}{5} + 5 \times 0$. Then, simplify the fraction, $5 + 5 \times 0$. Finally, multiply, then add, resulting in 5.

Example 5   Evaluate the expression, $\dfrac{(5 + 5 \times 7)}{(40 - 20)} + 2^2$.

   A. 0
   B. 2
   C. 3
   D. 5
   E. 6

ANSWER: E. Begin by simplifying all parentheses first. So $5 + 5 \times 7 = 40$, and $40 - 20 = 20$. Then divide these terms: $\frac{40}{20} = 2$. Then do the exponent $2^2 = 4$. Finally, add $2 + 4$ to get 6.

Example 6   Evaluate the expression, $\dfrac{5 \times 10 - 40 + 90 \div 10}{(100 - 99)}$.

   A. 16
   B. 17
   C. 18
   D. 19
   E. 20

ANSWER: D. First, perform the subtraction inside the parentheses in the denominator, $\frac{5 \times 10 - 40 + 90 \div 10}{1}$. Next, perform the multiplication in the numerator, $\frac{50 - 40 + 90 \div 10}{1}$. Then, perform the division in the numerator, $\frac{50 - 40 + 9}{1}$. Now, add and subtract the numbers in the numerator from left to right, $\frac{19}{1}$. Finally, simplify the fraction, to 19.

Example 7 Evaluate the expression, $2 \times [(100 - 25) + 200] \div 10$.

- A. 55
- B. 67
- C. 86
- D. 102
- E. 134

ANSWER: A. Begin by performing operations inside of the inner most grouping symbol, $2 \times [(75) + 200] \div 10$. Next, perform the operation inside of the brackets, $2 \times 275 \div 10$. Finally, multiply then divide from left to right, to arrive at 55.

Example 8 Evaluate the expression, $22 + \frac{24}{2} \times \frac{50}{5} - \frac{100}{10} + \frac{20}{20} \times 4$.

- A. 133
- B. 134
- C. 135
- D. 136
- E. 137

ANSWER: D. First, simplify all fractions (fractions can act as grouping symbols), $22 + 12 \times 10 - 10 + 1 \times 4$. Then multiply, $22 + 120 - 10 + 4$. Lastly, add and subtract from left to right to get 136.

Example 9 Evaluate the expression, $\frac{(2+2)^3}{2} + 0.5(10)$.

| A. 31 | B. 33 | C. 35 | D. 37 | E. 39 |

ANSWER: D. First, add within the parentheses, $\frac{4^3}{2} + 0.5(10)$. Then, simplify all exponents, $\frac{64}{2} + 0.5(10)$. Next, simplify all fractions, $32 + 0.5(10)$. Now, multiply, $32 + 5$. Finally, add, to arrive at 37.

Example 10 Evaluate the expression, $\dfrac{(45 \div 9)}{(6 + 4)} \times 6^3$.

    A. 108

    B. 110

    C. 134

    D. 1,567

    E. 10,756

ANSWER: A. First, perform all operations inside parentheses, $\dfrac{(5)}{(10)} \times 6^3$. Then, simplify all exponents, $\dfrac{(5)}{(10)} \times 216$. Next, simplify all fractions, $\frac{1}{2} \times 216$. Finally, multiply to get 108.

Practice Problems

1. Evaluate the expression, $(1.3 + 5.9) \div (6.8 - 4.4) =$
   A. 0
   B. 1
   C. 2
   D. 3
   E. 4

2. Evaluate the expression, $3 \times 6 + 10 + 10 \div 1 + 8 - 3 + 9 \times 5 =$
   A. 88
   B. 97
   C. 98
   D. 120
   E. 121

3. Evaluate the expression, $(5 \times 6 + 15) + (100 \div 2) + (8 - 3 + 9 \times 5) =$
   A. 122
   B. 134
   C. 141
   D. 145
   E. 153

4. Evaluate the expression, $\left(\dfrac{4}{3} \times \dfrac{1}{3} + \dfrac{7}{5} \right) \div 1 =$
   A. $\dfrac{12}{32}$
   B. $\dfrac{14}{35}$
   C. $\dfrac{17}{76}$
   D. $\dfrac{45}{83}$
   E. $\dfrac{83}{45}$

5. Evaluate the expression, $\left(2 - \dfrac{1}{4}\right)(4 - 2) =$

    A. $1\dfrac{3}{4}$

    B. $2\dfrac{3}{4}$

    C. $2\dfrac{1}{8}$

    D. $3\dfrac{1}{2}$

    E. $3\dfrac{4}{5}$

6. Evaluate the expression, $\left(\dfrac{7}{1} \times \dfrac{7}{7}\right) \div \left(\dfrac{28}{4}\right) =$

    A. 1

    B. 7

    C. 8

    D. 9

    E. 10

7. Evaluate the expression, $\dfrac{9}{3} \div \left(3 - \dfrac{4}{4}\right) =$

    A. $1\dfrac{1}{2}$

    B. $2\dfrac{1}{2}$

    C. $3\dfrac{2}{3}$

    D. $4\dfrac{5}{7}$

    E. $7\dfrac{4}{5}$

8. Evaluate the expression, $100 - 10(2 + 3) + 4 =$

    A. 23

    B. 36

    C. 54

    D. 59

    E. 72

9. Evaluate the expression, $4 + 6(8 + 2) - 3 =$
   A. 61
   B. 63
   C. 78
   D. 79
   E. 83

10. Evaluate the expression, $\dfrac{(5 \times 4)}{(100 \div 20)} =$
    A. 0
    B. 1
    C. 2
    D. 3
    E. 4

11. Evaluate the expression, $1100 - 10(2 + 3) + 400 =$
    A. 1,450
    B. 1,467
    C. 1,534
    D. 1,897
    E. 2,123

12. Evaluate the expression, $36 \div 4(5 - 2) + 6 =$
    A. 9
    B. 33
    C. 45
    D. 67
    E. 79

13. Evaluate the expression, $30 - 3 \times 4 + 2 =$
    A. 5
    B. 10
    C. 20
    D. 23
    E. 56

14. Evaluate the expression, $3,000 \div 300 - 5 + 1,000 =$
    A. 1,005
    B. 1,010
    C. 1,100
    D. 1,400
    E. 1,450

15. Evaluate the expression, $\dfrac{[(30-3) \times 4 + 2]}{2} =$
    A. 10
    B. 55
    C. 75
    D. 110
    E. 123

Solutions to Practice Problems

1. **D.** First, simplify the operations inside the parentheses, $(7.2) \div (2.4)$. Finally, divide, to obtain 3.

2. **A.** First, simplify all multiplication and division operations from left to right, $18 + 10 + 10 + 8 - 3 + 45$. Next, simplify all addition and subtraction operations from left to right, to obtain 88.

3. **D.** First, simplify the multiplication and division operations inside the parentheses, $(30 + 15) + (50) + (8 - 3 + 45)$. Now, simplify the addition and subtraction operations within the parentheses, $45 + 50 + 50$. Next, add the numbers from left to right, to arrive at 145.

4. **E.** First, simplify all multiplication operations inside the parentheses, $\left(\frac{4}{9} + \frac{7}{5}\right) \div 1$. Now, simplify the addition operation inside the parentheses, $\left(\frac{83}{45}\right) \div 1$. Next, divide the fraction in the numerator by 1, to arrive at $\frac{83}{45}$.

5. **D.** First, simplify the operations inside the parentheses, $\left(1\frac{3}{4}\right)(2)$. Now, multiply, to arrive at $3\frac{1}{2}$.

6. **A.** Perform the operation in parentheses first. Simplify the multiplication operation in parentheses in the numerator, $(7) \div \left(\frac{28}{4}\right)$. Now, simplify the fraction in the other parenthesis. $(7) \div (7)$. Next, divide, to arrive at 1.

7. **A.** Simplify the fraction in the parenthesis, $3 \div (3 - 1)$. Now subtract to obtain $3 \div 2$. Finally, put the fraction in simplest terms, $\frac{3}{2}$, to get $1\frac{1}{2}$

8. **C.** First, simplify operations inside the parentheses, $100 - 10(5) + 4$. Now, multiply from left to right, $100 - 50 + 4$. Next, complete addition and subtraction operations from left to right, 54

9. **A.** First, simplify the operations inside the parentheses, $4 + 6(10) - 3$. Now, complete all multiplication operations from left to right, $4 + 60 - 3$. Next, complete all addition and subtraction operations from left to right, to arrive at 61.

10. **E.** First, simplify the multiplication operation in the numerator, $\frac{20}{(100 \div 20)}$. Now, simplify the division operation in the denominator, $\frac{20}{5}$. Next, simplify the fraction, to arrive at 4.

11. **A.** First, simplify the operations inside the parentheses, $1100 - 10(5) + 400$. Now, multiply from left to right, $1,100 - 50 + 400$. Next, add and subtract from left to right, to arrive at $1,450$.

12. **A.** First, simplify the operations inside the parentheses, $36 \div 4(3) + 6$. Now multiply the 4 by 3 to obtain $36 \div 12 + 6$. Then divide, $3 + 6 = 9$.

13. **C.** First, multiply and divide from left to right, $30 - 12 + 2$. Now, add and subtract from left to right, to arrive at 20.

14. **A.** First, divide from left to right, $10 - 5 + 1,000$. Now, add and subtract from left to right, to arrive at $1,005$.

15. **B.** First, complete all operations inside of parentheses in the numerator, $\dfrac{[27 \times 4 + 2]}{2}$. Next, multiply within the brackets in the numerator, $\dfrac{[108 + 2]}{2}$. Then, add within the brackets in the numerator, $\dfrac{110}{2}$. Finally, divide 110 by 2, to arrive at 55.

Chapter 4

Negative Numbers

Negative numbers are all numbers that are less than zero. On a number line, the negative number integers or non-integers such as fractions are all numbers to the left of zero. The numbers that are further to the left of zero on a number line are more negative and have a smaller value than those numbers closer to zero. For example, -11 is less than -5. Another example, $-\frac{1}{2}$ is less than $-\frac{1}{3}$.

Addition, subtraction, multiplication, and division of negative numbers are similar to those same operations for positive numbers. Below are rules for the operations involving negative numbers that you should learn.

Addition of Negative Numbers

We first need to define absolute value. Absolute value, shown by the symbol $|x|$, where x is a specific number, is the value of a number without regard to its sign. For example, $|3| = 3, |-3| = 3, |\frac{1}{2}| = \frac{1}{2}, |-\frac{1}{2}| = \frac{1}{2}$. In other words, if you plug in a positive number into x, you also get a positive number. If you plug in a negative number, you also get a positive number. The absolute value of 0, or $|0| = 0$. The absolute value of a positive number is that positive number. The absolute value of a negative number is its corresponding positive value.

A way to think of absolute value is the distance between x and 0. So if $x = 3$, the distance between 3 and 0 is 3, so the absolute value of 3 equals 3. The distance between -3 and 0 is also 3, so the absolute value of -3 is also 3.

When adding two negative numbers together, add the absolute values together first, then make the sign negative. Accordingly, adding two negative numbers results in a negative number.

$$Example: -2 + -4 = -(2 + 4) = -6$$
$$Example: -12 + -10 = -(12 + 10) = -22$$

Addition of Negative and Positive Numbers

In adding negative and positive numbers together, learn the following two rules and study the corresponding examples.

Case One: If the |Negative Number| > |Positive Number|

In adding negative and positive numbers together, if the absolute value of the negative number is greater than the absolute value of the positive number, subtract the positive number from the absolute value of the negative number. Then, make the result negative to arrive at the correct answer.

$$Example : -15 + 4 = -(|-15| - |4|) = -(15 - 4) = -11$$
$$Example : 3 + -10 = -(|-10| - |3|) = -(10 - 3) = -7$$
$$Example : 5 + -19 = -(|-19| - |5|) = -(19 - 5) = -14$$

Case Two: If the |Positive Number| > |Negative Number|

In adding negative and positive numbers together, if the absolute value of the positive number is greater than the absolute value of the negative number, subtract the absolute value of the negative number from the positive number.

$$Example : 9 + -5 = 9 - |-5| = 9 - 5 = 4$$
$$Example : 12 + -11 = 12 - |-11| = 12 - 11 = 1$$
$$Example : -18 + 24 = 24 - |-18| = 24 - 18 = 6$$

Subtraction

Subtracting a negative number is the same as adding a positive number.

$$Example : 3 - (-5) = 3 + 5 = 8$$
$$Example : -4 - (-2) = -4 + 2 = -2$$
$$Example : -4 - 2 = -6$$

Multiplication

Multiplying an odd number of negative numbers together (for example 3 negative numbers) results in a negative number.

$$Example : -2 \times -2 \times -2 = -8$$

Multiplying an even number of negative numbers together results in a positive number.

$$Example: -2 \times -2 = 4$$

Just remember:

$$negative \times negative = positive$$
$$negative \times positive = negative$$
$$positive \times negative = negative$$

Division

Rules for multiplication also apply for division. Division involving a negative number and a positive number results in a negative number.

$$Example: 2 \div -2 = -1$$

Division involving two negative numbers together results in a positive number.

$$Example: -2 \div -2 = 1$$

Just remember:

$$negative \div negative = positive$$
$$negative \div positive = negative$$
$$positive \div negative = negative$$

Exponents

Any negative number when raised to an odd power results in a negative number.

$$Example: (-2)^3 = -2 \times -2 \times -2 = -8 \; because -2 \times -2 = 4 \; and \; 4 \times -2 = -8.$$

Any negative number when raised to an even power results in a positive number.

$$Example: (-2)^2 = -2 \times -2 = 4$$

Example 1   Which of the following statements is <u>true</u>?

   I. $-5 > -4$
  II. $-5 < -4$
 III. $-5 < 4$
 IV. $5 > -4$

  A. I only
  B. II only
  C. III only
  D. I and II
  E. II, III, and IV

ANSWER: E.

  I. False. This is because -5 is more negative than -4 and is therefore less than -4 and not greater than -4.

  II. True. This is because -5 is more negative than -4 and is therefore less than -4.

  III. True. This is because a negative number is always less than a positive number. In this case -5 is less than the positive value of 4.

  IV. True. This is because a positive number is always greater than a negative number.

Example 2   Which of the following is <u>greatest</u>?

  A. -5
  B. -8
  C. 0
  D. -3
  E. -2

ANSWER: C. Zero is a number greater than all other negative numbers, and the answer choices other than C are all negative numbers.

Example 3   Compute $-5 + -3$.

ANSWER: -8. $-5 + -3 = -(5 + 3) = -8$. Imagine a number line at -5. Because we are adding -3 to -5, we are becoming more negative. We, therefore, move 3 spaces to the left of -5 and arrive at our answer, -8. Add the absolute values together first, then make the sign negative.

Example 4 Compute $-6 - 3$.

ANSWER: -9 $-6 - 3 = -6 + -3 = -(6 + 3) = -9$. Subtracting negative numbers is the same as adding a negative number. Therefore, subtracting -3 from -6 is the same as adding -3 to -6. Once again, imagine a number line. Because we are adding -3 to -6, we move 3 spaces to the left of -6 and arrive at our answer, -9. Also, when adding these two negative numbers together, add the absolute values together first, then make the sign negative.

Example 5 Which of the following is <u>greatest</u>?

    A. $(-2)^1$
    B. $(-2)^3$
    C. $(-2)^2$
    D. $-(-2)^2$
    E. $-(-2)^3$

ANSWER: E. Compute the value of each choice to arrive at the answer.

    A. $(-2)^1 = -2$. A negative number when raised to the power of one equals that negative number.

    B. $(-2)^3 = -2 \times -2 \times -2 = -8$. A negative number when raised to an odd power results in a negative number.

    C. $(-2)^2 = -2 \times -2 = 4$. A negative number when raised to an even power results in a positive number.

    D. $-(-2)^2 = -(-2 \times -2) = -(4) = -1 \times 4 = -4$. The operation involving exponents is performed before operations involving multiplication. The negative sign to the left of the parenthesis is equivalent to muliplying by -1. Accordingly, we first perform the operation $(-2)^2$ and then multiply the result by -1, to arrive at -4

    E. $-(-2)^3 = -(-2 \times -2 \times -2) = -(-8) = -1 \times -8 = 8$. As with answer choice D, the operation involving exponents is performed before operations involving multiplication, and the negative sign to the left of the parenthesis is equivalent to muliplying by -1. Accordingly, we first perform the operation $(-2)^3$ and then multiply the result by -1. 8 is the greatest value of the all the answer choices. Answer E is therefore the correct answer.

Example 6   On an elevator, going up is the same as moving in a positive direction and going down is the same as going in a negative direction. With that in mind, which of the following is the greatest number of floors traveled in the positive direction?

A. Moving from floor 5 to floor 8
B. Moving from floor 10 to floor 5
C. Moving from floor 2 to floor 6 then to floor 3
D. Moving from floor 9 to floor 6 and then to floor 2
E. Moving from floor 1 to floor 8 and then to floor 10

ANSWER: E.

A. Moving from floor 5 to floor 8 is a movement in a positive direction. That is, you are moving 3 floors in a positive direction.

B. Moving from floor 10 to floor 5 is a movement in a negative direction. That is, you are moving 5 floors in a negative direction.

C. Moving from floor 2 to floor 6 is movement of 4 floors in a positive direction. The movement from floor 6 back to floor 3 is a movement of 3 floors in a negative direction. As a result, you have moved 1 floor in a positive direction.

D. Moving from floor 9 to floor 6 is a movement of 3 floors in a negative direction. The movement from floor 6 to floor 2 is a movement of 4 floors in a negative direction. As a result, you have moved 7 floors in a negative direction.

E. Moving from floor 1 to floor 8 is a movement of 7 floors in a positive direction. The movement from floor 8 to floor 10 is a movement of 2 floors in a positive direction. As a result, you have moved 9 floors in a positive direction. This is the largest numbers of floors traveled in the positive direction and is therefore the correct answer.

Example 7   Compute $-7 + 2 - (-8)$.

ANSWER: 3. $-7 + 2 - (-8) = (-7 + 2) - (-8) = -5 - -8 = -5 + 8 = 3$. In solving this problem, we solve the left part first and move right. That is, we perform $-7 + 2$ first. $-7 + 2$ is the same as adding 2 to -7 resulting in -5. We then subtract -8 from -5. Remember that subtracting a negative number is the same as adding a positive number. $-5 - (-8) = -5 + 8 = 3$.

Example 8   Compute $(-8 - [-2]) \div (-3 + -4)$.

ANSWER: $\frac{6}{7}$. $(-8 - [-2]) \div (-3 + -4) = (-8 + 2) \div (-3 + -4) = -6 \div -7 = \frac{6}{7}$. In solving this problem, we first solve inside the parenthesis and second perform the division operation. Remember that division involving two negative numbers together results in a positive number.

Example 9   Which of the following is <u>least</u>?

  A. -10
  B. $-20 \div -5$
  C. $-1 + -12$
  D. $(-4)^2$
  E. -3×3

ANSWER: C.

  A. -10

  B. $-20 \div -5 = 4$. Division involving two negative numbers together results in a positive number.

  C. $-1 + -12 = -13$. Adding negative numbers together results in a negative number. This is the most negative choice and therefore has the least value.

  D. $(-4)^2 = -4 \times -4 = 16$. Any negative number when raised to an even power results in a positive number.

  E. $-3 \times 3 = -9$ A positive number multiplied by a negative number equals a negative number.

Example 10   Alice has $20,000 in her checking account and writes a check for $25,000 to buy a new car. Which of the following mathematical steps can be used to calculate the final balance?

  A. $20,000 - 25,000 = |25,000| - |20,000|$
  B. $20,000 + 25,000 = 45,000$
  C. $20,000 - 5,000 = 15,000$
  D. $20,000 - 25,000 = -(25,000 - 20,000) = -5,000$
  E. $25,000 - 5,000 = 20,000$

ANSWER: D. You can calculate the balance mathematically by subtracting the amount of the check ($25,000) from the amount in Alice's account ($20,000). That is $20,000 - 25,000$. Because $|-25,000|$ is greater than $|20,000|$, subtract 20,000 from 25,000 and make the result negative to arrive at the correct answer (-5,000).

Practice Problems

1. Compute $-16 - (-11)$.

2. Which of the following negative numbers is the greatest?

   A. -45
   B. -9×4
   C. $-70 \div 10$
   D. $5 + -7$
   E. -1

3. Which of the following is closest to the number 0?

   A. -4×-2
   B. $(-5)^2$
   C. $(-6)^2 - (-3)^3$
   D. $-21 - (-9)$
   E. $-22 \div 11$

4. Compute -4×-20.

5. Which of the following is <u>false</u>?
   I. $-5 - (-15) < -15 - (-5)$
   II. $20 \times -6 > 120 \div -2$
   III. $0 > -4$

   A. I only
   B. II only
   C. III only
   D. I and II
   E. I, II, and III

6. Which of the following is equivalent to -1?

    A. $-30 + -7$
    B $(-4)^3 - 8^2$
    C. $-1 - 1$
    D. $125 \div -25$
    E. $-13 - (-12)$

7. Compute $-36 \div 6$.

8. Which of the following is the most negative number?

    A. -70
    B. $-69 - (-4)$
    C. $100 + -50$
    D. 0
    E. $4 - 80$

9. Tom has \$50,000 in his bank account and writes a check from that account in the amount of \$53,000. Which of the following mathematical steps can be used to calculate the final balance?

    A. $3,000 + 50,000 = 53,000$
    B. $50,000 - 53,000 = -(53,000 - 50,000) = -3,000$
    C. $50,000 - 3,000 = 47,000$
    D. $50,000 + 53,000 = 103,000$
    E. $50,000 - 53,000 = |53,000| - |50,000| = 3,000$

10. $(-2)^5 \div 2^2$.

11. $-17 + 4 - (-2)$. is equivalent to which of the answer choices below?

    A. -11
    B. -15
    C. 11
    D. 15
    E. 23

12. Which of the following is <u>greatest</u>?

    A. $3 - (-6)$
    B. $-7 + -8$
    C. 0
    D. $2 + -16$
    E. $16 + -2$

13. Compute $-10 + -17 + -2$.

14. Which of the following is <u>least</u>?

    A. $-3 \times -2 \times -1$
    B. $-15 \div 3$
    C. $-17 + -14$
    D. $12 - (-12)$
    E. $-20 - (-19)$

15. Is the following statement true?

$$(-2)^2 + 4 - (-7) < (3)^2 + \frac{15}{-3} - (-12)$$

Solutions to Practice Problems

1. **-5.** $-16 - (-11) = -16 + 11 = -5$. Subtracting a negative number is the same as adding a positive number.

2. **E.** In this case A is -45, B is $-9 \times 4 = -36$, C is $-70 \div 10 = -7$, and D is $5 + -7 = -2$, and E is -1. Of all the answer choices -1 is the closest to zero and therefore the least negative.

3. **E.** We calculate all the answer choices to arrive at the number that is closest to zero.

    A. $-4 \times -2 = 8$.
    B. $(-5)^2 = -5 \times -5 = 25$.
    C. $(-6)^2 - (-3)^3 = (-6 \times -6) - (-3 \times -3 \times -3) = 36 - (-27) = 36 + 27 = 63$.
    D. $-21 - (-9) = -21 + 9 = -12$.
    E. $-22 \div 11 = -2$.

4. **80.** $-4 \times -20 = 80$. Multiplying an even number of negative numbers together results in a positive number.

5. **D.**

    I. False. $-5 - (-15) = -5 + 15 = 10$ and $-15 - (-5) = -15 + 5 = -10$. 10 is greater than and not less than -10.

    II. False. $20 \times -6 = -120$ and $120 \div -2 = -60$. -120 is more negative than -60 and is therefore less than and not greater than -60.

    III. True. 0 is greater than -4.

6. **E.**
    A. $-30 + -7 = -37$.
    B. $(-4)^3 - 8^2 = (-4 \times -4 \times -4) - (8 \times 8) = -64 - 64 = -64 + -64 = -128$.
    C. $-1 - 1 = -1 + -1 = -2$.
    D. $125 \div -25 = -5$.
    E. $-13 - (-12) = -13 + 12 = -1$.

7. **-6.** $-36 \div 6 = -6$. Division involving a negative number and a positive number results in a negative number.

8. **E.** A is -70, B is $-69 - (-4) = -65$, C is $100 + -50 = 50$, D is 0, E is $4 - 80 = 4 + -80 = -76$. Of all the answer choices -76 is the negative number furthest away from zero and is therefore the most negative among the choices.

9. **B.** You can calculate the balance mathematically by subtracting the amount of the check ($53,000) from the amount in Tom's account ($50,000). That is $50,000 - 53,000$. Because $|-53,000|$ is greater than $|50,000|$, subtract 50,000 from 53,000 and make the result negative to arrive at the correct answer (-3,000).

10. **-8.** $(-2)^5 \div 2^2 = (-2 \times -2 \times -2 \times -2 \times -2) \div (2 \times 2) = -32 \div 4 = -8$.

11. **A.** $-17 + 4 - (-2) = -(17 - 4) - (-2) = -13 - (-2) = -13 + 2 = -(13 - 2) = -11$.

12. **E.**

    A. $3 - -6 = 3 + 6 = 9$

    B. $-7 + -8 = -(7 + 8) = -15$

    C. 0

    D. $2 + -16 = -(16 - 2) = -14$

    E. $16 + -2 = 16 - 2 = 14$

13. **-29.** When adding negative numbers together, add the absolute values together first then make the sign negative. $-10 + -17 + -2 = -(10 + 17 + 2) = -29$.

14. **C.**

    A. $-3 \times -2 \times -1 = -6$.

    B. $-15 \div 3 = -5$.

    C. $-17 + -14 = -(17 + 14) = -31$.

    D. $12 - (-12) = 12 + 12 = 24$.

    E. $-20 - (-19) = -20 + 19 = -1$.

15. **True.** $(-2)^2 + 4 - -7 < (3)^2 + \frac{15}{-3} - -12$ is a true statement.

    $(-2)^2 + 4 - (-7) = 4 + 4 + 7 = 15$ which is less than $(3)^2 + \frac{15}{-3} - (-12) = 9 + -5 + 12 = 9 + (12 - 5) = 9 + 7 = 16$.

Section III: Algebra

Chapter 5

Simplifying Expressions

Oftentimes an expression, or a mathematical quantity that may be composed of variables and coefficients, is written in a form that can be made simpler and more concise. Consider the expression:

$$\frac{22x}{11} + \frac{17x}{17}$$

This expression can be rewritten in more concise form. $\frac{22x}{11}$ can be simplified and rewritten as $2x$. The second part, $\frac{17x}{17}$, can be rewritten as x. Substituting these values will yield:

$$\frac{22x}{11} + \frac{17x}{17} = 2x + x$$
$$= 3x$$

Rewriting an expression in its most concise form is known as simplifying the expression. For more complicated expressions there are complex methods of simplifying; however, because the Praxis exam is designed to be light on computation, we can expect less complicated expressions for which the following methods should suffice.

Simplifying Fractions

Any fractions should be reduced to simplest form when simplifying expressions. To reduce a fraction, find any common factors between the numerator and the denominator, and divide by those common factors until the only common factor between numerator and denominator is 1. Ideally, we want to find the GCD (the greatest common factor) of the numerator and denominator. The example above involves fractions that can be simplified in this manner. To start, we will only look at the first part:

$$\frac{22x}{11}$$

11 is a common factor, so divide numerator and denominator by 11.

$$= \frac{2x}{1}$$

$$= 2x$$

A second example:

$$\frac{12(x+2)y}{4(x+2)}$$

4 is a common factor, so divide numerator and denominator by 4.

$$= \frac{3(x+2)y}{1(x+2)}$$

$(x+2)$ is a common factor so divide numerator and denominator by $(x+2)$

$$= \frac{3y}{1}$$

$$= 3y$$

Example 1 Simplify the following completely: $\dfrac{18x}{6x}$

A. $3x$

B. 3

C. $\dfrac{3x}{x}$

D. $\dfrac{18}{6}$

E. $\dfrac{3}{x}$

ANSWER: B. The coefficients (numbers) in the fraction can be reduced from $\dfrac{18}{6}$ to $\dfrac{3}{1}$, or just 3. The x's in the fraction cancel each other out, reducing to $\dfrac{1}{1}$ or just 1. We are left with 3 times 1, which is equal to 3.

Example 2 Simplify the following completely: $\dfrac{2+2}{16x}$

A. $4x$

B. $\dfrac{1+1}{8x}$

C. $\dfrac{3x}{x}$

D. $\dfrac{1}{4x}$

E. $\dfrac{4}{16x}$

ANSWER: D. First note that both 2's in the numerator must be combined: $2 + 2 = 4$. The expression simplifies to $\dfrac{4}{16x}$. Next, we can reduce the numbers in the fraction by dividing both numerator and denominator by 4, which leaves us with $\dfrac{1}{4x}$.

Example 3 Simplify the following fraction completely: $\dfrac{32x}{8}$

A. $\dfrac{16x}{4}$

B. $8x$

C. $4x$

D. $\dfrac{8x}{2}$

E. $\dfrac{12x}{3}$

ANSWER: C. Divide the numerator and denominator by 8 to get $\dfrac{4x}{1}$, or $4x$. Note that while $\dfrac{16x}{4}$ and $\dfrac{8x}{2}$ are mathematically equivalent, they are not completely simplified as there are still common factors between numerator and denominator in both fractions.

Combining like terms

A **term** is an expression containing a numerical coefficient that multiplies a variable, such as x or y, raised to a certain exponent. When a term is raised to the 1st power, we do not need to write the exponent. The following examples are all terms:

$$8 \qquad 2x \qquad 5x^2 \qquad -4y^3$$

Like terms are any terms that have the same variable raised to the same power. Terms without variables (those containing only numbers) are also considered like terms. Only like terms can be combined through addition and subtraction; unlike terms cannot. For example:

$$3 + 8 - 4x + 2x^2 - 5x^2$$

In the above expression, there are two pairs of like terms: 3 and 8 are like terms, and $2x^2$ and $-5x^2$ are like terms. The first pair, 3 and 8, both have no variable. The second pair, $2x^2$ and $-5x^2$, share the same variable **and** the variable is raised to the same power. For each of these pairs the like terms, placed in parentheses and boldfaced below for emphasis, can be combined:

$$(\mathbf{3 + 8}) - 4x + (\mathbf{2x^2 - 5x^2}) = 11 - 4x - 3x^2$$

Note that the $4x$ and $3x^2$ have the same variable, but different exponents and cannot be combined by addition or subtraction.

By combining like terms, we have simplified the expression into its most concise form, $11 - 4x - 3x^2$. The final step is to convert the expression to standard form, in which the terms with the highest exponents are placed furthest to the left, and lowest exponents furthest to the right:

$$11 - 4x - 3x^2 = \mathbf{-3x^2 - 4x + 11}$$

The right side of the equation is equivalent to the left because of the commutative property of addition and subtraction: for any set of terms that are added and subtracted, the order does not matter. Care should be taken to ensure that all terms retain their original positive or negative signs.

Example 4   Which of the following contains all like terms?

A. $3, 3x$
B. $2x, 5x, 5x^2$
C. x, y, z
D. $8n, 3m, 3$
E. $a, 3a, -2a, 9a$

ANSWER: E. Each of the terms contains an a with the same exponent (if no exponent is written, the number is assumed to be raised to the 1st power).

Example 5   Which of the following expressions can be simplified?

A. $8 + 4$
B. $4x + 1$
C. $13x^2 + x + 1$
D. $-7x$
E. $3a + 2b$

ANSWER: A. Only A contains terms that can be combined. In B, the term $4x$ has an x while the term 1 does not, so they cannot be combined. In C, the first term contains x^2, which has a different exponent on the x (2) than the second term, which has an x with no exponent (which is equivalent to an exponent of 1). The third term has no x in the term. In D, there is only one term that cannot be simplified further. In E, the expression cannot be further reduced, so it is already in simplest form.

Example 6   Simplify the following: $3 + 5 + 8x - 2x$

A. $3 + 5 + 8x - 2x$
B. $8 + 8x - 2x$
C. $8 + 6x$
D. $8 + 10x$
E. $11 + 3x$

ANSWER: C. The 3 and 5 can be combined to make 8. The $8x$ and $-2x$ can be combined to make $6x$. This leaves $8 + 6x$.

Example 7 Simplify the following: $x + 3 + y - 2 + 3x$

    A. $x + 1 + y + 3x$
    B. $x + y$
    C. $4x + y + 1$
    D. $x + 3y + 2$
    E. $x + 3 + 3y$

ANSWER: C. Combining the x's gives us $x + 3x = 4x$. Combining the numbers gives us $3 - 2 = 1$. We are left with $4x + y + 1$. Note that the simplified terms can be written in any order: $4x + y + 1$ is equivalent to $y + 1 + 4x$.

The Distributive Property

Another useful tool for simplifying expressions is the distributive property, which can help to get rid of parentheses that may be in the way of finding and combining like terms. The distributive property can be illustrated as follows:

$$3(4 + 5)$$

To evaluate this without using the distributive property, we would first evaluate the inside of the parentheses: $4 + 5$, which equals 9. We can then rewrite the original expression as $3(9)$, giving us a final result of 27.

Using the distributive property, we will arrive at the same result since mathematically it does not change the expression. The distributive property allows us to distribute the coefficient 3 to the numbers inside the parentheses, thus getting rid of the parentheses:

$$3(4 + 5) = 3(4) + 3(5)$$
$$= 12 + 15$$
$$= 27$$

The distributive property can be used to help simplify expressions, particularly if the terms inside the parentheses are unlike terms. Consider:

$$-5 + 3x + 2(5x - 3)$$

We cannot combine the terms inside the parentheses, $5x$ and -3, because they are unlike terms. We also cannot combine terms from outside the parentheses with terms inside the parentheses.

However, using the distributive property, we can get rid of the parentheses and then find like terms to simplify the expression:

$$\begin{aligned}
-5 + 3x + 2(5x - 3) &= -5 + 3x + 2(5x) - 2(3) &&\text{Distribute the 2 to the } 5x \text{ and the } 3 \\
&= -5 + 3x + 10x - 6 &&\text{Multiply } 2(5x) \text{ and } -2(3) \\
&= -11 + 13x &&\text{Combine like terms} \\
&= 13x - 11 &&\text{Rewrite in standard form}
\end{aligned}$$

In the final step we convert to standard form, since the exponent on $13x$ (implied to be x^1) is greater than the exponent on 11 (implied to be x^0).

Multiplying Variables

Example 8   Apply the distributive property to expand the following expression: $3(5x^2 + 3x - 3)$

    A. $15x^2 + 3x - 3$
    B. $8x^2 + 6x + 6$
    C. $15x^2$
    D. $15x^2 + 9x - 3$
    E. $15x^2 + 9x - 9$

ANSWER: E. The 3 on the outside must be distributed to all terms inside the parentheses. This yields $3(5x^2) + 3(3x) - 3(3)$, which yields $15x^2 + 9x - 9$.

Example 9   Which of the following is equivalent to $2(3x^2 + 9x - 1)$?

    A. $6x^2 + 18x - 2$
    B. $6x^2 + 9x - 1$
    C. $3x^2 + 18x - 1$
    D. $3x^2 + 9x - 2$
    E. $23x$

ANSWER: A. Apply the distributive property: all terms within the parentheses must be multiplied by 2.

Example 10 Simplify the following expression completely: $2x + 3 + 3(2x + 3)$

    A. $2x + 3 + 6x + 9$

    B. $8x + 12$

    C. $6x + 6$

    D. $4x + 9$

    E. None of the above

ANSWER: B. First apply the distributive property to get $2x + 3 + 6x + 9$. Then combine like terms to get $8x + 12$. Note that while choice A is mathematically equivalent, it is not simplified because like terms have not been combined.

Multiplying and Dividing Variables

What would you get by multiplying x by x? Well, the rule is that $x(x) = x^2$. This is because you have 2 x's in the multiplication. It works just as $2(2) = 2^2$ does.

Example 11 Apply the distributive property to the following: $6x(3x - 2)$

    A. $6x^2 - 2$

    B. $12x^2 - 18$

    C. $18x^2 - 2$

    D. $18x^2 - 12x$

    E. None of the above.

ANSWER: D. First multiply $6x$ by $3x$ to obtain $18x^2$. Then multiply $6x$ by -2 to obtain $-12x$. Now add the two to obtain $18x^2 - 12x$.

Example 12 What is $\dfrac{x^2}{x}$?

ANSWER: x. We have: $\dfrac{(x)(x)}{x}$. One of the x's in the numerator cancels with the x in the denominator, so we simply have $\dfrac{(x)(x)}{x} = x$

Example 13 What is $\dfrac{x^3}{x^2}$?

ANSWER:x. We have $\dfrac{(x)(x)(x)}{(x)(x)} = x$.

Example 14   What is $\dfrac{(y^4)(x^2)}{(y^2)(x)}$?

ANSWER: y^2x First divide y^4 by y^2 to obtain y^2, then divide x^2 by x to obtain x. Then multiply those terms by each other to obtain y^2x.

Practice Problems

1. Apply the distributive property to the following: $8x(2x + 3)$

    A. $16x^2 + 24x$
    B. $16x + 24$
    C. $40x$
    D. $26x$
    E. $16x^2 + 3x$

2. Which of the following sets of terms are all like terms?

    A. $x, 3x, 3x^2$
    B. $2, 2a, 2b, 2c$
    C. $6m, mn, 3np$
    D. $8x^2, 8x^3$
    E. $3y^2, 9y^2, y^2$

3. Which of the following is in simplest form?

    A. $\dfrac{12}{4}$
    B. $\dfrac{8x}{16}$
    C. $\dfrac{6x^2}{2x^4}$
    D. $\dfrac{7x^2y^3}{21xy^2}$
    E. $\dfrac{3x}{8y}$

4. Simplify the following: $n - 8 + 4n + 12 - n$

    A. $5n + 20$
    B. $n - 8 + 3n + 12$
    C. $-4n + 4$
    D. $4n + 4$
    E. None of the above

5. Simplify the following expression completely: $3 + 3(3x + 3)$

    A. $3 + 9x + 9$
    B. $3 + 3x$
    C. $9 + 3x$
    D. $9x + 12$
    E. $3 + 12x$

6. Simplify the following expression completely: $\dfrac{21y}{7x}$

    A. $3y$

    B. $\dfrac{3y}{x}$

    C. $\dfrac{3y}{7x}$

    D. $\dfrac{3x}{y}$

    E. 3

7. Which fraction is already in simplest form?

    A. $\dfrac{20xy}{5x}$

    B. $\dfrac{10n}{15n}$

    C. $\dfrac{x}{9x}$

    D. $\dfrac{2}{3xy}$

    E. $\dfrac{7(a+b)}{21(a+b)}$

8. Simplify the following expression completely: $3(2x + 2) + 4(x + 1)$

    A. $10x + 10$
    B. $32x + 8$
    C. $7x + 10$
    D. $10x + 3$
    E. $3x + 10$

9. Simplify the following expression completely: $\dfrac{x + 3x}{2x + 2x}$

    A. $\dfrac{4x}{4x}$

    B. $\dfrac{4}{4}$

    C. 1

    D. $\dfrac{3x}{4}$

    E. $\dfrac{4}{2}$

10. Simplify the following expression completely: $\dfrac{30b}{15} + \dfrac{6b}{2}$

    A. $\dfrac{2b}{1} + \dfrac{6b}{1}$

    B. $5b$

    C. $\dfrac{5}{b}$

    D. $\dfrac{2b}{1} + \dfrac{3b}{2}$

    E. $\dfrac{30b}{15} + \dfrac{6b}{2}$

11. Apply the distributive property to simplify the following: $3(x + 8) + 3x$

    A. $3x + 8$
    B. $6x + 24$
    C. $3x + 8x$
    D. $3x + 24$
    E. $6x + 8$

12. Simplify the following expression completely: $\dfrac{9h}{3h}$

    A. $\dfrac{3}{h}$

    B. $3h$

    C. 3

    D. $\dfrac{9}{3h}$

    E. $\dfrac{3h}{h}$

13. Which of the following is NOT in simplest form?

    A. $3a + 8y + 2z$

    B. $5b + 17 + 2x + 3b$

    C. $\dfrac{5c}{19}$

    D. $\dfrac{3d}{2} + 1$

    E. $e + f - g$

14. Which of the following contains ALL like terms?

    A. $1, x, 3x, 4x$
    B. $5b, 5, 5c, 5d$
    C. $a, 3a, 9a, 9$
    D. x, y, z
    E. $2, 4, 9, 124, 291$

15. Simplify the following expression completely: $\dfrac{18(b + c)}{6(b + c)}$

    A. 3 B. $3b + 3c$ C. $\dfrac{6(b + c)}{2}$ D. $\dfrac{18b + 18c}{6b + 6c}$ E. Cannot be factored

Solutions to Practice Problems

1. **A.** Multiplying $8x$ with the first term in parentheses, $2x$, yields $16x^2$, because $(8)(2) = 16$ and $(x)(x) = x^2$. Multiplying $8x$ by the second term in parentheses, 3, yields $24x$. So we are left with $16x^2 + 24x$.

2. **E.** Only in choice E do all terms have the same variable raised to the same power.

3. **E.** Only in choice E are there no common factors between the numerator and the denominator.

4. **D.** Combining like terms yields $4n + 4$.

5. **D.** Using the distributive property yields $3 + 9x + 9$. Combining like terms results in $9x + 12$.

6. **B.** Factoring 7 from the numerator and denominator yields $\dfrac{3y}{x}$. There are no other common factors.

7. **D.** In all the other choices there is at least one common factor between numerator and denominator.

8. **A.** Apply the distributive property to get $6x + 6 + 4x + 4$. Combine like terms to get $10x + 10$.

9. **C.** Combining like terms yields $\dfrac{4x}{4x}$, which can be simplified to 1 since $4x$ is a common factor between numerator and denominator.

10. **B.** First factor out common factors in both fractions (15 in the first and 2 in the second), which will yield $\dfrac{2b}{1} + \dfrac{3b}{1}$, or $2b + 3b$. Combine like terms to get $5b$.

11. **B.** Apply the distributive property by multiplying each term in the parentheses by 3:

$$3(x + 8) + 3x = 3x + 24 + 3x$$

Then combine like terms to get $6x + 24$.

12. **C.** Factoring 3 from both the numerator and denominator yields $\dfrac{3h}{h}$, which is answer choice E; however, it is not factored completely, as the h can also be factored out, leaving $\dfrac{3}{1}$ or just 3.

13. **B.** The terms with b can be combined from $5b + 17 + 2x + 3b$ to yield $8b + 17 + 2x$. None of the terms in the other answer choices can be combined.

14. **E.** Only $2, 4, 9, 124, 291$ are all like terms because they all do not contain any variables.

15. **A.** Factoring 6 out of both the numerator and denominator leaves us with $\dfrac{3(b+c)}{(b+c)}$. We can then factor out the quantity $(b+c)$ out of both the numerator and denominator as well, leaving us with 3.

Chapter 6

Exponents and Roots

Exponents

An exponent refers to repeated multiplication of a number by itself. The number of times the number is multiplied by itself is determined by the value of the power. For example, 2 to the power of 3 or 2^3 is 2 multiplied by itself 3 times. That is $2^3 = 2 \times 2 \times 2$. In this example, 2 is called the base, and 3 is known as the exponent.

Squaring a negative number

Note that there is a difference between $-x^2$ and $(-x)^2$. With $-x^2$ you square x to obtain x^2, then multiply by a negative sign. With $(-x)^2$ you are squaring $-x$ to obtain $(-x) \times (-x) = +x^2$.

Examples:

$$(-2)^2 = (-2) \times (-2) = 4$$
$$-2^2 = -(2 \times 2) = -4$$
$$-(-2)^2 = -(-2 \times -2) = -(4) = -4$$

Learn the following three rules about exponents: Any number when raised to the power of 1 equals that number. Examples:

$$x^1 = x$$
$$2^1 = 2$$

Any non-zero number when raised to the exponent of zero equals 1.

Examples:

$$x^0 = 1$$
$$2^0 = 1$$

Any non-zero number when raised to a negative exponent equals one divided by that number raised to the positive exponent.

Examples:

$$x^{-2} = \frac{1}{x^2} \qquad\qquad 2^{-2} = \frac{1}{2^2} = \frac{1}{4}$$

Square Roots

A root of a number is the opposite of a power or exponent. The symbol for a square root is the radical sign " $\sqrt{}$ ". The square root of a number is a number which, when multiplied by itself, yields that original number. For example, $2 \times 2 = 4$, so the square root of 4 is 2.

Every positive number has only one square root, another positive number. However, consider the equation $x^2 = 4$. In this case, there are two square roots of x^2: one positive and one negative. You solve for the two values of x by taking the square roots of both sides of the equation. $\sqrt{x^2} = \sqrt{4}$. The square root of x^2 is x and the square root of 4 is 2. Because $(2)^2 = 4$ and $(-2)^2 = 4$, there are two values for x, 2 and -2.

Simplifying the Square Root of a Fraction

The square root of a fraction equals the square root of the numerator over the square root of the denominator.

$$\sqrt{\frac{a}{b}} = \frac{\sqrt{a}}{\sqrt{b}}$$

Example 1 $\quad \sqrt{\frac{25}{36}} = \frac{\sqrt{25}}{\sqrt{36}} = \frac{5}{6}$

Tables for Powers and Roots

MEMORIZE THIS TABLE!

x (Number)	x^2 (Powers)	$\sqrt{x^2}$ (Square Roots)
1	$1^2 = 1$	$\sqrt{1} = 1$
2	$2^2 = 4$	$\sqrt{4} = 2$
3	$3^2 = 9$	$\sqrt{9} = 3$
4	$4^2 = 16$	$\sqrt{16} = 4$
5	$5^2 = 25$	$\sqrt{25} = 5$
6	$6^2 = 36$	$\sqrt{36} = 6$
7	$7^2 = 49$	$\sqrt{49} = 7$
8	$8^2 = 64$	$\sqrt{64} = 8$
9	$9^2 = 81$	$\sqrt{81} = 9$
10	$10^2 = 100$	$\sqrt{100} = 10$
11	$11^2 = 121$	$\sqrt{121} = 11$
12	$12^2 = 144$	$\sqrt{144} = 12$

Example 2 Which of the following is greatest?

   A. 3^0
   B. 3^1
   C. 3^{-2}
   D. 3^2
   E. 3

ANSWER: D. This problem applies the rules of powers discussed in this chapter. First, glance at the answer choices and find the answer that appears to yield the largest number. That answer is D, since $3^2 = 9$. All the other answer choices are less than 9 and can be eliminated. In A, $3^0 = 1$ applying the rule that any non-zero number when raised to the power of zero equals 1. In B, $3^1 = 3$ applying the rule that any number when raised to the power of 1 equals that number. In C, $3^{-2} = \frac{1}{3^2} = \frac{1}{9}$ applying the rule that any non-zero number when raised to a negative exponent equals one divided by that number raised to the positive exponent.

Example 3 Compute 4^3.

ANSWER: 64. The base is 4. The exponent is 3. Therefore, 4 is multiplied by itself 3 times. $4^3 = 4 \times 4 \times 4 = 64$.

Example 4 Which statement is <u>true</u>?

   I. $\sqrt{2^2} = 2$
  II. $2^4 = 2^{-4}$
 III. $\sqrt{2^{-4}} = \frac{1}{4}$

  A. I only
  B. II only
  C. III only
  D. I and II
  E. I and III

ANSWER: E.

I. True. This is because $\sqrt{2^2} = \sqrt{2 \times 2} = \sqrt{4} = 2$.

II. False. This is because $2^4 = 2 \times 2 \times 2 \times 2 = 16 \neq 2^{-4} = \frac{1}{2^4} = \frac{1}{2 \times 2 \times 2 \times 2} = \frac{1}{16}$. This applies the rule that any non-zero number when raised to a negative exponent equals one divided by that number raised to the positive exponent.

III. True. This is because $\sqrt{2^{-4}} = \sqrt{\frac{1}{2^4}} = \sqrt{\frac{1}{16}} = \frac{\sqrt{1}}{\sqrt{16}} = \frac{1}{4}$. The applicable rule is that the square root of a fraction equals the square root of the numerator over the square root of the denominator. $\sqrt{\frac{a}{b}} = \frac{\sqrt{a}}{\sqrt{b}}$.

Example 5 Compute $\sqrt{81}$.

ANSWER: 9. $\sqrt{81} = \sqrt{9 \times 9} = 9$

Example 6 Solve for x when $x^2 = 16$.

  A. -4
  B. 0
  C. 2
  D. 4
  E. -4 and 4

ANSWER: E. Take the square roots of both sides. $\sqrt{x^2} = \sqrt{16}$. The square root of x^2 is x. The square root of 16 is 4. However, $(4)^2 = 16$ and $(-4)^2 = 16$. Therefore, there are two values for x, 4 and -4, leading to answer choice E.

Example 7 Compute 9^{-2}.

ANSWER: $\frac{1}{81}$. $9^{-2} = \dfrac{1}{9^2} = \dfrac{1}{81}$

Example 8 Solve for x when $x^2 = 121$.

   A. -11
   B. 10
   C. 11
   D. 12
   E. 11 and -11

ANSWER: E. This problem is similar to problem 5. Take the square roots of both sides. $\sqrt{x^2} = \sqrt{121}$. The square root of x^2 is x. The square root of 121 is 11. However, $(11)^2 = 121$ and $(-11)^2 = 121$. Therefore, there are two values for x, 11 and -11, leading to answer choice E.

Example 9 Which of the following is <u>false</u>?
   I. $\sqrt{144} = 12$
   II. $\sqrt{7^2} = 49$
  III.   If $x^2 = 25, x = 5$ or $x = -5$

   A. I only
   B. II only
   C. III only
   D. I and II
   E. II and III

ANSWER: B. I. True. The square root of 144 equals 12. II. False. $\sqrt{7^2} = \sqrt{49} = 7$ III. True. When $x^2 = 25$, there are two solutions for $x, 5$ or -5.

Example 10   Which of the following is <u>smallest</u>?

    A. 0
    B. 5^0
    C. 4^3
    D. 4^{-3}
    E. $\sqrt{64}$

ANSWER: A.

A. This answer choice has the smallest value because all of the other answer choices are of a greater value.

B. $5^0 = 1$. Any non-zero number when raised to the power of zero equals 1.

C. $4^3 = 4 \times 4 \times 4 = 64$.

D. $4^{-3} = \frac{1}{4^3} = \frac{1}{64}$.

E. The square root of 64 equals 8.

Example 11   Compute $(\sqrt{100})^{-2}$.

ANSWER: $\frac{1}{100}$. $(\sqrt{100})^{-2} = 10^{-2} = \frac{1}{10^2} = \frac{1}{100}$. We perform the operation inside the parenthesis first. Accordingly, we first take the square root of 100 and then perform the exponent operation. We then apply the rule that any non-zero number when raised to a negative exponent equals one divided by that number raised to the positive exponent.

Practice Problems

1. Compute $(\sqrt{64} + \sqrt{16})^2$.

2. Which of the following is <u>true</u>?

     I. $1^2 = 1$
    II. $2^2 = \sqrt{4}$
   III. $10^2 = \sqrt{10^2}$

  A. I only
  B. II only
  C. III only
  D. I, II, and III
  E. I and III

3. Solve for x when $x^2 = \sqrt{1}$.

4. In which of the following are the two numbers equivalent?

  A. $5^0 = 6^0$
  B. $1^5 = 5$
  C. $7^{-2} = 49$
  D. $\sqrt{49} = 7^2$
  E. $\sqrt{144} = 11$

5. Compute $(\sqrt{100} - \sqrt{81})^2$.

6. Which of the following is closest to the number 91?

  A. 7^2
  B. 16^1
  C. $\sqrt{1}$
  D. 3^{-2}
  E. $(\sqrt{121})^2$

7. Compute 7^2 .

8. Which of the following is <u>false</u>?

  I. $(-4)^2 = 4^{-2}$
  II. $5^1 = 1^5$
  III. $3^3 = 9$

  A. I only   B. II only   C. III only   D. I and II   E. I, II, and III

9. Compute $1^2 + 5^0 + \sqrt{16}$.

10. Sam hired 2 new employees every day for 4 days. What is the equivalent expression below that represents the number of employees he has hired?

    A. 8^0
    B. 8^{-2}
    C. 4^2
    D. 2^3
    E. 2^4

11. Compute $7^2 + 9^2 - 6^2$.

12. Which of the following is <u>false</u>?

    I. $6^2 + 3^2 = 81$
    II. $2^{-3} - 2^0 + 1 < 0$
    III. $\sqrt{25} = 5$

    A. I only
    B. II only
    C. III only
    D. I and II
    E. I and III

13. Compute $\sqrt{144} - \sqrt{16} + \sqrt{7^2}$.

14. In which of the following are the two numbers equivalent?

    A. $1^5 = 5$
    B. $8^2 = \frac{1}{64}$
    C. $\sqrt{11^2} = 121$
    D. $1^0 = 1^{-2}$
    E. $\frac{1}{4} = 4^{-2}$

15. Compute $\dfrac{3^0}{9^2}$.

Solutions to Practice Problems

1. **144.** $(\sqrt{64} + \sqrt{16})^2 = (8 + 4)^2 = (12)^2 = 144$. First perform the operations within the parenthesis and then perform the exponent operation outside the parenthesis.

2. **A.** I. True. $1^2 = 1$ and $\sqrt{1} = 1$. These are equivalent values. II. False. $2^2 = 4$ and $\sqrt{4} = 2$. These are not equivalent values. III. False. $10^2 = 100$ and $\sqrt{10^2} = 10$. These are not equivalent values.

3. **1 or -1**. Take the square roots of both sides. $\sqrt{x^2} = \sqrt{1}$. x can be 1 and x can be -1 because $1^2 = 1$ and $(-1)^2 = 1$.

4. **A.**

   A. $5^0 = 1$ and $6^0 = 1$. These are equivalent values. The applicable rule is that any non-zero number when raised to the power of zero equals 1.
   B. $1^5 = 1$ which is not equivalent to 5. 1 to any power is equal to 1.
   C. $7^{-2} = \frac{1}{7^2} = \frac{1}{49}$ which is not equivalent to 49. The applicable rule is that any non-zero number when raised to a negative exponent equals one divided by that number raised to the positive exponent.
   D. $\sqrt{49} = 7$ which is not equivalent to $7^2 = 49$.
   E. $\sqrt{144} = 12$ and not 11.

5. **1.** $(\sqrt{100} - \sqrt{81})^2 = (10 - 9)^2 = (1)^2 = 1$.

6. **E.**
   A. $7^2 = 49$.
   B. $16^1 = 16$.
   C. $\sqrt{1} = 1$.
   D. $3^{-2} = \frac{1}{3^2} = \frac{1}{9}$.
   E. $(\sqrt{121})^2 = 11^2 = 121$. 121 is the closest number to 91.

7. **49.** $7^2 = 49$.

8. **E.** I. False. $(-4)^2 = -4 \times -4 = 16 \neq 4^{-2} = \frac{1}{4^2} = \frac{1}{16}$. II. False. $5^1 = 5 \neq 1^5 = 1$. III. False. $3^3 = 3 \times 3 \times 3 = 27 \neq 9$.

9. **6.** $1^2 + 5^0 + \sqrt{16} = 1 + 1 + 4 = 6$.

10. **D.** Sam has hired 8 employees.

    A. $8^0 = 1$. Any non-zero number when raised to the power of zero equals 1.
    B. $8^{-2} = \frac{1}{8^2} = \frac{1}{64}$. Any non-zero number when raised to a negative exponent equals one divided by that number raised to the positive exponent.
    C. $4^2 = 16$.
    D. $2^3 = 2 \times 2 \times 2 = 8$.
    E. $2^4 = 16$.

11. **94.** $7^2 + 9^2 - 6^2 = 49 + 81 - 36 = 94$.

12. **D.** I. False. $6^2 + 3^2 = 36 + 9 = 45 \neq 81$.
    II. False. $2^{-3} - 2^0 + 1 = \frac{1}{2^3} - 1 + 1 = \frac{1}{8}$ which is greater than zero and not less than zero.
    III. True. $\sqrt{25} = 5$

13. **15.** $\sqrt{144} - \sqrt{16} + \sqrt{7^2} = 12 - 4 + 7 = 15$.

14. **D.**

    A. $1^5 = 1$ and $\neq 5$.
    B. $8^2 = 64$ and $\neq \frac{1}{64} = \frac{1}{8^2} = 8^{-2}$.
    C. $\sqrt{11^2} = 11$ and $\neq 121$.
    D. $1^0 = 1$ and $1^{-2} = \frac{1}{1^2} = \frac{1}{1} = 1$. This statement is equivalent. Any non-zero number when raised to the power of zero equals 1, and 1 when raised to any power equals 1.
    E. $\frac{1}{4} \neq 4^{-2} = \frac{1}{4^2} = \frac{1}{16}$.

15. $\frac{1}{81} \cdot \frac{3^0}{9^2} = \frac{1}{9^2} = \frac{1}{81}$. In computing the numerator, remember that any non-zero number when raised to the power of zero equals 1.

Chapter 7

Algebraic Manipulation

Algebraic Manipulation is the process of manipulating and solving equations for an unknown quantity. An equation is an algebraic sentence with an equals sign such as, $3x - 5 = 8$. It states that the value of both sides of the equals sign are the same. Algebra uses variables, usually letters such as x and y, to represent unknown quantities. When we solve equations, we find the value of the variable that makes the equation a true statement. For example, in the simple equation $2 + x = 5$, the value of the variable x must be 3, because $2 + 3 = 5$ is a true statement.

The most important thing to remember when solving equations is that you must always do the same operation with the same quantity (number or variable) to both sides of the equation. This way, the two sides of the equation remain equal. An equation is like a balance; if we subtract 5 ounces from one side, we must subtract 5 ounces from the other side for the two sides to remain equal.

Solving One-Step Equations Involving Addition and Subtraction

The first type of equation we will learn to solve is called a one-step equation because it only takes one step to solve it. One-step equations with a constant added to or subtracted from the variable are solved by adding or subtracting the constant term from both sides of the equation. We do the opposite operation so that the result will be zero.

Example 1 What is the value of x in the equation $x - 7 = 6$?

   A. 6
   B. -1
   C. 1
   D. 7
   E. 13

ANSWER: E. Since the constant term 7 is subtracted from x, we do the opposite and add 7 to each side of the = sign to get x all by itself on the left side, as follows:

$$x - 7 = 6$$
$$x - 7 + 7 = 6 + 7$$
$$x + 0 = 13$$
$$x = 13$$

Example 2 If $x + 11 = 15$, then what is the value of x?

   A. 26
   B. 4
   C. -4
   D. 15
   E. 11

ANSWER: B. Here the constant term is added to the variable, so we subtract 11 from both sides to get x all by itself on the left side of the equation:

$$x + 11 - 11 = 15 - 11$$
$$x + 0 = 4$$
$$x = 4$$

Solving One-Step Equations Involving Multiplication

The other type of one-step equation contains a constant multiplied by the variable such as $5x = 15$. The x term is already isolated on the left side of the equation. So all we need to do is to make the coefficient of the x term a 1. We can do this by dividing each side of the equation by the coefficient of x, because any number divided by itself equals 1. Note that x is the same as $1x$ and we usually don't write the 1. Here are some examples and their solutions.

Example 3   What is the value of x in the equation $-3x = 18$?

   A. 21
   B. 15
   C. 6
   D. -6
   E. 54

ANSWER: D. We solve this equation by dividing both sides of the equation by -3, so that the coefficient of x becomes 1.

$$\frac{-3x}{-3} = \frac{18}{-3}$$
$$1x = -6$$
$$x = -6$$

Example 4   Solve the following equation for a: $\dfrac{2a}{3} = 14$.

   A. 21
   B. 42
   C. 28
   D. 7
   E. 11

ANSWER: A. In this equation the coefficient of the variable is a fraction. We want the coefficient to be a 1. So we multiply both sides of the equation by the reciprocal of $\dfrac{2}{3}$, which is $\dfrac{3}{2}$, because any number multiplied by its reciprocal is 1.

$$\frac{3}{2} \cdot \frac{2a}{3} = 14 \cdot \frac{3}{2}$$
$$1a = 21$$
$$a = 21$$

Example 5   What is the value of the variable in the equation $\dfrac{z}{4} = -7$?

   A. -3   B. $-\dfrac{7}{4}$ C. -28   D. -11   E. 28

ANSWER: C. In this equation the variable is divided by 4. But remember that z is equivalent to $1z$. So $\frac{z}{4}$ is the same as $\frac{1z}{4}$. Therefore, the coefficient of z is the fraction $\frac{1}{4}$, and this equation can be solved by multiplying by the reciprocal of the coefficient, just like in example 2. Note that the reciprocal of $\frac{1}{4}$ is $\frac{4}{1}$, which is the same as 4.

$$\frac{4}{1} \cdot \frac{1z}{4} = -7 \cdot \frac{4}{1}$$
$$z = -28$$

Solving Two-Step Equations

Solving two-step equations is just a combination of solving the two types of one-step equations that we have solved so far. The process must always be done in a specific order. First, add or subtract any constant term that is on the same side of the equals sign as the variable term from both sides of the equals sign. This will isolate the variable term on one side of the equals sign (note that it does not matter which side). Next, make the coefficient of the variable term equal to 1 by dividing (if it is a whole number), or multiplying by the reciprocal (if it is a fraction). So, adding or subtracting always comes first, then multiplication or division second. And all operations are always performed on both sides of the equation so that the sides remain equal.

Example 6 What is the value of x in the equation $8x + 9 = 33$?

A. 13   B. 3   C. 5   D. 24   E. $\dfrac{33}{8}$

ANSWER: B. The first step in solving this equation is to subtract the constant term 9 from both sides of the equation. Then we divide by 8 to make the coefficient of the x term a 1.

$$8x + 9 - 9 = 33 - 9$$
$$\frac{8x}{8} = \frac{24}{8}$$
$$x = 3$$

Example 7 Solve the following equation for x: $14 - 2 = \dfrac{-3x}{8} + 17$.

A. $\dfrac{5}{3}$ B. -8   C. $-\dfrac{15}{8}$ D. -5   E. $\dfrac{40}{3}$

ANSWER: E. There are two constant terms on the left side of this equation. We need to combine these like terms $(14 - 2 = 12)$, before proceeding with the two steps for equation solving. First, subtract 17 from both sides to isolate the x term. Next, multiply by the reciprocal of $\frac{3}{8}$ to make the coefficient a 1. Notice that the variable is on the right side of this equation, but this does not change the solving process. We simply isolate the variable on the right side of the equation instead of the left.

$$12 = \frac{-3x}{8} + 17$$
$$12 - 17 = \frac{-3x}{8} + 17 - 17$$
$$-5 = \frac{-3x}{8}$$
$$\frac{-8}{3} \cdot -5 = \frac{-3x}{8} \cdot \frac{-8}{3}$$
$$x = \frac{40}{3}$$

Solving More Complex Equations

Sometimes the equations we need to solve are more complex, involving fractions with variable expressions in them such as $\frac{x+5}{6} = 22$, or expressions containing parentheses like $7(x+4) = 35$. The next two example problems will explain how to solve these types of equations.

Example 8 What is the value of x in the equation $\dfrac{x-7}{3} = -13$?

A. $\dfrac{13}{3}$ B. -18   C. 46   D. -32   E. -39

ANSWER: D. In this equation the variable x is contained within a fraction. To solve this type of equation we first need to eliminate the fraction. We do this by multiplying both sides of the equation by the denominator of the fraction. Then the equation is just a simple one-step problem that is solved by adding 7 to both sides.

$$3 \cdot \frac{x-7}{3} = -13 \cdot 3$$
$$x - 7 = -39$$
$$x - 7 + 7 = -39 + 7$$
$$x = -32$$

Example 9 Solve the following equation for x: $3(x - 5) = 6$.

A. $\dfrac{11}{3}$ B. 2 C. 7 D. -3 E. 13

ANSWER: C. In this equation the variable x is contained within parentheses. To solve this type of equation we divide both sides of the equation by 3. Then we add five to both sides of the equal sign, to obtain $x = 7$.

$$3(x - 5) = 6$$
$$x - 5 = 2$$
$$x = 7$$

Solving an Equation for One Variable in Terms of Another

Sometimes an equation contains more than one variable. For example, the formula for converting degrees farenheit to degrees Celsius contains two variables: $C = \frac{5}{9} \times (F - 32)$. This equation is solved for C in terms of F because C is all by itself on one side of the equation. "In terms of F" means that we can't solve this equation for a numerical value for C; instead, we have an expression with the variable F in it. Once we know the value of F, we can plug it into the equation and get a numerical value for C. An equation containing two variables can be solved for either one of the variables by the same process we use to solve an equation with one variable. The variable you are solving for is isolated on one side of the equation, and the other variable is manipulated just like a constant term. This is illustrated in the following example.

Example 10 If $12x - 3y = 18$, what is the value of y in terms of x?

A. $4x - 6$
B. $12x - 18$
C. $3x + 12$
D. -2
E. $10x$

ANSWER: A. This equation contains two variables, x and y. We are asked to solve the equation for y in terms of x. Therefore, we want to isolate the y term. Since $12x$ is on the same side of the equation as $3y$, we subtract $12x$ from both sides, just like we would if it was a constant term. Note that the effect of this is that we now have the opposite of $12x$, or $-12x$, on the other side of the equation. This is why this process is sometimes referred to as moving the x term to the other side of the equation. Next, we divide both sides of the equation by -3 to make the coefficient of the y term a 1. Notice that these are the same steps we used to solve single variable equations.

$$12x - 3y = 18$$
$$12x - 3y - 12x = 18 - 12x$$
$$\frac{-3y}{-3} = \frac{-12x + 18}{-3}$$
$$1y = \frac{-12x}{-3} + \frac{18}{-3}$$
$$y = 4x - 6$$

Solving Equations for a Specific Expression

Equations can also be solved for a specific algebraic expression such as $(x - 4)$ or $(3a + 12)$. Our goal is to isolate the expression we are solving for on one side of the equation. We use the exact same methods as we have been using to solve equations for a single variable. However, when we are solving for an expression, we might not want the variable coefficient to be a 1, like we always do when solving for just one variable. For example, if we are solving for the expression $6b - 5$, then we want the variable coefficient to be a 6, not a 1. We will need to divide by the appropriate value to get the coefficient we want, as illustrated in the following example.

Example 11   If $4(y + 3) = 6x - 8$, then what is the value of $2y - 3x$?

A. $\dfrac{5}{2}$ B. $\dfrac{-11}{2}$ C. 2   D. -10   E. 20

ANSWER: D. First, notice that this equation contains two variables, x and y. We are asked to solve the equation for the expression $2y - 3x$. Order of operations tells us to take care of parentheses first, so our first step is to distribute. Next, we need to get both the x and y terms on the same side of the equation, and all constant terms on the other side. Remember, we can move terms around by adding or subtracting them from both sides of the equation. Our last step is to divide both sides of the equation by 2 to get the desired coefficients for x and y. Notice that when we divide both sides of the equation by 2, that means we must divide each term on each side of the equation by 2.

$$4(y + 3) = 6x - 8$$
$$4y + 12 = 6x - 8$$
$$4y + 12 - 12 = 6x - 8 - 12$$
$$4y = 6x - 20$$
$$4y - 6x = 6x - 20 - 6x$$
$$4y - 6x = -20$$
$$\frac{4y - 6x}{2} = \frac{-20}{2}$$
$$\frac{4y}{2} - \frac{6x}{2} = -10$$
$$2y - 3x = -10$$

Manipulating Equations Using Number Properties

We can manipulate equations using number properties such as the *Commutative Property, the Associative Property, and the Distributive Property over Addition and Multiplication.*

The **Commutative Property of Addition** means that when we add two quantities, we will get the same answer no matter what order we add them in. For example, $a + b = b + a$. This property applies to multiplication as well, but not to subtraction or division.

The **Associative Property of Multiplication** states that we can change the grouping (parentheses), and not change the answer. For example, $(a \cdot b) \cdot c = a \cdot (b \cdot c)$. In other words, we can multiply a times b first, then multiply by c, or we can multiply b times c first, then multiply by a, and we will get the same answer either way. The Associative Property applies to addition as well, but not to subtraction or division.

The **Distributive Property of Multiplication over Addition** states that $a(b+c) = a \cdot b + a \cdot c$. The a is distributed through the parentheses and multiplies first times b and then times c. We can use these properties to manipulate equations and determine if two equations are equal as shown in the example below.

Example 12   If x, y, and z are positive integers, which of the following equations must be true?

A. $x \cdot y + z = x + y \cdot z$
B. $x(y + z) = x \cdot y + x \cdot z$
C. $x + y + z = x \cdot y - x \cdot z$
D. $z - y + x = y - z + x$
E. $(x - y) - z = x + (y - z)$

ANSWER: B. To solve this problem we need to determine which equation makes correct usage of number properties, so that both sides are equal.

A. False. This equation violates the order of operations.
B. True. This equation demonstrates correct use of the distributive property. The x is distributed through the parentheses, multiplying first times the y and then times the z.
C. False. There is no multiplication on the left side of this equation, so the distributive property has been incorrectly applied.
D. False. The order of the z and y terms have been reversed, but this is not valid because the commutative property does not apply to subtraction.
E. False. This is an attempt to apply the associative property, but the first subtraction sign was changed to addition. Also, the associative property does not apply to subtraction.

Practice Problems

1. What is the value of the variable in the equation $x + 8 = 15$?

    A. 23
    B. 7
    C. $\frac{15}{8}$
    D. -7
    E. 12

2. Solve the following equation for x: $-6x = 24$.

    A. 4
    B. 30
    C. 18
    D. -18
    E. -4

3. What is the value of x in the equation $\dfrac{-4x}{5} = 12$?

    A. 15
    B. -48
    C. 3
    D. -15
    E. -3

4. If $4x - 11 = -3$, what is the value of x?

    A. 8
    B. $\frac{-7}{2}$
    C. 2
    D. -8
    E. -12

5. What is the value of x in the equation $\dfrac{3x}{5} - 6 = 9$?

    A. 25
    B. 5
    C. 9
    D. -5
    E. 15

6. Solve the equation $4(9 - 5x) = 16$ for x.

    A. -20
    B. 4
    C. $\dfrac{-7}{5}$
    D. $\dfrac{13}{5}$
    E. 1

7. What is the value of x when $11x - 14 = 7x + 22$?

    A. 9
    B. -7
    C. -2
    D. 36
    E. 2

8. If $9(x - 3) = 18$, what is the value of x?

    A. 45
    B. -2
    C. -1
    D. 5
    E. 21

9. Solve the equation $-5(x - 6) = 10$ for x.

    A. -8
    B. 4
    C. $\frac{-16}{5}$
    D. 16
    E. -4

10. What is the value of x in the equation $\dfrac{x + 17}{5} = 6$?

    A. 13
    B. -11
    C. 43
    D. -6
    E. 7

11. What is the value of the variable in the following equation: $\dfrac{14}{x - 4} = 2$?

    A. 11
    B. $\frac{3}{7}$
    C. 8
    D. 24
    E. -6

12. If $8x - 15 = 3(y - 7)$, then what is the value of $8x - 3y$?

    A. 36
    B. -6
    C. 8
    D. 6
    E. 3

13. If $\dfrac{7}{x} + 6 = y$, what is the value if x in terms of y?

    A. $\dfrac{y + 6}{7}$ B. $7(y - 6)$ C. $7y - 6$ D. $\dfrac{7}{y - 6}$ E. $13y$

14. Solve the equation $8x - 2y + 7 = 21$ for y in terms of x.

    A. $8x - 13$
    B. $-4x + 14$
    C. $4x - 7$
    D. $8x + 7$
    E. $2x - 21$

15. What is the value of $2x + y$ in the equation $6x + 3(y + 4) = 27$?

    A. 15
    B. 9
    C. 5
    D. 14
    E. -9

Solutions to Practice Problems

1. **B.** This is a one-step equation involving addition because a constant term is added to the variable. We need to isolate x on the left side of the equation, so we subtract 8 from 8, giving us zero. And whatever we do to one side of the equation, we must do to the other side as well.

$$x + 8 = 15$$
$$x + 8 - 8 = 15 - 8$$
$$x = 7$$

2. **E.** This is a one step equation where the variable is multiplied by -6. We want the coefficient of x to be 1, so we divide both sides of the equation by -6.

$$\frac{-6x}{-6} = \frac{24}{-6}$$
$$1x = -4$$
$$x = -4$$

3. **D.** This is a one-step equation where the coefficient of the variable is a fraction. We want the coefficient of x to be 1, so we multiply both sides of the equation by the reciprocal.

$$\frac{-4x}{5} = 12$$
$$\frac{-5}{4} \cdot \frac{-4x}{5} = 12 \cdot \frac{-5}{4}$$
$$1x = -15$$
$$x = -15$$

4. **C.** This is a two-step equation. First we isolate the x by adding 11 to both sides. Then we divide by the coefficient of x to make it a 1.

$$4x - 11 = -3$$
$$4x - 11 + 11 = -3 + 11$$
$$\frac{4x}{4} = \frac{8}{4}$$
$$1x = 2$$
$$x = 2$$

5. **A.** This is a two-step equation with a fractional coefficient. First, we eliminate the constant term from the left side of the equation by adding 6 to each side. Next, we multiply by the reciprocal of $\frac{3}{5}$, which gives us a coefficient of 1.

$$\frac{3x}{5} - 6 = 9$$
$$\frac{3x}{5} - 6 + 6 = 9 + 6$$
$$\frac{3x}{5} = 15$$
$$\frac{5}{3} \times \frac{3x}{5} = 15 \times \frac{5}{3}$$
$$1x = 5 \cdot 5$$
$$x = 25$$

6. **E.** We divide both sides of the equation by 4, then subtract 9 from both sides, then divide by -5 to obtain $x = 1$.

$$4(9 - 5x) = 16$$
$$9 - 5x = 4$$
$$-5x = -5$$
$$x = 1$$

7. **A.** This equation contains variable terms and constant terms on both sides of the equation. So first we need to get all the x terms on one side, and all the constant terms on the other side. Then we can combine like terms on each side. The last step is to make the coefficient of the x term a 1 by dividing both sides by 4.

$$11x - 14 = 7x + 22$$
$$11x - 14 - 7x = 7x + 22 - 7x$$
$$4x - 14 = 22$$
$$4x - 14 + 14 = 22 + 14$$
$$\frac{4x}{4} = \frac{36}{4}$$
$$x = 9$$

8. **D.** We divide both sides of the equation by 9, then add 3 to both sides.

$$9(x - 3) = 18$$
$$x - 3 = 2$$
$$x = 5$$

9. **B.** We divide both sides of the equation by -5, then add 6 to both sides.

$$-5(x - 6) = 10$$
$$x - 6 = -2$$
$$x = 4$$

10. **A.** In this equation the variable is contained within the numerator of a fraction. First we clear the fraction by multiplying both sides by the denominator. This leaves us with a simple one-step equation that is solved by subtracting 17 from both sides.

$$\frac{x + 17}{5} = 6$$
$$\frac{x + 17}{5} \cdot 5 = 6 \cdot 5$$
$$x + 17 = 30$$
$$x + 17 - 17 = 30 - 17$$
$$x = 13$$

11. **A.** In this equation the variable is contained in the denominator of a fraction. The first thing we need to do is eliminate the fraction by multiplying both sides of the equation by the denominator, which is the quantity $(x - 4)$. Notice that this expression is enclosed in parentheses to ensure that we multiply by the entire expression, not just the x term. Next we distribute, then isolate the variable term, followed by dividing by the variable coefficient.

$$\frac{14}{(x - 4)} \cdot (x - 4) = 2 \cdot (x - 4)$$
$$14 = 2x - 8$$
$$14 + 8 = 2x - 8 + 8$$
$$\frac{22}{2} = \frac{2x}{2}$$
$$11 = x$$
$$x = 11$$

12. **B.** We are asked to solve the equation for a specific expression, so we need to isolate this expression on one side of the equation. We start by distributing through the parentheses. Then we move the y term over to the left side of the equation by subtracting $3y$ from both sides. Now we have the desired expression $8x - 3y$ on the left side of the equation, but there is also a constant term there. So we eliminate it from the left side by adding 15 (to both sides), and finish by combining like terms.

$$8x - 15 = 3(y - 7)$$
$$8x - 15 = 3y - 21$$
$$8x - 15 - 3y = 3y - 21 - 3y$$
$$8x - 3y - 15 = -21$$
$$8x - 3y - 15 + 15 = -21 + 15$$
$$8x - 3y = -6$$

13. **D.** This equation needs to be solved for one variable in terms of another. So we isolate the variable we are solving for (x), and treat the other variable (y) as we would a constant term. First we eliminate the constant term 6 from the left side of the equation by subtracting 6. Next we must get the variable x out of the denominator of the fraction by multiplying both sides by x. Now we divide both sides by the expression $y - 6$ in order to get x all by itself.

$$\frac{7}{x} + 6 = y$$
$$\frac{7}{x} + 6 - 6 = y - 6$$
$$\frac{7}{x} = y - 6$$
$$\frac{7}{x} \cdot x = (y - 6) \cdot x$$
$$\frac{7}{y - 6} = \frac{(y - 6)}{(y - 6)} \cdot x$$
$$\frac{7}{y - 6} = x$$

14. **C.** This equation needs to be solved for y in terms of x. So we need to isolate the y term on the left side of the equation. We move the other two terms to the right side by adding their opposite to both sides of the equation. The final step is to divide by -2 to make the coefficient of y a 1.

$$8x - 2y + 7 = 21$$
$$8x - 2y + 7 - 7 = 21 - 7$$
$$8x - 2y = 14$$
$$8x - 2y - 8x = 14 - 8x$$
$$\frac{-2y}{-2} = \frac{14 - 8x}{-2}$$
$$1y = -7 + 4x$$
$$y = 4x - 7$$

15. **C.** We need to solve this equation for the expression $2x + y$, so that is what we need to isolate. First, distribute through the parentheses. Then bring the constant term to the right side of the equation, leaving us with just the x and y terms on the left side. Last, divide both sides by 3 to get the coefficients to equal the ones in the expression we are solving for.

$$6x + 3(y + 4) = 27$$
$$6x + 3y + 12 = 27$$
$$6x + 3y + 12 - 12 = 27 - 12$$
$$6x + 3y = 15$$
$$\frac{6x + 3y}{3} = \frac{15}{3}$$
$$2x + y = 5$$

Chapter 8

Inequalities

Inequalities are comparisons between two quantities that are not definitely equal. Where an equation states that one quantity is equal to another, inequalities compare two quantities using one of five relationships: less than, greater than, less than or equal to, greater than or equal to, and finally, not equal to. On a number line, they can be represented as follows:

In this example, a number is less than 2 (the number could be 1.99, 0, -5, or any other number less than 2). The part of the number line in bold represents possible values of the number.

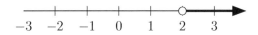

This example demonstrates a number is greater than 2. Note that an open circle means that number cannot be where the circle is. In both of the above examples, the open circle at 2 means the number in question cannot be 2.

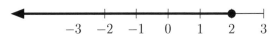

This example shows a number is less than or equal to 2. Note that a closed, filled-in circle means that number could be where the circle is. In this example and the one below, the closed circle at 2 means that it is possible for the number in question to be 2.

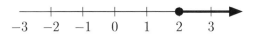

The line above shows a number is greater than or equal to 2.

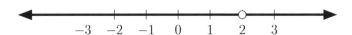

This example shows a number is not equal to 2. The open circle means that the number in question cannot be 2. That the number cannot be equal to 2 is the only fact given by this statement. It is possible for the number to be any other number either greater or less than 2 (see figure above).

The symbols used to represent less than, greater than, less than or equal to, greater than or equal to, and not equal to are as follows:

Symbol	Meaning	Example	Meaning of Example
$<$	Less than	$x < 2$	An unknown number x is less than 2
$>$	Greater than	$x > 2$	An unknown number x is greater than 2
$\leq$	Less than or equal to	$x \leq 2$	An unknown number x is less than or equal to 2
$\geq$	Greater than or equal to	$x \geq 2$	An unknown number x is greater than or equal to 2
$\neq$	Not equal to	$x \neq 2$	An unknown number x is not equal to 2

Just as the quantities on either side of an equation can be switched, the quantities on either side of an inequality can also be switched. It is important to note however, that for $<$, $>$, $\leq$, and $\geq$, the direction of the comparison symbol must be switched as well. For example, we could state the inequality 1 is less than 2, or

$$1 < 2$$

If we merely switch the quantities, and not the symbol, the new statement is incorrect:

$$2 < 1$$

But if we switch both the numbers and the comparison symbol from $<$ to $>$, we maintain the meaning of the original inequality:

$$2 > 1$$

or 2 is greater than 1, which is equivalent to stating that 1 is less than 2. Think of $<$ or $>$ as a "pacman" It is always eating the smaller number.

For inequalities involving the not equal to sign, $\neq$, the quantities on either side may be switched without having to change the not equal to sign, $\neq$.

Example 1   Which of the following best expresses the following statement: "A number is greater than or equal to 15?"

   A. $x < 15$
   B. $x = 15$
   C. $x > 15$
   D. $x \geq 15$
   E. $x \leq 15$

ANSWER: D. The $\geq$ symbol stands for "greater than or equal to."

Example 2   Which of the following best expresses the following inequality: $x + 1 < 5$?

   A. A number x is greater than 5 plus 1.
   B. A number x plus 1 is less than 5.
   C. 5 is greater than 1.
   D. 1 is greater than 5 plus a number.
   E. A number x is less than 5 plus 1.

ANSWER: B. The $<$ symbol stands for "less than."

AND vs. OR

Inequalities can be combined using "and" or "or." For our purposes, we do not need to consider inequalities using the $\neq$ sign.

In our first example, we will consider the "or" case:

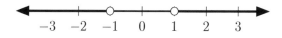

This number line represents an unknown number being either less than -1 OR greater than 1. This can also be written as two inequalities:

$$x < -1 \quad \text{or} \quad x > 1$$

Note that inequalities related by "or" (as above) are not combined into a single statement, as x cannot be simultaneously two different values. In the next example, the unknown number is greater than 1 AND less than 5.

This can also be written using two inequalities in either of two ways:

$$x > 1 \ \text{and} \ x < 5 \qquad\qquad 1 < x < 5$$

Note that the second way of writing these inequalities only works because it is possible for x to satisfy both inequalities at the same time: x can be both greater than 1 and less than 5. If we had started with the inequalities:

$$x < 1 \quad \text{and} \quad x > 5$$

...we cannot combine them, as it is impossible for x to be simultaneously less than 1 and greater than 5. If x is less than 1, then it cannot be greater than 5; likewise, if x is greater than 5, it is not possible for it to be less than 1.

Also note that if our inequalities are:

$$x > 1 \quad \text{and} \quad 2x < 5$$

...we must first isolate x in the inequality on the right by dividing both sides by 2. Since $\frac{5}{2}$ equals 2.5, dividing both sides by 2 yields $x < 2.5$. We can then combine the inequalities as:

$$1 < x < 2.5$$

Since it is possible for x to be greater than 1 and less than 2.5 at the same time, the inequality can be correctly written this way.

Example 3 Which of the following is equivalent to the pair of inequalities, $x > 0$ and $x < 7$?

    A. $x > 0$ or $x < 7$
    B. $x > 7$
    C. $0 < x < 7$
    D. $0 < x$ or $x < 7$
    E. None of the above

ANSWER: C. The first inequality, $x > 0$, can be rewritten as $0 < x$. Thus we can combine with $x < 7$ to make $0 < x < 7$.

Solving Inequalities

Solving inequalities is accomplished in almost exactly the same way as equations. Like equations, inequalities contain a quantity on the left, a comparison symbol (= for equations, $<, >, \leq, \geq$ for inequalities), and a quantity on the right. Using inverse operations, the variable can be isolated for either equations or inequalities.

Example 4 What is the solution to $x + 5 = 3$? To solve this equation, we subtract 5 from both sides of the = sign:

$$x + 5 - 5 = 3 - 5$$
$$x + 0 = -2$$
$$x = -2$$

The solution is $x = -2$. An inequality can be solved in the same manner:

Example 5 Find the solution to the inequality $x + 5 > 3$.

$$x + 5 - 5 > 3 - 5$$
$$x + 0 > -2$$
$$x > -2$$

The solution is $x > -2$.

If the comparison symbol is $\neq$, or not equal to, the same rules apply:

Example 6   Find the solution to the equation $x + 5 \neq 3$.

$$
\begin{array}{r}
x + 5 \neq 3 \\
-5 \quad -5 \\
\hline
x + 0 \neq -2
\end{array}
$$

The solution is $x \neq -2$.

In the case of two inequalities combined with "and," there are two ways of writing the inequalities, and we will explain how to solve both. When both inequalities are written separately, solve both inequalities separately. For example:

$$x + 3 < 6 \quad \text{and} \quad x + 3 > 1$$

We subtract 3 from both sides of the inequality:

$$
\begin{array}{cc}
x + 3 < 6 \quad \text{and} & x + 3 > 1 \\
-3 \quad -3 & -3 \quad -3 \\
\hline
x + 0 < 3 \quad \text{and} & x + 0 > -2
\end{array}
$$

This yields $x < 3$ and $x > -2$, which is the solution. This can be rewritten as $-2 < x < 3$.

If we were to begin with the inequalities:

$$x + 3 < 6 \quad \text{and} \quad x + 3 > 1$$

It could be rewritten as:

$$1 < x + 3 < 6$$

For this type of inequality, all operations must be carried out on all quantities. In other words, any operation must be carried out on the 1, the $x + 3$, and the 6. In order to isolate x, we will subtract 3 from each:

$$
\begin{array}{r}
1 < x + 3 < 6 \\
-3 \quad -3 \quad -3 \\
\hline
-2 < x + 0 < 3
\end{array}
$$

The solution is $-2 < x < 3$, will be is the same result obtained from solving the original inequalities separately.

Example 7 Solve the following inequality for x: $x + 7 < 12$

    A. $x < 5$
    B. $x > 5$
    C. $x = 5$
    D. $x < 19$
    E. $x > 19$

ANSWER: A. Subtract 7 from both sides to isolate x.

Example 8 Solve the following inequality for x: $x + 3 < 1$ or $x - 5 > 10$

    A. $x < -2$ and $x > 15$
    B. $x < 1$ and $x > 5$
    C. $x = -2$ or $x = 15$
    D. $x < 2$ or $x > 15$
    E. $x < -2$ or $x > 15$

ANSWER: E. For each inequality, isolate x. In the first part of the inequality, subtract 3 from both sides to get $x < -2$. In the second part to the problem, add 5 to both sides to get $x > 15$.

Example 9 Solve the following inequality: $x + 2 \neq 11$

    A. $x < 9$
    B. $x \leq 9$
    C. $x = 13$
    D. $x \neq 9$
    E. $x > 13$

ANSWER: D. Subtract 2 from both sides to get $x \neq 9$. The comparison symbol $\neq$ does not change.

Example 10 Solve the following inequality: $x - 5 \neq 1$

    A. $x < 6$ B. $x \leq 6$ C. $x = 6$ D. $x \neq 6$ E. $x > 6$

ANSWER: D. Add 5 to both sides to get $x \neq 6$. The comparison symbol $\neq$ does not change.

Example 11   Solve the following inequality for x: $3x > 12$

   A. $x = 3$
   B. $x > 4$
   C. $x = 4$
   D. $x < 4$
   E. $x > 12$

ANSWER: B. Divide both sides by 3 to get $x > 4$.

Example 12   Solve the following inequality for x: $x + 4 \leq 2$

   A. $x \leq -2$
   B. $x \leq 6$
   C. $x = -2$
   D. $x < -2$
   E. $x \geq 6$

ANSWER: A. Subtract 4 from both sides to get $x \leq -2$.

Multiplying or Dividing by -1 Flips the Symbol

One important concept to know is that multiplying or dividing both sides by any negative number flips the symbol: "less than" must be changed to "greater than," and vice versa; "less than or equal to" must changed to "greater than or equal to," and vice versa. For example, to solve the following inequality:

$$-x < 1$$

This inequality is equivalent to $x > -1$. Note that the $-x$ became x, the 1 became -1, and the comparison symbol $<$ became $>$. Why?

We must multiply both sides by -1 in order to isolate x, and when we do we must flip the comparison symbol. One way to think of this is to imagine the comparison symbol being negated:

Step (1) $-x$ $<$ 1 Multiply both sides by -1, and negate the $<$ sign

Step (2) $-1 \cdot -x$ (-<) $1 \cdot -1$ The comparison symbol will be flipped

Step (3) x >-1

We can check this result by choosing a number for x and seeing whether it holds true for both the original inequality (step 1) above, and the solved inequality (step 3) above. In step (3), we can choose any number larger than -1; for the sake of simplicity we can choose 0 for x. Substituting 0 for x gives us $0 > -1$ in step (3), which is true; when substituting 0 for x in the original step (1), yields $0 < 1$, which is also true.

If we did not change the sign when multiplying by -1, we would instead have arrived at the solution $x < -1$. Substituting 0 for x, which held true for the original inequality, would yield $0 < -1$ for inequality (3), which is incorrect.

Example 13 Solve the following inequality for x: $-x + 3 \leq 4$

A. $x < -1$
B. $x \leq -1$
C. $x = -1$
D. $x \geq -1$
E. $x > -1$

ANSWER: D. We can subtract 3 from both sides first to get $-x \leq 1$, and then multiply by -1, flipping the comparison symbol, to get $x \geq -1$.

Alternatively, we can either multiply both sides by -1 as the first step or the last step. If we multiply -1 as the first step, this will yield $x - 3 \geq -4$. Note the flipping of the comparison symbol from $\leq$ to $\geq$. We then add 3 to both sides to get $x \geq -1$.

Practice Problems

1. In words, how might one express the inequality: $n \neq 10$?

   A. n might be 10
   B. 10 is equal to n
   C. n is equal to 10
   D. n does not equal 10
   E. None of the above

2. If $a < b$, which of the following statements must be true?

   A. b is greater than a
   B. a is greater than b
   C. a is equal to b
   D. a could be equal to b
   E. b is smaller than a

3. Solve the following inequality for x: $x + 3 < 10$

   A. $x \leq 13$
   B. $x < 7$
   C. $x < 13$
   D. $x \geq 3$
   E. $x = 9$

4. Solve the following inequality for t: $6t \leq -36$

   A. $t = 6$
   B. $t = -6$
   C. $t < 6$
   D. $t \geq 6$
   E. $t \leq -6$

5. If $y \geq 2$, which of the following could y equal?

  A. -2
  B. 1
  C. 0
  D. 1
  E. 2

6. Solve the following inequality for m: $-2m < -10$

  A. $m < 5$
  B. $m > 5$
  C. $m > -5$
  D. $m < -5$
  E. $m = 5$

7. In the inequality $4x \neq 12$, which of the following values COULD NOT be equal to x?

  A. -5
  B. 0
  C. 3
  D. 4
  E. 8

8. Due to poor penmanship, a reporter cannot tell whether the number written is 1 or 7. If the reporter knows that the number > 4, which number must it be?

  A. 1
  B. 7

9. Solve the following inequality for x: $2x < x - 9$

  A. $x < 3$
  B. $x < 4.5$
  C. $x < 9$
  D. $x < -9$
  E. None of the above

10. Which of the following could be equal to x if $x > 3$ and $x < 9$?

    A. -2
    B. 3
    C. 7
    D. 9
    E. 15

11. If $x < 1$ or $x > 10$, which of the following answer choices contain values that ALL could be equal to x?

    A. $-10, -4, -2, 0, 2$
    B. $0, 4, 12, 18, 19$
    C. $2, 5, 8, 9$
    D. $-5, 0, 1, 12, 19, 25$
    E. $-10, -5, 0, 11, 15, 19$

12. If $x > 3$ and $x < 13$, which of the following numbers could equal x?

    A. -3
    B. 0
    C. 1
    D. 3
    E. 4

13. Which of the following MUST be true if $x < 9$ or $x > 9$?

    A. $x \geq 9$
    B. $x \leq 9$
    C. $x = 9$
    D. $x \neq 9$
    E. $x < 9$ and $x > 9$

14. Solve the following inequality for x: $x + 5 \leq 15$?

    A. $x < 10$
    B. $x \leq 10$
    C. $x \geq 10$
    D. $x < 15$
    E. $x \leq 15$

15. If $p \geq 10$, then p could be:

    A. -2
    B. 10
    C. -8
    D. 4
    E. -1

Solutions to Practice Problems

1. **D.** The inequality $n \neq 10$ can be written as n does not equal 10.

2. **A.** If $a < b$, then b must be greater than a.

3. **B.** Subtract 3 from both sides to get $x < 7$

4. **E.** Divide both sides by 6 to get $t \leq -6$. Note that we are not dividing by a negative number, so the comparison symbol $\leq$ does not have to change.

5. **E.** Because y is greater than or equal to 2, it could be equal 2 or anything greater than 2.

6. **B.** Divide both sides by -2. Because we are dividing by a negative number, the comparison symbol must be flipped from $<$ to $>$, so we will get $m > 5$.

7. **C.** Dividing both sides by 4 yields $x \neq 3$, so x could not be 3.

8. **B.** If the number > 4, it is greater than 4 so it cannot be 1. The only other choice is 7.

9. **D.** Subtract x from both sides, to get $2x - 1x < x - 1x - 9$ or $x < -9$

10. **C.** If $x > 3$ and $x < 9$, x must be between 3 and 9 and cannot be either 3 or 9.

11. **E.** If $x < 1$ or $x > 10$, x must either be less than 1 or greater than 10. Thus the numbers $-10, -5, 0$ (less than 1), $11, 15, 19$ (greater than 10) are ALL possible values of x.

12. **E.** If $x > 3$ and $x < 13$, x must be between 3 and 13, not including either 3 or 13.

13. **D.** If $x < 9$ or $x > 9$, then x can be any number less than 9 or greater than 9; in other words, x can be any number but 9. So the only statement that must be true is $x \neq 9$.

14. **B.** Subtract 5 from both sides and maintain the original comparison symbol to get:

$$x + 5 \leq 15$$
$$x \leq 10$$

15. **B.** If $p \geq 10$, then p must be either equal to 10 or greater than 10. It cannot be less than 10.

Section IV: Word Problems

Chapter 9

Proportions

A ratio, or rate, is a comparison of two things. A proportion sets two ratios equal to each other. We see ratios and proportions everyday all around us. Three dollars per gallon, $4.50 per pound, $30 per hour, and 10 cents per minute are all expressions involving ratios and proportions. When we use one of these known rates to find a specific unknown amount, we are using a proportion. For example, if a cell phone rate is 10 cents per minute, how much will I be charged for a 5 minute call? The answer, just by multiplying it, is 50 cents. This can be written in mathematical form as $\frac{10}{1} = \frac{x}{5}$. The terms on each side of the equal sign are ratios, or rates, and the entire mathematical equation is a proportion. On each side of the equal sign are ratios, or rates, and the entire mathematical equation is a proportion. To solve it, we cross multiply: $1 \times x = 5 \times 10$, and finally $x = 50$ cents. Every ratio, rate, and proportion word problem involves substituting the given values into some stage of an operation similar to the one above.

Rates

Ratios represent the comparison of one quantity to another. Ratios are expressed as c:d, where c is one quantity and d is another.

Example 1 Jason traveled between Los Angeles and San Francisco by car. The distance between those cities is 396 miles. The gas gauge in Jason's car was on full when he started. He filled his tank twice during the trip. Once he arrived, it was empty again. His car's tank holds 11 gallons of gas. How many miles per gallon did the car average on the trip?

   A. 12
   B. 14
   C. 15
   D. 22
   E. 26

ANSWER: A. Jason traveled 396 miles (given). He used up three gas tanks. Since the gas tank holds 11 gallons, Jason used $11 \times 3 = 33$ gallons. So he got 396 miles per 33 gallons. We write the ratio as: $\frac{396 \text{ miles}}{33 \text{ gallons}} = 12$. He got 12 miles per gallon. To solve using a proportion, we write: $\frac{396 \text{ mi}}{33 \text{ gallons}} = \frac{x \text{ miles}}{1 \text{ gallon}}$. Then we cross multiply to obtain $33x = 396 \times 1$, so $x = \frac{396 \times 1}{33} = 12$.

Example 2 Jonathan bought three bags of apples, each weighing 4 pounds. The price of apples is \$1.50 per pound. He paid the cashier \$20 for the apples. How much change should he receive?

   A. \$0
   B. \$1
   C. \$2
   D. \$2.5
   E. \$3.49

ANSWER: C. Three bags weighing 4 pounds each total 12 pounds. Since the price of apples is \$1.50/ pound, we set up the proportion:

$$\frac{1.5 \text{ dollars}}{1 \text{ lb}} = \frac{x \text{ dollars}}{12 \text{ lbs}}$$
$$12 \times 1.5 = 1 \times x$$
$$x = 18$$

We can read this equation as "If one has to pay \$1.50 for one pound, how many dollars will one have to pay for 12 pounds?" So if he paid \$20, and it costed him 18 dollars, he should get \$2 back.

Proportions

A proportion is an equation in which two ratios are compared. To solve a proportion, cross multiply.

Example 3 Boneless chicken breasts at Fresh Foods are \$3.69 per pound. How much will Peter be charged for a 3 pound package?

   A. \$10.84
   B. \$10.92
   C. \$11.02
   D. \$11.07
   E. \$11.34

ANSWER D. We set up the proportion:

$$\frac{\$3.69}{1 \text{ lb}} = \frac{\$x}{3 \text{ lbs}}$$
$$x = 3 \times \frac{3.69}{1}$$
$$x = \$11.07$$

You can read this statement as "if 1 pound costs \$3.69, how much will 3 pounds cost?" In other words, the ratio of the price to 1 pound of chicken breasts, is the same as the ratio of the price to 3 pounds of chicken breasts.

Example 4   Janet made a downpayment of \$73,000 on a house. If the house cost five times the downpayment amount, how much does the house cost?

   A. \$112,000
   B. \$198,000
   C. \$262,000
   D. \$365,000
   E. \$505,000

ANSWER: D. We solve by setting up the equation:

$$\frac{x}{\$73,000} = \frac{5}{1}$$
$$x = \$73,000 \times 5$$
$$x = \$365,000$$

Above we see that the total price of the house, x, divided by the downpayment amount equals five. The "1" in the denominator equals one downpayment.

Example 5   Solve for x:

$$\frac{4}{5} = \frac{x}{25}$$

   A. 18
   B. 20
   C. 30
   D. 36
   E. 42

ANSWER: B. We multiply each side of the equation by 25 to obtain: $25 \times \frac{4}{5} = x$. So $x = 5 \times 4 = 20$.

Example 6 Solve for x: $\dfrac{16}{x} = \dfrac{32}{50}$

    A. 15
    B. 20
    C. 25
    D. 30
    E. 35

ANSWER: C. We cross multiply to obtain:

$$
\begin{aligned}
16 \times 50 &= x \times 32 \\
\frac{16 \times 50}{32} &= x \\
x &= \frac{50}{2} \\
x &= 25
\end{aligned}
$$

Example 7 On a map of Florida, a scale is used in which 3 inches equals 45 miles. If the distance on the map between Orlando and Miami is 20 inches, what is the actual distance between the two cities in miles?

    A. 300   B. 310   C. 320   D. 330   E. 340

ANSWER: A. We set up the proportion:

$$
\begin{aligned}
\frac{45 \text{ mi}}{3 \text{ in}} &= \frac{x \text{ mi}}{20 \text{ in}} \\
20 \times \frac{45}{3} &= x \\
x &= 20 \times 15 \\
x &= 300 \text{ mi}
\end{aligned}
$$

An alternative is to write:

$\frac{3 \text{ in}}{20 \text{ in}} = \frac{45 \text{ mi}}{x \text{ mi}}$ This proportion can be read as "the ratio between 3 inches on the map and 20 inches on the map is the same ratio as 45 actual miles to x actual miles." We cross multiply:

$$3x = 20 \times 45$$
$$x = \frac{20 \times 45}{3}$$
$$= 20 \times \frac{45}{3}$$
$$= 20 \times 15$$
$$= 300$$

Example 8 What divided by 2500 is the same as 3 times one half?

   A. 750   B. 1000   C. 2150   D. 3500   E. 3750

ANSWER: E. We set up the equation:

$$\frac{x}{2500} = 3 \times \frac{1}{2}$$
$$\frac{x}{2500} = \frac{3}{2}$$
$$2x = 2500 \times 3$$
$$x = \frac{3 \times 2500}{2}$$
$$= 3 \times 1250$$
$$= 3750$$

Ratios

A ratio between two quantities represents the comparison of one quantity to the other.

Example 9 There are 30 balloons in a bag. Twelve are red, 8 are blue, and the rest are green. What is the ratio of green balloons to red balloons?

   A. 1:4   B. 1:3   C. 1:2   D. 2:3   E. 5:6

ANSWER: E. If $12 + 8 = 20$ balloons are not green and there are a total of 30 balloons, then there are $30 - 20 = 10$ green balloons. The ratio of green balloons to red balloons is 10:12, which simplified is 5:6.

Example 10 In Washington, DC it snows an average of 18 days per year and it rains an average of 108 days per year. What is the ratio of snowy days to rainy days?

    A. 1:6
    B. 1:7
    C. 2:9
    D. 2:13
    E. 3:14

ANSWER: A. The ratio is 18 snowy:108 rainy, which simplified is 1:6.

Practice Problems

1. Solve for x: $\dfrac{39}{x} = \dfrac{13}{14}$

   A. 48
   B. 50
   C. 42
   D. 54
   E. 62

2. What is the value of $\dfrac{x}{y}$ if $\dfrac{x}{210} = \dfrac{y}{14}$?

   A. 15
   B. 20
   C. 25
   D. 30
   E. 35

3. 27 divided by 810 is the same as two thirds of what number?

   A. $\dfrac{3}{100}$
   B. $\dfrac{3}{50}$
   C. $\dfrac{2}{25}$
   D. $\dfrac{1}{20}$
   E. $\dfrac{1}{15}$

4. A map of Switzerland is 6 inches long. If the scale of the map is 2 inches to 75 actual miles, how long is Switzerland in miles?

   A. 225
   B. 275
   C. 300
   D. 330
   E. 375

5. Broccoli is on sale for $1.69/lb. Martha paid $8.45 for broccoli. How many pounds did she purchase?

   A. 3.5
   B. 4.25
   C. 4.75
   D. 5
   E. 5.5

6. The exchange rate is one dollar for 0.69 Euros. How many dollars can Joseph get for 69 Euros?

   A. 50
   B. 60
   C. 75
   D. 92
   E. 100

7. A recipe calls for half a teaspoon of vanilla for every 7 eggs. Maria used 70 eggs. How many teaspoons of vanilla must she use?

   A. 3
   B. 4
   C. 4.5
   D. 5
   E. 5.5

8. If Alex read a third of a book on Monday and one fifth of the book on Tuesday, what is the ratio of the part of the book he read to the part he did not read?

   A. 2:3
   B. 3:4
   C. 4:5
   D. 8:7
   E. 9:6

9. Jessica put a $50,000 downpayment on a house valued at $400,000. What is the ratio of the downpayment to the amount she still owes on her house?

   A. 1:10   B. 1:9   C. 1:8   D. 1:7   E. 1:6

10. Jenny originally bought her car for $42,000. Four years later, she sold it to a used car salesman for $14,000. What is the ratio of the amount she sold it for to the amount that it depreciated?

    A. 1:2
    B. 2:3
    C. 3:4
    D. 4:5
    E. 5:6

11. Tim has a large credit card debt. He pays a third of the outstanding balance. What is the ratio of the amount he still owes to the amount he paid off?

    A. 1:1
    B. 2:1
    C. 3:1
    D. 4:1
    E. 5:1

12. The Washington Pinkskins lost the first three of five games in the beginning of the season. At that rate, how many more games will they have to play in order to win 90 games?

    A. 145
    B. 150
    C. 155
    D. 220
    E. 225

13. At the University of Southwestern Akron only 1 in 8 applicants were accepted for admission in 2010. At that rate, how many applicants will be accepted if 6,480 applied?

    A. 810
    B. 840
    C. 860
    D. 880
    E. 910

14. In an international screenplay competition, 3,686 screenplays were entered. There were first, second, and third place awards in each of six genres and one grand prize winner. What is the ratio of winners to non-winners?

    A. 1:92
    B. 1:102
    C. 1:141
    D. 1:182
    E. 1:193

15. In a hat there are 18 red and blue balloons. If the ratio of blue balloons to red balloons is 5, how many red balloons are there?

    A. 2
    B. 3
    C. 5
    D. 12
    E. 15

Solutions to Practice Problems

1. **C.** We have $\frac{39}{x} = \frac{13}{14}$. Cross multiply to solve:

$$
\begin{aligned}
x \times 13 &= 39 \times 14 \\
x &= \frac{39 \times 14}{13} \\
&= \frac{39}{13} \times 14 \\
&= 3 \times 14 \\
&= 42
\end{aligned}
$$

2. **A.** Cross multiply to solve:

$$
\begin{aligned}
14 \times x &= 210 \times y \\
\frac{14 \times x}{y} &= 210 \\
\frac{x}{y} &= \frac{210}{14} \\
&= 15
\end{aligned}
$$

3. **D.** We have $\frac{27}{810} = \frac{2}{3} \times x$. Multiplying both sides of the equation by the reciprocal of $\frac{2}{3}$, which is $\frac{3}{2}$, we then have:

$$
\begin{aligned}
\frac{3}{2} \times \frac{27}{810} &= \frac{2}{3}x \times \frac{3}{2} \\
x &= \frac{81}{2 \times 810} \\
&= \frac{1}{2 \times 10} \\
&= \frac{1}{20}
\end{aligned}
$$

4. **A.** We are comparing 6 inches to two inches, and therefore, the length of Switzerland to 75 miles. So we have $\frac{6 \text{ in}}{2 \text{ in}} = \frac{x \text{ mi}}{75 \text{ mi}}$. So $3 = \frac{x}{75}$. So $x = 3 \times 75 = 225$ miles.

5. **D.** We have $\frac{\$1.69}{1\ lb} = \frac{\$8.45}{x\ lb}$. So $1.69 \times x = 8.45 \times 1 \times x = \frac{8.45}{1.69} = 5$.

135

6. **E.** We have $\frac{.69 \text{ Euros}}{1 \text{ dollar}} = \frac{69}{x \text{ dollars}}$. So $.69 Euros \times x = 69 \times 1$. $x = \frac{69}{.69} = 100$. In order to calculate this last step, notice that 69 is .69 with the decimal moved to the right two spaces, which indicates that 69 is exactly 100 times .69.

7. **D.** We have $\frac{70}{7} = \frac{x}{\frac{1}{2}}$. $7x = 70 \times \frac{1}{2}$. $x = \frac{70}{7} \times \frac{1}{2} = 10 \times \frac{1}{2} = 5$. She would use 5 teaspoons.

8. **D.** We have $\frac{1}{3} + \frac{1}{5} = \frac{5+3}{15} = \frac{8}{15}$. Therefore he didn't read $\frac{7}{15}$. The ratio therefore is 8:7.

9. **D.** The amount still owed on the house is $\$400,000 - \$50,000 = \$350,000$. The ratio of paid to unpaid amount is $\frac{50,000}{350,000} = \frac{1}{7}$ The ratio therefore is 1:7.

10. **A.** The amount that the car depreciated is $\$42,000 - \$14,000 = \$28,000$. So we have the ratio of the amount sold to depreciated as $\frac{14,000}{28,000} = \frac{1}{2}$. The ratio is therefore 1:2.

11. **B.** If he paid off a third of his credit card debt, he still owes two thirds. The ratio he owes to the paid off amount is: $\frac{\frac{2}{3}}{\frac{1}{3}} = \frac{2}{3} \times \frac{3}{1} = 2$. The ratio therefore is 2:1. We can see here that we don't need to know how much money he owes to find the ratio.

12. **D.** If the Pinkskins lost 3 in 5 games, that means they won 2 in 5 games. We have $90 = \frac{2}{5} \times x$, where x is the total number of games played. To understand this equation, notice that the equation states that 90 games won is two fifths of the total number of games played. What is x? That is the total number of games. So we multiply both sides of the equation by $\frac{5}{2}$ to obtain $90 \times \frac{5}{2} = \frac{2}{5} \times x \times \frac{5}{2}$. $x = 90 \times \frac{5}{2} = 225$. They already played 5 games, so they have 220 more games to go.

13. **A.** We have the ratio $\frac{1}{8} = \frac{x}{6480}$. $\frac{1}{8} \times 6480 = 810$.

14. **E.** We have a total of $3 \times 6 + 1 = 19$ winners. If 3686 screenplays were entered and there were 19 winners, that means that there are $3686 - 19 = 3667$ non-winners. The ratio of winners to non-winners is $\frac{19}{3667} = \frac{1}{193}$. How do we get 193? Divide 19 into 3,667 to obtain 193, then put the 193 in the denominator.

15. **B.** We label Blue, B, and Red, R. So we have B=5×R, and $B + R = 18$. In the first equation, we plug 5R into the second equation to obtain: $5R + R = 18$, so $6R = 18$, so $R = 3$.

Chapter 10

Percent

The Latin word "cent" means 100. So "percent" means "per hundred," or "divided by 100." Percentages are represented by the symbol %, and can easily be translated into fractions or decimals by dividing by 100. For example, 50% translates to $\frac{50}{100}$, which reduces to $\frac{1}{2}$. Likewise, you can make a percent from a decimal by multiplying by 100 and adding the percent sign. For example, 0.2 translates to 0.2 x 100%=20%.

Rule 1: To make a percent, you multiply by 100 and add the percent sign.

Rule 2: To drop a percent, you divide by 100 and drop the percent sign.

To illustrate:

Example 1: Convert 0.4 to percent.

ANSWER: We calculate this from Rule 1: $0.4 \times 100\% = 40\%$

Example 2: Convert 35% to a fraction.

ANSWER: By Rule 2, we drop a percent by dividing by 100%: $\frac{35\%}{100\%} = \frac{35}{100} = \frac{7}{20}$. Here, we see that the percent sign disappeared.

To understand percent intuitively, let us consider a family of four sharing a pizza with 8 slices. The four members each eat one slice – the family finished exactly half of the total pizza. What percent of the pizza did they finish? We know that one-half is the same as 50% (recall the expression, "fifty-fifty", which literally means "half-half"). But how did we get from "one half" to "50%?" We apply Rule 1: $\frac{1}{2} \times 100\% = 50\%$. If the family were to collectively finish two more slices, only two would remain – which is one-quarter of the pizza, or 25% of the pizza. We get from "one-quarter"

137

to "25%" as follows: $\frac{1}{4} \times 100\% = 25\%$.

Let's try going backwards, to find the fraction equivalent of a percent. If George eats 30% of a sandwich, what fraction of the sandwich does he eat? Using Rule 2, we calculate: $\frac{30\%}{100\%} = \frac{3}{10}$. In decimal form, we have $\frac{3}{10} = 0.3$.

The following table provides some percents and their fraction and decimal equivalents. The below fractions and percents are some of the most common, and we recommend they be memorized to save time while taking the test.

Fraction	Decimal	Percent
$\frac{0}{2}=\frac{0}{3}=\frac{0}{4}=\frac{0}{5}\ldots$	0	0%
$\frac{1}{10}$	0.1	10%
$\frac{1}{8}$	0.125	12.5%
$\frac{1}{5}=\frac{2}{10}$	0.2	20%
$\frac{1}{4}=\frac{2}{8}$	0.25	25%
$\frac{3}{10}$	0.3	30%
$\frac{1}{3}$	0.333...	33.3%
$\frac{3}{8}$	0.375	37.5%
$\frac{2}{5}=\frac{4}{10}$	0.4	40%
$\frac{1}{2}=\frac{2}{4}=\frac{4}{8}=\frac{5}{10}$	0.5	50%

Fraction	Decimal	Percent
$\frac{3}{5}=\frac{6}{10}$	0.6	60%
$\frac{5}{8}$	0.625	62.5%
$\frac{2}{3}$	0.666...	66.7%
$\frac{7}{10}$	0.7	70%
$\frac{3}{4}=\frac{6}{8}$	0.75	75%
$\frac{4}{5}=\frac{8}{10}$	0.8	80%
$\frac{7}{8}$	0.875	87.5%
$\frac{9}{10}$	0.9	90%
$\frac{2}{2}=\frac{3}{3}=\frac{4}{4}=\frac{5}{5}\ldots$	1.0	100%
$\frac{2}{1}=\frac{4}{2}=\frac{6}{3}=\frac{8}{4}\ldots$	2.0	200%

Example 3   What is 15% of 340?

A. 4   B. 45   C. 49   D. 51   E. 765

ANSWER: D. Translate the percent into a fraction to solve the problem. Also, keep in mind that "of" means "times". 15% of 340 translates to $\frac{15}{100} \times 340$. The result is 51.

The PRAXIS exam does not allow the use of calculators. Some problems, like **Example 3** above, will require some arithmetic. The solution to **Example 3** is found by reducing the fraction in stages:

$$\begin{aligned}
\frac{15}{100} \times 340 &= \frac{15 \times 340}{100} \\
&= \frac{15 \times 34}{10} \\
&= \frac{3 \times 34}{2} \\
&= 3 \times 17 \\
&= 51
\end{aligned}$$

Fractions, ratios, and proportions can be converted into percentages by determining the decimal equivalent. This can require a bit of work – the fraction may need to be divided out.

$$\begin{aligned}
\frac{2}{5} &= 0.4 = 40\% \\
\frac{21}{60} &= \frac{7}{20} = 0.35 = 35\% \\
\frac{8}{13} &\approx 0.6154 \approx 62\%
\end{aligned}$$

Example 4 If in a group of 84 people, 36 are men, approximately what percentage of the group are men?

    A. 30%
    B. 43%
    C. 48%
    D. 54%
    E. 57%

ANSWER: B. There are 36 men out of a total of 84 people. This is represented by the fraction: $\frac{36}{84}$. Without a calculator, the fraction can first be reduced and then divided out to determine the decimal equivalent. $\frac{36}{84} = \frac{3}{7} \approx 0.4286$, which is closest to 43%.

Practice translating between fractions and percentages below by filling in the empty cells in the following table.

Fraction	Percent
$\frac{3}{4}$	75%
	80%
$\frac{12}{25}$	
	42%
$\frac{1}{3}$	

Fraction	Percent
$\frac{15}{5}$	
	165%
$\frac{27}{73}$	
	0.4%
$\frac{6}{900}$	

ANSWERS: $80\% = \frac{80}{100} = \frac{8}{10} = \frac{4}{5}$; $\frac{12}{25} = \frac{48}{100} = 48\%$; $42\% = \frac{21}{50}$; $\frac{1}{3} = 33.333\ldots\%$; $\frac{15}{5} = 3 = 300\%$; $165\% = \frac{165}{100} = \frac{33}{20}$; $\frac{27}{73} = 36.986\ldots\%$; $0.4\% = \frac{1}{250}$; $\frac{6}{900} = 0.666\ldots\%$.

In the calculations above .4% is converted to $\frac{1}{250}$. How do we know this? We have $\frac{\frac{4}{10}}{100} = \frac{4}{1000}$. Dividing both the denominator and numerator by 4 we obtain $\frac{1}{250}$.

Similarly, to convert $\frac{6}{900}$ to a percent we have, $\frac{6}{900} \times 100 = \frac{6}{9} = \frac{2}{3} = .666\%$.

Understanding percentages is necessary to obtaining a good score on the PRAXIS math exam. A few questions, like the first two in this chapter, will focus solely on calculating percentages. But percentages will be incorporated into several other question types as well. Take the following, for example:

Grade	Number of Students
A	14
B	13
C	8
D	5
F	2

Example 5 The table above represents the grades received by a class of students on a test. Approximately what percentage of the students did not receive an A on the test?

   A. 33%   B. 50%   C. 67%   D. 83%   E. 95%

ANSWER: C. From the table, we can calculate the total number of students in the class, and how many students did not receive an A. The class has a total of $14 + 13 + 8 + 5 + 2 = 42$ students.

Of these, $13+8+5+2 = 28$ students did not receive an A. $\frac{28}{42} = \frac{2}{3} \approx 0.6667$ which is closest to C, 67%.

There are only a few limited ways in which a percentage word problem may be phrased. Almost all percentage problems can be reduced to one of the questions below. If we understand how to translate these problems into math, we can solve practically any percent problem in the PRAXIS. Use the table below to help you translate the English word into symbolic form.

English Word	Symbolic Form
is	= sign
of	×
What	x variable

Example 6 What is 40% of 60?

Translation: What (x) is (=) 40% (which converts to .40) of (×) 60:

$$x = .40 \times 60$$
$$= 24$$

Example 7 What percent of 60 is 40? **Translation:** What percent (x) of (×) 60 is = 40?

$$x \times 60 = 40$$
$$x = \frac{40}{60}$$
$$= \frac{4}{6}$$
$$= \frac{2}{3}$$
$$= 66.6\%$$

Percent Change

Percent change is the difference between the new value and the original value, divided by the original value. The result of this operation is a fraction, which is converted to a percent by multiplying by 100%.

$$\text{Percent Change} = \frac{\text{New Value} - \text{Original Value}}{\text{Original Value}} \times 100\%$$

A negative value indicates a *Percent Decrease* and a positive value a *Percent Increase*.

Example 8 A store owner changes the price of a product from \$25 to \$29. Which of the following represents the percent increase in the cost?

    A. 14%
    B. 16%
    C. 20%
    D. 25%
    E. 86%

ANSWER: B. The original price is \$25. The new price is \$29. The difference is \$4. The percent increase, therefore, is $\frac{29-25}{25} = \frac{4}{25} = 0.16$, which converts to 16%.

Example 9 32 inches is removed from a length of rope. If the rope is now 96 inches long, what was the percent decrease in the length of the rope?

    A. 25%
    B. 28%
    C. 30%
    D. 33%
    E. 36%

ANSWER: A. The original length of the rope must be calculated from the information. If the rope is 96 inches long after 32 inches were removed, then the original length of the rope is $96 + 32 = 128$. The percent decrease is the fraction of the difference over the original amount. $\frac{32}{128} = \frac{1}{4} = 0.25$, which translates to a 25% decrease.

Practice Problems

1. Which of the following is equal to 25% of 736?

   A. 29
   B. 175
   C. 184
   D. 368
   E. 2,944

2. 63 is approximately what percent of 81?

   A. 56%
   B. 63%
   C. 70%
   D. 78%
   E. 97%

3. The price of a toy is increased by 20%. The resulting price is later decreased by $40. If the original price of the toy is $60, what is the final price of the toy?

   A. $8
   B. $16
   C. $24
   D. $32
   E. $40

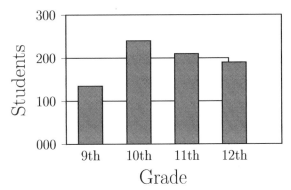

4. The chart above shows the distribution of students across each grade for a given high school. Approximately what percent of the students are not in 12th grade?

   A. 18%   B. 26%   C. 30%   D. 75%   E. 82%

5. A number is decreased by 50%, and the result is increased by 50% to yield 99. What is the original number?

    A. 25
    B. 50
    C. 74
    D. 99
    E. 132

6. $40\% \times \frac{1}{4} =$

    A. 10

    B. 4

    C. 1

    D. $\dfrac{1}{2}$

    E. $\dfrac{1}{10}$

7. The area of square A is 40 ft^2. The area of square B is 250% of the area of square A. What is the length of one *side* of square B?

    A. 2 ft
    B. 5 ft
    C. 10 ft
    D. 12 ft
    E. 20 ft

Color	Percent
Red	35%
Blue	22%
White	16%
Black	15%
Green	12%

8. 1,100 dresses at a store come in 5 colors, as shown by the distribution in the table above. How many dresses in the store are white?

   A. 160
   B. 176
   C. 220
   D. 242
   E. 924

9. Which of the following values is greatest?

   A. 15% of 480
   B. 20% of 480
   C. 30% of 320
   D. 35% of 320
   E. 40% of 120

10. If $T \div 3 = R$, then $60\% \times R =$

   A. $T \div 5$
   B. $T \div 2$
   C. $T \times \frac{6}{5}$
   D. $T \times 20$
   E. $T \times 180$

11. Ninety percent of X is 198. What is X?

   A. 178.2
   B. 217.8
   C. 220
   D. 222
   E. 376.2

12. A glass container contains 22 blue marbles and 18 green marbles. If 5 marbles are removed from the container, what is the percentage decrease in the total number of marbles?

    A. 29.4%
    B. 27.8%
    C. 22.7%
    D. 14.3%
    E. 12.5%

13. 90 is what percent of 150?

    A. 16.7%
    B. 40%
    C. 60%
    D. 66.6%
    E. 90%

Group	Men	Women	Total
A	8	5	13
B	7	5	12
C	9	6	15
D	7	7	14
Total	31	23	54

14. A medical study is conducted with 54 people. The individuals are assigned to 4 different groups as shown in the table above. Approximately what percent of Group B are women?

    A. 9.3%
    B. 21.7%
    C. 38.5%
    D. 41.7%
    E. 58.3%

15. What is 37.5% of the fraction $\frac{4}{9}$?

    A. $\frac{4}{3}$ B. $\frac{5}{9}$ C. $\frac{2}{9}$ D. $\frac{1}{6}$ E. $\frac{1}{7}$

Solutions to Practice Problems

1. **C.** 25% of 736 can be written as $\frac{25}{100} \times 736$ which is equal to $\frac{1}{4} \times 736 = 184$.

2. **D.** The problem is asking for the percent equivalent of the fraction $\frac{63}{81}$. First, reduce the fraction to $\frac{7}{9}$. Divide through to obtain the decimal equivalent: 0.777. Finally, multiply by 100% to get 77.777%. The closest answer is 78%, D.

3. **D.** The initial price is $60. 20% of $60 is $\frac{20}{100} \times 60 = \frac{60}{5} = \$12$. Therefore the price of the toy is $60 + 12 = 72$ dollars after the increase. If we subtract $40 from this price, we get $72 - 40 = 32$ dollars.

4. **D.** Solving this problem requires reading a chart. The number of students in each grade must be estimated from reading the chart so that a total may be calculated to derive the percentage of students not in the 12th grade. The number of students in the 9th grade looks close to 140. The 10th grade population looks close to 230. The average of the 11th and 12th grades appear to have about 200 students. The total number of students is about $140 + 230 + 200 + 200 = 770$, and those that are not in 12th grade is about $140 + 230 + 210 = 580$. The percentage is

$$\frac{580}{770} = \frac{58}{77} \approx 75\%$$

5. **E.** A number is decreased by 50% and then increased by 50%. If x is the original number, this can be expressed mathematically by $(50\% \times x) \times 150\% = 99$. Using the decimal equivalents, $0.5 \times x \times 1.5 = 0.75 \times x = 99$. So, $x = \frac{99}{0.75} = \frac{99 \times 4}{3} = 132$.

6. **E.** To solve this problem, just convert the percentage into a fraction and multiply through:

$$40\% \times \frac{1}{4} = \frac{40}{100} \times \frac{1}{4} = \frac{40}{400} = \frac{4}{40} = \frac{1}{10}$$

7. **C.** The area of square B is 250% that of square A. So, the area of square B is $\frac{250}{100} \times 40 = 100$ ft^2. The length of one side of a square is equal to the square root of the area. $\sqrt{100} = 10$, so the length of each side of square B is 10 ft.

8. **B.** According to the table, 16% of the dresses are white. There are a total of 1,100 dresses in the store. Therefore, the number of white dresses is $16\% \times 1,100 = \frac{16}{100} \times 1,100 = \frac{16 \times 1100}{100} = 16 \times 11 = 176$.

9. **D.** Just from looking at the answer choices, before doing any calculation, we should be able to eliminate A. (15% of 480) because it is obviously less than B. (20% of 480). Similarly, we can eliminate C. (30% of 320) because it is obviously less than D. (35% of 320). We calculate each of the remaining answer choices:

B. $\frac{20}{100} \times 480 = \frac{480}{5} = 96$;

D. $\frac{35}{100} \times 320 = \frac{7 \cdot 320}{20} = 7 \times 16 = 112$;

E. $\frac{40}{100} \times 120 = \frac{2 \cdot 120}{5} = 48$.

The largest value is D: 112.

10. **A.** We are trying to find 60% of R. The value 60% is equal to $\frac{60}{100} = \frac{3}{5}$. We can substitute R in the equation $\frac{3}{5} \times R$ with $R = \frac{T}{3}$. This gives $\frac{3}{5} \times \frac{T}{3} = \frac{T}{5}$.

11. **C.** The percent can be first translated into a fraction in the problem $\frac{90}{100}X = 198$. From this, we can see that $X = 198 \times \frac{100}{90} = 198 \times \frac{10}{9} = \frac{1,980}{9} = 220$.

12. **E.** Percentage change is given by the difference divided by the original total. The original total is $18 + 22 = 40$ marbles. The decrease is 5 marbles. The percentage change is then

$$\frac{5}{40} = \frac{1}{8}$$
$$= 12.5\%$$

13. **C.** The percentage is found by just dividing

$$\frac{90}{150} = \frac{9}{15}$$
$$= \frac{3}{5}$$
$$= 60\%$$

14. **D.** The table provides more information than is necessary to solve this problem. The total number of people in Group B (12) and the number of women in Group B (5) are the only two numbers needed from the table. The percent of women in Group B can be calculated from these two numbers: $5/12 = 41.666\ldots\% \approx 41.7\%$.

15. **D.** 37.5% is equivalent to the fraction $\frac{3}{8}$. Multiply through to find the answer:

$$\frac{3}{8} \times \frac{4}{9} = \frac{3 \times 4}{8 \times 9} = \frac{1 \times 1}{2 \times 3} = \frac{1}{6}$$

Chapter 11

Miscellaneous Word Problems

Word problems in the math Praxis I exam ask you to figure out the underlying mathematics behind a few lines of text and to find the solution. The key to solving them is to translate the problems into mathematics. A bit of creativity is necessary to solve problems that take multiple steps. While this book doesn't teach you how to be creative, it does provide some strategies to solve many of the word problems that you will encounter on the Praxis exam. To solve word problems, several steps are needed:

1. Read the problem very carefully.

2. Determine what data you know.

3. Determine what you need to solve for.

4. Determine what steps you need to take.

5. Implement your plan.

The most common type of word problem will ask you to translate the problem into algebraic equations and then manipulate these equations until you find a solution. Often this involves solving two equations with two variables simultaneously. Once you are ready to implement your plan, the first step is to choose English letters to represent the variables in question.

Example 1 At Ricardo's Tacos, four tacos and two orders of chips cost the same as two tacos and four orders of chips. If Ricardo's Tacos charges $2.00 for a single order of chips, how much does Ricardo's charge for one taco?

A. $1.00   B. $1.50   C. $2.00   D. $2.50   E. $3.00

ANSWER C. In order to solve this problem you must first write an equation representing the relationship between tacos and chips described in the above problem. If we let T stand for tacos, and C stand for chips, we obtain the following equation:

$$4T + 2C = 2T + 4C$$

Subtracting $2T$ and subtracting $2C$ from both sides of the equal sign we obtain:

$$2T = 2C$$
$$T = C$$

Therefore the price of tacos and chips are equal. Since chips cost $2, then tacos must also cost $2.

Example 2 Marie is b years old. April is 10 years younger than Marie. Claudia is three quarters as old as April. Which of the following represents the age of Claudia?

A. $10b - \dfrac{3}{4}$

B. $\dfrac{3}{4}b - \dfrac{15}{2}$

C. $\dfrac{4}{3}b + 10$

D. $2b + 9$

E. $10 + \dfrac{3}{4}$

ANSWER: B. If Marie is b years old, April is $b - 10$ years old. Claudia is three quarters of $b - 10$. So we have: Claudia's age $= \frac{3}{4} \times (b - 10)$. Distributing the three quarters, we obtain: $\frac{3}{4}b - \frac{3}{4}(10) = \frac{3}{4}b - \frac{15}{2}$.

Example 3 A duty free book store owner accepts only twenty dollar bills and one dollar bills. He sells large books for $10 and small books for 3 for $2. If Ralph wishes to purchase two large books and nine small books from this bookstore, how many bills does Ralph need to use in order to pay the owner the exact cost of the books?

ANSWER: 7 or 26. We label a large book as L and a small book as S. Therefore $L = 10$ and $S = \frac{2}{3}$. (3 for \$2 means that with \$2 you can buy 3 book, or each book cost $\frac{\$2}{3}$). Now we have $2L + 9S$ books that Ralph wants to purchase. Substituting 10 into L and $\frac{2}{3}$ into S, we obtain for the cost, C:

$$C = 2 \times 10 + 9 \times \frac{2}{3}$$
$$= 20 + 6$$
$$= 26$$

Therefore he needs a \$20 bill and 6 \$1 bills or 26 \$1 bills.

Some word problems involve proportions. See the proportion chapter for more information. We are including one proportion problem in this chapter for review purposes.

Example 4   The Empire State building in New York City is two hundred forty miles from Harvard Square in Boston. On a map of the East Coast, the scale used is 1 cm: 30 miles. How many centimeters apart are the two sites on the map in centimeters?

A. $\frac{1}{240}$ cm
B. 8 cm
C. 20 cm
D. 40 cm
E. 240 cm

ANSWER: B. We set up the following proportion: $\frac{1\text{cm}}{30\text{ miles}} = \frac{x\text{ cm}}{240\text{ miles}}$. We want to find the value of x. Multiplying both sides of the equal sign by 240 we obtain: $x = \frac{240}{30} = 8$. To understand this proportion, the equation asks, "If one centimeter equals 30 miles, how many centimeters on the map are there in 240 miles?"

Some word problems involve adding rates together, as in the below case:

Example 5   It takes Michael 3 hours to clean his house. It takes Dorothy 4 hours to clean that same house. If both Michael and Dorothy work together, how long will it take them to clean the house in hours and minutes, rounded to the nearest minute?

A. 1:43   B. 1:52   C. 2:00   D. 5:23   E. 7:00

ANSWER: A. In one hour, Michael can clean one third of the house. In one hour, Dorothy can clean one fourth of the house. Together, in one hour, they can clean $\frac{1}{3} + \frac{1}{4}$ of the house. Adding the two fractions, we obtain $\frac{7}{12}$ of the house. But we want $\frac{12}{12}$ of the house, since that fraction equals one (one house), or the entire house. If x represents the total time in hours it takes to clean the whole house, we can say that in x hours, we can clean 1 house. In one hour, we can clean $\frac{7}{12}$ of the house. We want to find x. So we set up the proportion:

$$\frac{x}{1} = \frac{\frac{12}{12}}{\frac{7}{12}}$$
$$\frac{x}{1} = \frac{1}{\frac{7}{12}}$$
$$x = \frac{12}{7}$$
$$x = 1.71 \text{ hours}$$

If you look back at the fractions chapter, when dividing a fraction by a fraction, we multiply by the inverse of the denominator. If you do not recall this, go back to the chapter on fractions.

So the time it takes to clean the house, x, is 1.71 hours. To convert to minutes, we obtain $1.71 \times 60 = 102.6$ minutes, or 1 hour and 43 minutes.

Since this is a timed test, remember that the trick is to take the sum of the hourly rates of the workers, to arrive at a fraction (In this case $\frac{7}{12}$), and then invert the fraction (in this case $\frac{12}{7}$).

Some word problems on the Praxis exam are meant to test logical reasoning, rather than purely math related skills, as in the cases below:

Example 6   At Tillman High School, a senior class has 102 students. 30 of them take French, 62 take Spanish, and 14 take both. How many students take neither?

   A. 4
   B. 8
   C. 18
   D. 24
   E. 36

ANSWER: D. If there are a total of 30 students who take French and 14 who take both French and Spanish, then there are $30 - 14 = 16$ students who take French only. Similarly, if 62 students take Spanish, and 14 take both, then $62 - 14 = 48$ students take Spanish only. Together, we have $16 + 14 + 48 = 78$ students who take French, Spanish, or both. Since there are 102 students total, then $102 - 78 = 24$ students don't take either subject.

Example 7 Three facts: Some bloopers are zoomies. No zoomies are ploopmats, but some bloopers are ploopmats. Based on those facts, all of the following must also be true, <u>Except</u>:

    A. No zoomies can be both bloopers and ploopmats.
    B. All ploopmats must be bloopers.
    C. No bloopers can be both zoomies and ploopmats.
    D. There are no ploopmats that are zoomies.
    E. Some ploopmats are bloopers.

ANSWER B. Draw a Venn Diagram. (See below) The intersection of zoomies and bloopers are zoomies that are also bloopers. The intersection of bloopers and ploopmats, are bloopers that are also ploopmats. There is no intersection of ploopmats and zoomies because we are told that no zoomies are ploopmats.

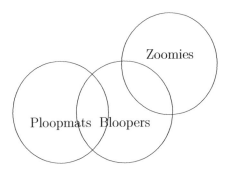

Let's examine each of the five choices. Choice A is a true statement, according to the diagram. Similarly choices C, D, and E, are all true statements. Choice B is false because only some of Ploopmats are Bloopers, not all.

Some word problems involve examining numbers and their properties, as in the case below:

Example 8 Which of the following numbers disproves the statement: For every integer, adding its reciprocal to itself is greater than the integer?

    A. -2
    B. 0
    C. $\frac{1}{2}$
    D. 2
    E. All of the above

ANSWER: A. We are asked to <u>disprove</u> the statement. Any positive number added to its reciprocal is greater than the original number. For example, as in choice D, $\frac{1}{2}$ is the reciprocal of 2. Adding the two numbers, $2 + \frac{1}{2} = 2\frac{1}{2}$, we see that the sum is greater than the original number. The reciprocal of zero, $\frac{1}{0}$ is undefined. The reciprocal of $\frac{1}{2}$ is 2, and so we obtain $\frac{1}{2} + 2 = 2\frac{1}{2}$ again. The reciprocal of a negative number such as in choice A, -2, is also negative: $-2 + -\frac{1}{2} = -2\frac{1}{2} < -2$. So the new number is smaller than the original number.

Some word problems require calculations that involve percent, as in the problem below:

Example 9 Sarah invests $1000 every year in a mutual fund yielding a 6% return. Her husband, Jim, invests $1000 every year in a fund that pays 8% interest. How much money does the couple profit in mutual funds in two years if the money compounds?

A. $280.00   B. $290.00   C. $394.45   D. $430.00   E. $512.77

ANSWER: D. After one year, Sarah has $1060. Since the problem states that the money compounds, a year later, she has an additional 6% of $1060 (Not of $1000!), or $63.6. She also makes $60 in interest on the money she invests in year 2. For the two years, she earned $60 + $63.6 + $60= $183.6 in interest. Jim made $80 in the first year, and an additional 8% of $1080 or $86.40 + $80 on money deposited in year 2. For the two years, he earned $80 + $86.4 +$80 = $246.4. In sum, they made $183.6 + $246.4 = $430.00.

In some word problems, several statements are given as facts, and the problem asks for determining the answer to a question assuming those facts.

Example 10 David is given the following data:

I. Gloria watches television an average of 3 hours per day during a 7 day period.
II. There are 10 commercials per every 3 hour period of television.
III. There are a total of 560 commercials in a week.

Which of the above items does David need to consider in order to calculate the number of commercials Gloria watches during the week in question?

A. I only
B. II only
C. III only
D. I and II only
E. I, II, and III

ANSWER: D. If Gloria watches an average of 3 hours per day during a 7 day period, she watches 21 hours of television. Since she watches 10 commercials per every 3 hour period, she watches $7 \times 10 = 70$ commercials. We don't need to know that there are a total of 560 commercials because we calculated the answer based on the first 2 facts only.

Practice Problems

1. Twenty two trains pass a station, one every twenty minutes. The first train passes at 5:00 AM. At what time does the last train pass the station?

   A. 9:40 AM
   B. 10:20 AM
   C. 11:00 AM
   D. 12:00 PM
   E. 12:20 PM

2. Rita reads a book once a week in 2010, starting January 1st. Mark reads three books every week in 2010 starting January 2nd. In a year of 365 days, what is the minimum combined number of books Rita and Mark read?

   A. 196
   B. 208
   C. 235
   D. 258
   E. 269

3. Every Tuesday in February, Ralph plays tennis by himself. Every Monday his wife plays tennis together with him. How many days does Ralph play tennis in the month of February, if February has 28 days?

   A. 7
   B. 8
   C. 9
   D. Either 8 or 9
   E. Either 9 or 10

4. Two consecutive integers have a sum of 95. What are the integers?

   A. 45 and 46
   B. 44 and 45
   C. 47 and 48
   D. 48 and 49
   E. 49 and 50

5. When added, four consecutive integers have a sum of 30. What are the integers?

    A. 3, 4, 5, and 6
    B. 4, 5, 6, and 7
    C. 5, 6, 7, and 8
    D. 6, 7, 8, and 9
    E. 7, 8, 9, and 10

6. The Rhinos won three times as many games as they have lost. If they played a total of 16 games, how many games did the Rhinos lose?

    A. 2
    B. 3
    C. 4
    D. 5
    E. 6

7. A real estate agency charges \$35 for a home inspection. If the customer purchases a "new home buyers kit," then he receives a \$10 discount on the home inspection. If x equals the cost of the "new home buyers kit," which of the following equations represents the total cost to the customer?

    A. $(x + \$10 + \$35)$
    B. $(x - \$10 - \$35)$
    C. $(\$10 + \$35) - x$
    D. $(\$35 + \$10) + x$
    E. $(x + \$35) - \$10$

8. The total ticket sales for a hockey game are \$3,750 for 2,000 tickets sold. Adults paid \$2.50 for admission and students paid \$1.25. How many adult tickets were sold?

    A. 500
    B. 750
    C. 1,000
    D. 1,100
    E. 1,200

9. Lyla is looking at the snowboards in the window of High Plains Sport store. The Middle Mountain snowboard costs $400 more than the Little Mountain snowboard, but $200 less than the Big Mountain snowboard. The three snowboards together costs $1,900. How much does the Middle Mountain snowboard cost?

   A. $400
   B. $500
   C. $600
   D. $700
   E. $800

10. In a book club, 80 members like fiction, 60 members like non-fiction and 50 like both categories. How many members are there in the book club?

    A. 90
    B. 100
    C. 110
    D. 140
    E. 190

11. At a conference, 60 people wore blue hats, red coats, or both. 48 wore blue hats and 24 wore red coats. How many people wore BOTH blue hats and red coats?

    A. None
    B. 12
    C. 18
    D. 20
    E. There is an error in the data provided

12. Dr. Strathman is writing a prescription for a patient on a prescription pad. If each prescription pad holds seventy five prescription pages, and he is writing his seven hundredth prescription, what number prescription pad is he filling?

    A. 7th
    B. 8th
    C. 9th
    D. 10th
    E. 11th

13. Stuart reads d books for a year. It takes him an average of 17 hours to read a book. Which of the following choices represents the average number of books Stuart reads in a week?

    A. $\dfrac{c}{d}$

    B. $\dfrac{c}{52d}$

    C. $\dfrac{d}{52}$

    D. $\dfrac{52d}{c}$

    E. $\dfrac{c}{2d}$

14. Three facts: All Doopers are Gloopers. All Zoopers are Gloopers. Some Doopers are Zoopers. Based on those facts, which of the following is/are true?

    A. There are Zoopers that are both Doopers and Gloopers.
    B. Doopers that are Zoopers aren't Gloopers.
    C. There are no Doopers that are both Zoopers and Gloopers.
    D. No Glooper is both a Dooper and a Zooper.
    E. Zoopers that are not Doopers are also not Gloopers.

Solutions to Practice Problems

1. **D.** If a train passes the station every twenty minutes, then 3 trains pass per hour. If the first train passes at 5 AM, the next at 5:20 AM, etc, then the 4th train passes at 6 AM. We have 22-4 = 18 trains left to pass, and 18 divided by 3 (3 per hour) is six. Therefore, the 22nd train passes six hours after the 6:00 AM train, which is at 12:00 noon.

2. **B.** A year contains exactly 52 weeks plus one day (because 365 divided by 7 is 52 with a remainder of 1). If Rita starts a book on the 1st of the year, she will read at least 52 books. She may read 53 books on December 31st, but the question asks for the minimum number of books. Mark starts reading on January 2nd. He will have exactly 364 days left, and so he will have read for exactly 52 weeks. In 52 weeks, he read exactly $3 \times 52 = 156$ books. Adding the figures, we obtain $52 + 156 = 208$ books.

3. **B.** If the 1st of the month is a Monday, there are 4 Mondays (1st, 8th, 15th, 22nd) and 4 Tuesdays (2nd, 9th, 16th, 23rd). In this case he plays 8 days in the month of February. If the first day of the month is a Tuesday, there are 4 Mondays (7th, 14th, 21th, 28th) and 4 Tuesdays (1st, 8th, 15th, 22nd). If the first day of the month is after Tuesday, there are only 4 Mondays and 4 Tuesdays, and therefore, Ralph plays on only 8 days.

4. **C.** Let x be the first integer. Then $x + 1$ is the next integer in question. Adding the two we have: $x + (x + 1) = 2x + 1 = 95$. Therefore $x = 47$, and $x + 1 = 48$.

5. **D.** Similar to the above problem, we let the first integer be x. Then the next 3 integers are: $x+1$, $x+2$, and $x+3$. Adding the four, we obtain: $x+(x+1)+(x+2)+(x+3) = 4x+6 = 30$ Therefore, $x = 6$. The numbers then are 6, 7, 8, and 9.

6. **C.** If we let W to be the number of games the Rhinos won, and L to be the number they have lost, we can write 2 equations with 2 unknowns:

$$W = 3L$$
$$W + L = 16$$

If we take $3L$ and plug it into W in the 2nd equation we obtain:

$$3L + L = 16$$
$$4L = 16$$
$$L = 4$$

They lost 4 games.

7. **E.** The total cost without the discount would normally be $x + 35$. But since the customer receives a discount of \$10, his total cost would be $(x + 35) - 10$.

8. **C.** We let A stand for the number of adult tickets and S be the number of student tickets sold. We know, then, that $A + S$ represents the total number of tickets sold, which we are told is 2000. If an adult ticket sells for \$2.50, then $2.5A$ is the total price paid by all adults, and similarly $1.25S$ is the total price paid by students, and so $2.5A + 1.25S$ is the total price paid by both adults and students. Therefore, we write two equations and solve for them simultaneously:

$$2.5A + 1.25S = 3750$$
$$A + S = 2000$$

We use the second equation and subtract S from both sides, to obtain: $A = 2000 - S$. We then plug $2000 - S$ into A in the first equation to obtain:

$$2.5(2000 - S) + 1.25S = 3750$$
$$5000 - 2.5S + 1.25S = 3750$$
$$-1.25S = -1250$$
$$S = 1000$$

Since $A + S = 2000$, then $A = 2000 - S = 2000 - 1000 = 1000$.

9. **D.** We let M be the middle size, L be the little size, and B be the big size snowboard. We then write 3 equations with three unknowns:

$$M = L + 400$$
$$M = B - 200$$
$$M + L + B = 1900$$

Since M is common to both equations, we can equate the first two equations, and that yields:

$$L + 400 = B - 200$$
$$L + 400 + 200 = B$$
$$B = L + 600$$

Plugging $L + 400$ into M and $L + 600$ into B in the third equation, we obtain:

$$(L + 400) + L + (L + 600) = 1900$$
$$3L + 1000 = 1900$$
$$3L = 900$$
$$L = 300$$

Since $M = L + 400$, $M = 700$.

10. **A.** If 80 people like fiction, and 50 people like both categories, then 80-50 = 30 people like only fiction. If 60 members like non-fiction and 50 like both categories, then 60-50 = 10 people liked only non fiction. Adding them, we have 30 members who like only fiction + 50 members who like both fiction and non-fiction + 10 members who like nonfiction only = 90 members in the book club.

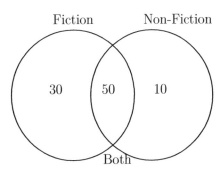

11. **B.** Let's represent the number of people who wore both blue hats and red coats as x. Then $48 - x$ people wore blue hats but not red coats, and $24 - x$ people wore red coats but no blue hats. Then $(48 - x) + x + (24 - x) = 60$. Combining like terms, we have $72 - x = 60$. Therefore $x = 12$.

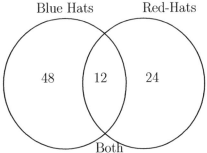

12. **D.** To solve this problem, we divide 75 into 700 to obtain 9 with a remainder of 25. Therefore, he has completed 9 prescription pads, and is now on his 10th one.

13. **C.** This question asks how many books he reads per year. The information about how long it takes him to read a book is not relevant, so we discard that data in attempting to solve the problem. Since there are 52 weeks in a year, and he reads d books in a year, he must read $\frac{d}{52}$ books a week.

14. **A.** Draw one large circle and call it Gloopers. Within that circle, draw two partially intersecting circles. One circle represents Doopers and the other represents Zoopers. You can see that all the Doopers and Zoopers are within the Gloopers circle, which means that all Doopers and Zoopers are also Gloopers, which is clearly stated in the problem. You will also see that the intersection of Doopers and Zoopers are both Doopers and Zoopers. This intersection is of course, within the Gloopers circle, and so that intersection represents those that are Doopers, Zoopers and Gloopers, which choice A states.

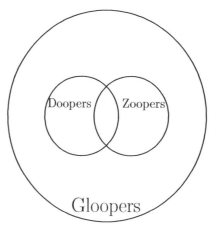

Section V: Geometry

Chapter 12

Angles and Triangles

Every Praxis exam has problems on angles and triangles. First, to understand what an angle is, a definition of a ray is important: A ray is a portion of a line that begins at one point and extends infinitely in one direction.

An angle is the formation of two rays that share an endpoint.

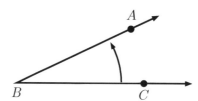

Above we have angle ABC, where the middle letter is the vertex, in this case, B. A vertex is the point at which the two rays that form an angle intersect.

Angles are measured in degrees, shown by a number and the degree symbol (°), or radians. For the Praxis exam, you will not need to understand radians.

A **right angle** measures 90° and forms a corner of a square. A right angle is indicated by a small square drawn inside it.

An **acute angle** is an angle that is greater than 0°, but smaller than 90°. For example, below is an angle of 45°:

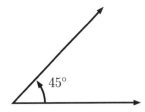

An **obtuse angle** is greater than 90°, but smaller than 180°. For example, here is an angle of 140°:

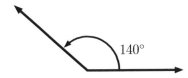

A **straight angle** measures 180°, as the following diagram shows:

A **reflex angle** has a measure greater than 180° but smaller than 360°. For example, here is an angle of 250°:

165

Rule 1: Complementary angles are two angles that add up to 90°:

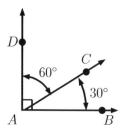

Angles DAC and CAB above are complimentary.

$$\angle DAC + \angle CAB = 90°$$

To find $\angle DAC$, if we know only $\angle CAB$, we subtract $\angle CAB$ from both sides of the equation:

$$\angle DAC = 90° - \angle CAB$$

Example 1 In Figure 12.1 below, find the measure of angle DAC.

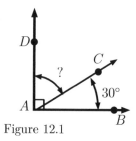

Figure 12.1

ANSWER 60° This is because $90° - 30° = 60°$.

Rule 2: Two supplementary angles add up to 180°

Example 2 In Figure 12.2, if $\angle 2 = 60°$, find the measure of angle 1:

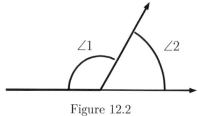

Figure 12.2

ANSWER: 120° We have:

$$\angle 1 + \angle 2 = 180°$$
$$\angle 1 = 180° - \angle 2$$
$$\angle 1 = 180° - 60°$$
$$= 120°$$

Example 3 Classify each angle as *acute, right, straight, obtuse,* or *reflex:*

1. 290°

2. 90°

3. 35°

4. 180°

5. 190°

6. 160°

ANSWER:

1. Reflex because 290° > 180°.
2. Right angle, since the angle equals 90°.
3. Acute, since 35° < 90°.
4. Straight, since the angle is 180°.
5. Reflex, since 190° > 180°.
6. Obtuse, since 90° < 160° < 180°.

Example 4 In Figure 12.3 below, find the measure of Angle 1 given $\angle 2 = 90°$ and $\angle 3 = 32°$.

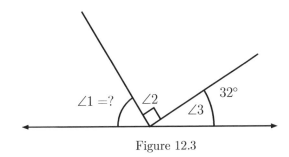

Figure 12.3

ANSWER: 58° We have

$$\angle 1 + \angle 2 + \angle 3 = 180°$$
$$\angle 1 = 180° - (\angle 2 + \angle 3)$$
$$= 180° - (90° + 32°)$$
$$= 180° - 122° = 58°$$

167

Example 5 Which of the following is a false statement?

A. The difference between a straight angle and an acute angle is an obtuse angle.
B. The sum of two obtuse angles is a reflex angle.
C. The sum of two right angles is a straight angle.
D. The sum of two straight angles measures 360°
E. The sum of two acute angles is greater than 90°.

ANSWER: E. Counter example: $20° + 30° = 50°$. Here both angles are acute, but the sum is also acute.

Triangles

A triangle is a closed three-sided figure:

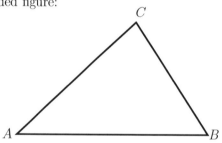

Figure 12.4 Triangle ABC

A triangle is named by writing its vertices in any order. In Figure 12.4, triangle ABC = triangle ACB = triangle CBA. Its sides are AB, BC, and AC. The sum of the angles of a triangle is 180°. Triangles can be classified by the lengths of their sides and by the measures of their angles. In Figure 12.5, all three angles and sides are equal:

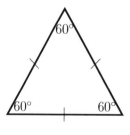

Figure 12.5

This triangle in Figure 12.5 is called an **equilateral triangle**.

168

In a **right triangle** (see Figure 12.6), one of the angles measures 90°.

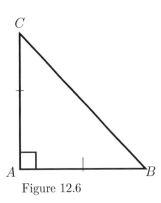

Figure 12.6

A **scalene triangle** (Figure 12.7) contains no equal sides or angles:

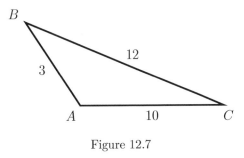

Figure 12.7

Figure 12.7 is also called an obtuse triangle, since one of the angles ($\angle A$) is greater than 90°. A scalene triangle can be right, acute, or obtuse. Try drawing a right scalene triangle and then an acute scalene triangle.

An **isosceles triangle** has two equal sides and two equal angles (see Figure 12.8 below).

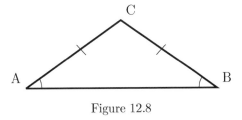

Figure 12.8

Example 6 In the Figure 12.9 below $\angle C = 40°$. What is the measure of $\angle B$?

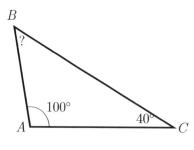

Figure 12.9

ANSWER: $40°$. We have:

$$\angle A + \angle B + \angle C = 180°$$
$$\angle B = 180 - \angle A - \angle C$$
$$= 180° - 100° - 40°$$
$$= 40°$$

Example 7 Which one of the following is/are possible in triangle ABC:

I. $\angle A = 40°$, $\angle B = 50°$, $\angle C = 90°$

II. $\angle A = 32°$, $\angle B = 49°$, $\angle C = 100°$

III. $\angle A = 30°$, $\angle B = 29°$, $\angle C = 121°$

A. I only
B. II only
C. I and II only
D. I and III only
E. I, II, and III

ANSWER: D I is true since $40 + 50 + 90 = 180$ and a triangle always measures $180°$. II is false since $32 + 49 + 100 = 181 \neq 180$. III is true since $30 + 29 + 121 = 180$.

Two triangles are congruent if the following corresponding parts are congruent:

Side-Side-Side (SSS) The side measures for both triangles are the same.
Angle-Side-Angle (ASA) Two angles and the side between them are the same.
Side-Angle-Side (SAS) Two sides and the angle between them are the same.

Example 9 In Figure 12.10, determine if the two triangles congruent?

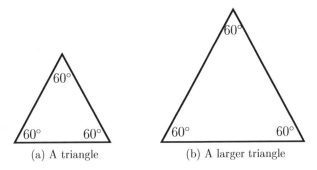

(a) A triangle   (b) A larger triangle

Figure 12.10

ANSWER: No. Because there is no rule AAA. Two triangles with the same angles are only congruent if the sides are also congruent as in the following:

Example 10 Are triangles ABD and CBD in Figure 12.11 (below) congruent?

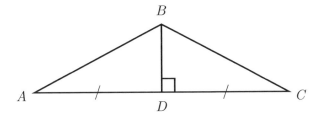

Figure 12.11

ANSWER: Yes. Because of SAS. Side BD is common to both triangles. Since it is shown that angle CDB is a right angle, it follows that angle ADB is also a right angle. It is also shown that AD = DC. So we have two sides and an angle in between the two sides that are all the same.

Similar triangles

Occur when the corresponding angles are congruent as in Figure 12.12 (below)

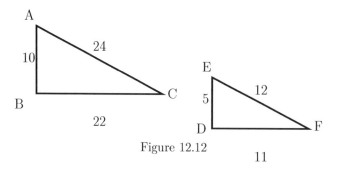

Figure 12.12

This is because side $AB = 2 \cdot DE$. Side $BC = 2 \cdot DF$, and $AC = 2 \cdot EF$.

Rule 3: If all corresponding sides are in the same ratio (as in the above case), the triangles are similar.

Rule 4: If all angles measures in the first triangle are equal to all angles measures in the second triangle, the triangles are also similar.

Pythagorean Theorem

In any right triangle (see Figure 12.13), the sum of the squares of the lengths of the smaller two sides (legs) is equal to the square of the length of the third side (hypotenuse). In algebra,

$$a^2 + b^2 = c^2$$

Simply put, the Pythagorean Theorem is used when trying to find a missing side of a *right triangle*.

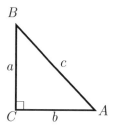

Figure 12.13

Example 11 Use the Pythagorean Theorem to find b in Figure 12.14 below.

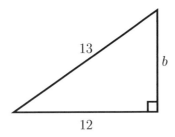

Figure 12.14

ANSWER: 5. To find the missing sides, use substitution and solve the equation for b.

$$a^2 + b^2 = c^2$$
$$(12)^2 + b^2 = (13)^2$$
$$144 + b^2 = 169$$
$$b^2 = 169 - 144$$
$$b^2 = 25$$
$$b = \sqrt{25}$$
$$b = 5$$

Example 12 Use the Pythagorean Theorem to find the missing length c, the hypotenuse, given that one leg, a is 3 and the other leg, b is 4.

ANSWER: 5. In this case, we are looking for the hypotenuse, the longest side, which makes this problem easier to solve. By substitution, we get

$$a^2 + b^2 = c^2$$
$$(3)^2 + (4)^2 = c^2$$
$$9 + 16 = c^2$$
$$25 = c^2$$
$$\sqrt{25} = c$$
$$5 = c$$

Practice Problems

1. In the Figure 12.15 below, side AC = BC and $\angle C = 40°$. What is the measure of angle A?

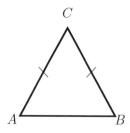

Figure 12.15

    A. 50°
    B. 60°
    C. 65°
    D. 70°
    E. 75°

2. Which of the following is/are true?

I. Bisecting an equilateral triangle produces two congruent triangles.
II. In a right triangle, at least two sides are congruent.
III. The sum of the measures of any two angles in a right triangle is always equal to the measure of the third angle.

    A. I only
    B. I and II only
    C. I and III only
    D. II and III only
    E. I, II, and III

3. What is the measure of each angle in an equilateral triangle?

    A. 40°
    B. 50°
    C. 60°
    D. 65°
    E. 70°

4. The triangle in Figure 12.16 is an example of:

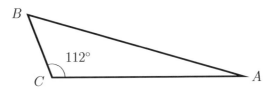

Figure 12.16

A. An acute triangle
B. An isosceles obtuse angle
C. A right equilateral triangle
D. A right isosceles triangle
E. An obtuse triangle

5. What is the measure of the third angle in a triangle if the first angle is equal to 89° and the second, 46°?

A. 45°
B. 54°
C. 65°
D. 73°
E. Cannot be determined from the information above

6. A reflex angle means that:

A. has a measure small than 90°.
B. has a measure greater than 90°.
C. has a measure greater than 120° but smaller than 180°.
D. has a measure greater than 180° but smaller than 360°.
E. has a measure greater than 270°, but smaller than 360°.

7. A right equilateral triangle:

   A. has two equal sides.
   B. has three equal sides.
   C. has an angle of 90°
   D. has an angle of 90° and all sides are equal
   E. Does not exist.

8. A right angle is bisected. What is the measure of each new angle?

   A. 45°
   B. 60°
   C. 90°
   D. 180°
   E. Cannot be determined by the information given.

9. Which of the following is/are true?

   I. An isosceles triangle cannot have as one of its angles, 75°.
   II. A triangle cannot have as any of its angles a measure greater than 180°
   III. When one combines two triangle into one, the sum of the angles of the new large triangle is 360°.

   A. I only
   B. II only
   C. I and II only
   D. II and III only
   E. I, II, and III

10. Which one of the following statements is false?

   I. The largest angle in a triangle can be 179°.
   II. An angle can have a measure greater than 360°
   III. In a right isosceles triangle, exactly two of its sides are congruent.

   A. I only
   B. II only
   C. I and II only
   D. II and III only
   E. I, II, and III

11. The following are two sides of a right triangle: 12 inches, 13 inches. What is the measure of the third side?

   A. 5 inches or $\sqrt{313}$
   B. 5 inches or $2\sqrt{10}$
   C. 6 inches or 9 inches
   D. 13 inches
   E. Cannot be determined from the information given.

12. All of the following triangles are similar except:

   A. Sides of triangle A are: 5, 10, 15 Sides of triangle B are 10,20, 30
   B. Sides of triangle A are: 5, 12, 13 Sides of triangle B are 10, 24, 26
   C. Sides of triangle A are: 11, 12, 19 Sides of triangle B are 22,24,38
   D. Sides of triangle A are: $\sqrt{2}$, $\sqrt{11}$, $\sqrt{13}$ Sides of triangle B are $2\sqrt{2}$, $2\sqrt{11}$, $2\sqrt{13}$
   E. Sides of triangle A are: 3,4,5 Sides of triangle B are 9,16,25

13. Which of the following is/are true?

   I. A reflex angle is always greater than an obtuse angle.
   II. The measure of an obtuse angle is no more than twice the measure of an acute angle.
   III. In an equilateral triangle, all sides are equal and all angles are not equal.

   A. I only
   B. I and II only
   C. I and III only
   D. II and III only
   E. I, II, and III

14. What is the side length a in the right triangle (Figure 12.17) below?

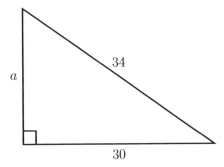

Figure 12.17

177

Solutions to Practice Problems

1. **D.** We have $\angle A = \angle B$. Since they are opposite to their respective equal sides. So:

$$\angle A + \angle B + \angle C = 180°$$
$$\angle A + \angle B + 40° = 180°$$
$$\angle A + \angle B = 140°$$

Since $\angle A = \angle B$, $\angle A$ is exactly half of $140° = 70°$.

2. **A.** II is false. Only in an isosceles right triangle are two sides congruent. III is false. In a right triangle, one of the angles equals 90°. The sum of the other two angles must add up to ninety degrees since the sum of all angles is 180°. So the right angle does equal the sum of the other two angles. However, one of the non right angles added to the right angle, does not equal the third angle. For example, $\angle A = 90°$, $\angle B = 60°$, and $\angle C = 30°$. Where we have $90° + 30° = 120° \neq 60°$. I is true. To "bisect" means to divide into two equal parts. Therefore this statement is true by definition.

3. **C.** We have $\angle A = \angle B = \angle C$ We also have $\angle A + \angle B + \angle C = 180°$. Therefore each angle is one third of $180° = 60°$.

4. **E.** Since the measure of one of the angles is greater than 90°, it is an obtuse triangle. B is incorrect since no two sides in this figure are equal.

5. **A.** We have:

$$\angle A + \angle B + \angle C = 180°$$
$$89° + 46° + x° = 180°$$
$$135° + x° = 180°$$
$$x° = 180° - 135° = 45°$$

6. **D.** By definition, D is true. See definition at the beginning of the chapter.

7. **E.** Try drawing one. You will see that it is not possible. In an equilateral triangle, the measure of each angle is 60°, and in a right triangle one of the angles is 90°. Figure 12.18 shows two kinds of right angles:

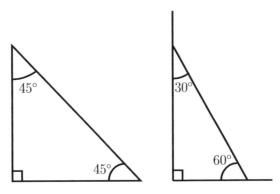

Figure 12.18

In neither of the cases above are all sides equal.

8. **A.** A right angle equals 90°. If you divide the angle into two equal angles ('bisect'), the measure of each resulting complimentary angle is half of ninety degrees, or 45°.

9. **B.** I is false. Counter example: $75° + 75° + 30° = 180°$. II is true: The largest measure of an angle in a triangle is smaller than 180° III is false. The sum of the angles of the new triangle is equal to 180° as is the case in all triangles.

10. **D.** I is false. Not all angles must be integers. For example $\angle A = 179.5°$, $\angle B = .25°$, and $\angle C = .25°$. These angles add up to 180°. II is true, as in the Figure 12.19:

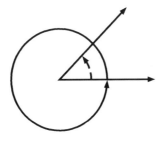

Figure 12.19

This angle has a measure of $360° + 45° = 405°$.

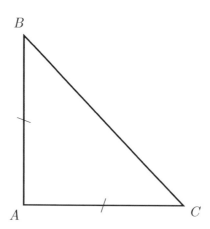

Figure 12.20

In Figure 12.20, we find that $AB = AC$, So III is true.

11. **A.** Draw a right triangle with two sides of dimension 12 and 13 like the two triangle in Figure 12.21.

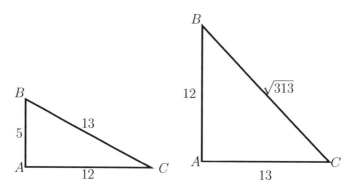

Figure 12.21

The hypotenuse is by definition the longest side. Using the Pythagorean theorem, $a^2 + b^2 = c^2$. In triangle 1, a is 12, c is 13, so we have $b^2 + 12^2 = 13^2$. So $b^2 = 13^2 - 12^2 = 169 - 144 = 25$. So b must be 5. In the other triangle, $c^2 = a^2 + b^2 = 12^2 + 13^2 = 144 + 169 = 313$. So C must be $\sqrt{313}$. Therefore there are two possibilities: 5 and $\sqrt{313}$.

12. **E.** Two triangles are similar when the corresponding sides are in proportion. In A-D, all corresponding sides of triangle B are exactly twice those of triangle A. This is not the case with choice E.

13. **A.** I is true because a reflex angle is greater than 180°, but smaller than 360°, while an obtuse angle is greater than 90° but smaller than 180°. II is false. As a counter example $\angle A = 30°$, $\angle B = 30°, \angle A + \angle B = 60°, \angle C = 120°$ and $120° > 60°$, So II is false. In an equilateral triangle all sides and all angles are equal.

14. **16.**

$$a^2 + b^2 = c^2$$
$$a^2 + 30^2 = 34^2$$
$$a^2 + 900 = 1,156$$
$$a^2 = 256$$
$$a = 16$$

Chapter 13

Lines

This chapter discusses parallel and perpendicular lines, as well as the angles that form when a line crosses another line(s). On most PRAXIS exams there are few problems dealing with lines, so this chapter is shorter than others. A line is a one-dimensional straight path that extends infinitely in two opposite directions (See Figure 13.1 below).

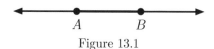

Figure 13.1

Line a or $\overleftrightarrow{AB}$ are two ways of naming a line. When two lines intersect, they form two pairs of vertical angles. The vertical angles are opposite each other.

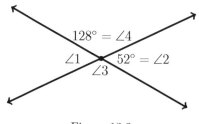

Figure 13.2

In Figure 13.2, ∠1 and ∠2 are a pair of vertical angles and congruent (equal measure with respect to each other), and ∠3 and ∠4 are also vertical angles and congruent to each other.

Rule Number 1: Vertical angles are congruent.

Example 1 ∠1 is 150° What is the measure of ∠2?

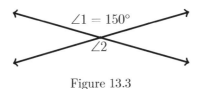

Figure 13.3

ANSWER: 150° Since ∠2 forms a vertical angle with ∠1 (see Figure 13.3), and vertical angles are equal, ∠2 is also 150°.

Intersecting lines also form adjacent angles. By definition, adjacent angles (in a plane) are formed when two angles share both a vertex and a side length but do not overlap. In Figure 13.2, ∠1 and ∠3 are adjacent to each other. Similarly ∠1 and ∠4, ∠4 and ∠2, and ∠2 and ∠3 are all adjacent to each other. The sum of two adjacent angles, when formed by two intersecting lines is always 180°.

Example 2 By congruency, ∠1 in Figure 13.2 is 52° (vertical angle with ∠2). What is the measure of ∠3?

   A. 118°
   B. 122°
   C. 128°
   D. 218°
   E. 248°

ANSWER: C. $52° + ∠3 = 180°$.

We subtract 52° from both sides to obtain $∠3 = 180° − 52° = 128°$

Parallel lines are lines that never intersect. The symbol for parallel is denoted as ∥ (two small parallel vertical segments). A transversal is a line that intersects two or more other lines, not necessarily parallel to each other. Here is an example of parallel lines:

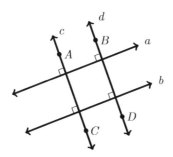

Figure 13.4

183

You can see that in Figure 13.4 line a and line b are parallel, and line c and line d are parallel. We can also see in Figure 13.4 that perpendicular lines are formed. When two angles intersect at a 90° angle, the angles are said to be perpendicular. Also, line c is perpendicular to line a and line b, and line d is perpendicular to line a and line b as well. The distance between points B and A is the same as point C and D, and the distance between B and C is the same as the distance between A and D. You may notice that the angle formed by crossing two perpendicular lines is 90°. The 90° angle is shown by a symbol that looks like a tiny square where the lines intersect.

In Figure 13.5 (below), the distance between points A and B is not equal to the distance between points C and D because Line a and Line b are not parallel to each other.

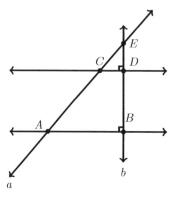

Figure 13.5

Rule Number 2: Lines that are not parallel to each other always intersect.

As Figure 13.5 shows, lines a and b intersect at point E.

When a transversal intersects two parallel lines, special angle relationships form. See Figure 13.6.

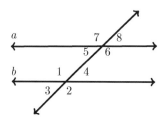

Figure 13.6

In Figure 13.6 the following are corresponding angles: $\angle 1$ and $\angle 7$, $\angle 3$ and $\angle 5$, $\angle 2$ and $\angle 6$, and finally $\angle 4$ and $\angle 8$. Corresponding angles have equal measure. Here, each angle matches another angle in the same position on the transversals.

184

Alternate interior angles are angles that lie on opposite sides of the transversals and are inside the parallel lines. These angles are congruent In Figure 13.6, one pair of alternate interior angles is $\angle 1$ and $\angle 6$. Another is $\angle 4$ and $\angle 5$. These sets of angles are located in between lines a and b.

Alternate exterior angles lie on opposite sides of the transversal and are outside the parallel lines. These angles are also congruent. In Figure 13.6, one pair of alternate exterior angles is $\angle 3$ and $\angle 8$, and the other is $\angle 2$ and $\angle 7$.

Example 3 In Figure 13.6, suppose $\angle 4 = 43°$. What is the measure of $\angle 7$?

   A. $43°$
   B. $110°$
   C. $120°$
   D. $137°$
   E. $140°$

ANSWER: D $\angle 4$ and $\angle 2$ are adjacent angles, therefore they are congruent. Thus, $\angle 2 = 180° - 43° = 137°$. $\angle 7$ and $\angle 2$ are alternate exterior angles, therefore they are congruent. Therefore, we can conclude that $\angle 7 = 137°$.

Example 4 In Figure 13.7, $\angle 8$ is $45°$. What is the measure of $\angle 1$?

ANSWER: $m\angle 1 = 135°$: By definition, $\angle 1$ and $\angle 6$ are alternate interior angles, and therefore are congruent. $\angle 6$ and $\angle 8$ are adjacent angles whose sum is $180°$ (supplementary). Therefore, $m\angle 6 = 180° - 45° = 135°$. Since $\angle 1 = \angle 6$, $m\angle 1 = 135°$.

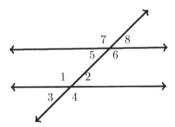

Figure 13.7

Example 5 In Figure 13.7, suppose $\angle 5$ is $43°$. What is the measure of $\angle 2$?

ANSWER: $43°$. If $\angle 5 = 43°$, then $\angle 2$ is also $43°$ because they are alternate interior angles.

Practice Problems

Problem 1-3 pertain to Figure 13.8:

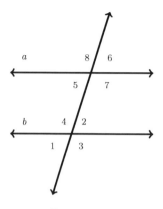

Figure 13.8

1. If $\angle 2 = 50°$ and Lines a and b are parallel. Which of the following angles cannot be determined?

    A. $\angle 1$
    B. $\angle 3$
    C. $\angle 4$
    D. $\angle 8$
    E. None of the above

2. $\angle 2 = 36°$. What is the measure of $\angle 7$?

    A. $16°$
    B. $26°$
    C. $36°$
    D. $126°$
    E. $144°$

3. If $\angle 4 = 144°$, What is $\angle 4 + \angle 8$?

    A. $110°$
    B. $214°$
    C. $282°$
    D. $268°$
    E. $288°$

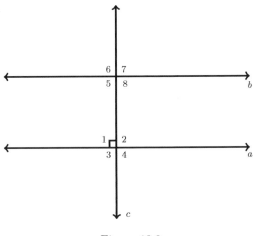

Figure 13.9

4. In Figure 13.9, line c is perpendicular to lines a and b. What is the sum of angles 1 through 8?

A. 440°   B. 540°   C. 660°   D. 720°   E. 900°

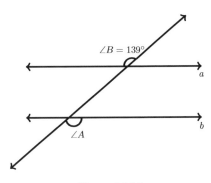

Figure 13.10

5. In Figure 13.10, what is the value of $\angle A$?(Assume that $\overleftrightarrow{a} \parallel \overleftrightarrow{b}$).

A. 41°
B. 101°
C. 139°
D. 161°
E. None of the above

Solutions to Practice Problems

1. **E.** Given any angle in this figure, we can determine all other angles.

2. **E.** $\angle 4$ is equal to 144° since $\angle 4 + \angle 1 = 180$ (supplementary angles). $\angle 7$ equals $\angle 4$ by definition of alternate interior angles. So $\angle 7 = 144°$.

3. **E.** $\angle 4 = 144°$ (Given). So we need to find $\angle 8$. Since $\angle 4 = 144°$, $\angle 8$ is also 144°. Now we have the two angles combined as $144° + 144° = 288°$.

4. **D.** Each of the eight angles has a measure of 90°. So we have $8 * 90 = 720$. In fact, in any drawing where a transversal passes through a set of two parallel lines, all the angles formed add up to 720°, regardless of the slant of the transversal.

5. **C.** $\angle A$ is equal to 139° because $\angle A$ and the 139° angle are alternate exterior angles.

Chapter 14

Circles, Quadrilaterals, Multiple Figures

Circles

Circumference of a Circle $= \pi \cdot d = 2\pi \dot{r}$
Area of a Circle $= \pi r^2$
Radius $= \frac{1}{2} \cdot d$

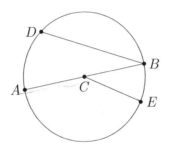

The circle, pictured above, has point C as its center. The circle itself represents all points that are on the same plane and are one radius length from the center, C. The radius is shown as line segment CE. As you can see, two radii make up the diameter, AB. The diameter is the longest chord, or a line segment connecting two points that lie on the circle. BD is another chord. Arcs are curves defined by two points on the circle. From point A to point D along the circle is an arc. AE is another arc. Finally, a section is the area within two radii and an arc. Visualize section ACE and shade it in.

Example 1 What is the area of Figure 14.1?

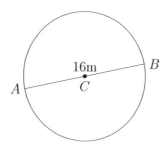

Figure 14.1

ANSWER: 200.96m^2 To find the area of the circle, we must find the radius r. The radius is half the diameter, $r = \frac{16}{2}$, or 8. Therefore, by substituting 8 into the area of circle formula, we get,

$$A = \pi r^2$$
$$= \pi(8)^2$$
$$= 64\pi$$
$$\approx 200.96\text{m}^2$$

Example 2 What is the area of section ABC pictured in Figure 14.2 below?

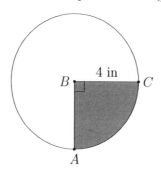

Figure 14.2

A. 2π in^2
B. 4π in^2
C. 8π in^2
D. 16π in^2
E. 64π in^2

ANSWER: B To calculate the area of the section, first calculate the area of the whole circle, and then divide by 4. The area of the whole circle is $\pi \times 4^2 = 16\pi$ in^2. The section's area is $\frac{90}{360}$ or $\frac{1}{4}$ of the circle's area. Therefore, one-fourth of sixteen is 4; $\frac{1}{4} \times 16\pi$ in$^2 = 4\pi$ in^2.

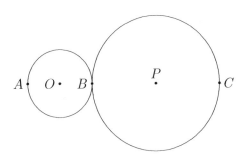

Figure 14.3

Example 3 In Figure 14.3 above, circles O and P touch at point B, and points A, O, B, P and C lie on the same line. If circle O has a radius of 2 cm and circle P has a radius of 5 cm, what is the distance from point A to point C?

A. 7   B. 8   C. 10   D. 12   E. 14

ANSWER: E To find the length of segment AC, we must find the diameter of Circles O and P. For Circle O, since the radius is 2, we know that $d = 2r$. Therefore the diameter of $O = 4$ and $P = 10$. By taking the sum $4 + 10$ we get 14. Therefore the length of $AC = 14$cm

Quadrilaterals

Quadrilaterals are shapes with four sides and four corners. Rectangles are one of the most common quadrilaterals. They have four right angles (90 degree angles) and opposite sides that are equal (and parallel). Squares are rectangles with four equal sides. Other common quadrilaterals include parallelograms, rhombuses, and trapezoids, pictured below.

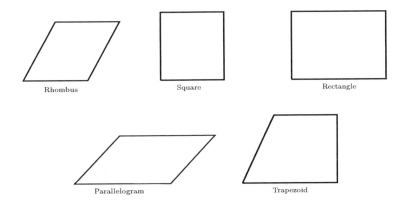

Example 4   How many total degrees are inside a rectangle?

A. $90°$
B. $180°$
C. $270°$
D. $360°$
E. $450°$

ANSWER: D. Each corner of a rectangle measures 90 degrees, and a rectangle has four corners. $4(90) = 360$.

The formula to calculate area of a parallelogram is the product of the base times its height, $A = bh$.

Example 5   What is the area of a parallelogram with a base of 5cm and a height of 3cm?

A. 15 cm^2
B. 20 cm^2
C. 25 cm^2
D. 50 cm^2
E. 125 cm^2

ANSWER: A. The base is 3 and the height is 5; $A = bh$ $3(5) = 15$.

Example 6   A large square with side length of 8 inches is split up into 16 equally sized smaller squares. What is the area of each small square?

A. 4 in^2 B. 8 in^2 C. 16 in^2 D. 32 in^2 E. 64 in^2

ANSWER: A. Area of a square is side times side, or side squared. $A = s^2$. The area of the larger square is 64 in.^{2} divided into 16 smaller squares, $\frac{64}{16} = 4 \text{ in}^2$.

Example 7   Compare the perimeter of a square with side length of 6m to the perimeter of a rhombus with side length of 6 m.

A. The perimeter of the square is greater
B. The perimeter of the rhombus is greater
C. The perimeters are equivalent
D. The relationship cannot be determined

ANSWER: C. A rhombus is like a square in that it has four equivalent sides. A rhombus differs from a square in that it does not have four right (90 degree) angles. When you sum the four side lengths, the perimeter of each figure is 24 m.

Mixed Figures

A mixed figure is a combination of any two common geometric figures. The two figures may overlap or share an adjacent side, or one figure may be circumscribed, or drawn completely inside, the other. When a figure is circumscribed, the corners of the shape inside touch the sides of the shape outside. There are no special formulas for multiple figures, since they can be broken down into more common shapes.

Example 8   In Figure 14.4, rectangle ABDC, has a length of 9 cm. Line segment EF bisects line segments AB and CD and creates two equivalent squares inside the rectangle. What is the area of one of these squares?

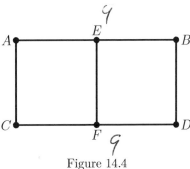

Figure 14.4

A. 9 cm^2
B. 12.5 cm^2
C. 15 cm^2
D. 18 cm^2
E. 20.25 cm^2

ANSWER: E. If the length of 9 cm is bisected, the result is two sides of a square with a length of 4.5 cm. To find the area of one of these squares, use

$$A = s^2$$
$$= (4.5)^2 \text{ cm}^2$$
$$= 20.25 \text{ cm}^2$$

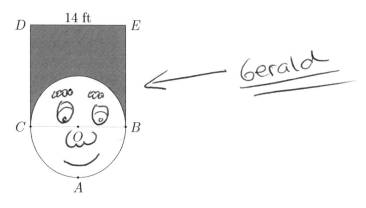

Figure 14.5

Example 9 What is the area of the shaded portion in Figure 14.5, considering square DEBC and Circle O?

   A. $24.5\pi\text{ft}^2$
   B. $62.5\pi\text{ft}^2$
   C. $96.5 - 7\pi\text{ft}^2$
   D. $129.5\pi\text{ft}^2$
   E. $196 - 24.5\pi\text{ft}^2$

ANSWER: E. Each side of the square measures 14 ft. The diameter of the circle is also 14 ft, making the radius 7 ft. The area of the shaded region is equal to the area of the square minus the area of half the circle. The area of the square is $14\text{ft}^2 = 196\text{ft}^2$. The area of the entire circle is $49\pi\text{ft}^2$. The area of half the circle is $\frac{49}{2}\pi\text{ft}^2 = 24.5\pi\text{ft}^2$. Therefore, subtracting half the circle from the area of the square, the area of the shaded region is $196 - \frac{49}{2}\pi$ ft^2.

Example 10 If a circle is circumscribed around a square, which of the following is equal to the diameter of the circle?

   A. The side length of the square
   B. The area of the square
   C. The diagonal of the square
   D. Two times the side length of the square

Answer: C. Draw a square and then a circle around it that touches the square at its four corners. Add the diagonal of the square connecting two opposite corners. This will also represent the diameter of the circle.

Practice Problems

1. John runs along a circular route around a lake. The jogging path has a radius of $\frac{1}{8}$mi., and he usually runs exactly 4 laps. Approximately how far does John run in one workout?

   A. 1.57 mi.
   B. 3.14 mi.
   C. 4.71 mi.
   D. 6.28 mi.
   E. 9.42 mi.

2. A woman needs to sow 80 percent of her lawn with grass seed. The lawn measures 10 meters in length and 25 meters in width. If 1,000 seeds have to be sown per square meter, how many seeds will she plant?

   A. 50,000 seeds
   B. 100,000 seeds
   C. 125,000 seeds
   D. 200,000 seeds
   E. 250,000 seeds

3. What is the fewest number of equally sized triangles that will fill up the space inside of a rectangle?

   A. 1
   B. 2
   C. 3
   D. 4
   E. 5

4. What is the diameter of a circle with a circumference of 15π in?

   A. 3 in
   B. 5 in
   C. 7.5 in
   D. 10 in
   E. 15 in

5. Three-quarters of the circumference of a circle represents how many degrees of that circle?

   A. 45°
   B. 90°
   C. 180°
   D. 270°
   E. 360°

6. Circle A has a radius of 7cm and circle B has a radius of 14cm. Which circle contains more degrees?

   A. Circle A
   B. Circle B
   C. They are an equal number of degrees
   D. Cannot be determined from the information given

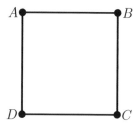

Figure 14.6

7. Take square ABCD in Figure 14.6 and draw a line segment from A to C. What is the measure of angle CAD?

   A. 30°
   B. 45°
   C. 60°
   D. 90°
   E. 135°

8. An equilateral triangle sits atop the short side of a rectangle that measures 8 in. by 10 in. What is the perimeter of the entire figure?

   A. 36 in   B. 44 in   C. 52 in   D. 60 in   E. 64 in

196

9. What is the longest line segment that connects two points on a circle?

   A. Chord
   B. Arc
   C. Radius
   D. Perimeter
   E. Diameter

10. Which of the following cannot be the area of a square if its side lengths are integers?

    A. 20in^2
    B. 25in^2
    C. 36in^2
    D. 64in^2
    E. 81in^2

11. In Figure 14.7, the diameter of Circle O is 10cm, what is the area of the rectangle?

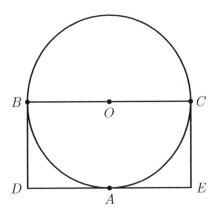

Figure 14.7

   A. 25 cm^2
   B. 30 cm^2
   C. 45 cm^2
   D. 50 cm^2
   E. 100 cm^2

197

12. Two rival pizza companies offer differently shaped pizza. Pizza A is a circular pizza with a radius of 10 in. and pizza B is a 20 in. by 17 in. rectangular pizza. If Pizza B costs twice as much as Pizza A and have the same amount of toppings, which pizza is the better deal?

    A. Pizza A
    B. Pizza B
    C. They are equal
    D. Cannot be determined from the information given

13. Figure 14.8 is a square. Points E and F lie at the midpoints of AB and BD respectively. Side AB = 8 inches. What is the area of Triangle EBF?

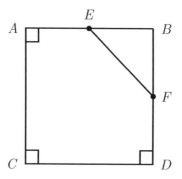

Figure 14.8

    A. 8 in^2
    B. 12 in^2
    C. 16 in^2
    D. 20 in^2
    E. 64 in^2

Solutions to Practice Problems

1. **B.** John is running around the circumference of his jogging trail. To figure out how far he runs in four laps, find the circumference of the path, then multiply by four. Calculate circumference from the formula $2\pi r$ to get $\frac{1}{4}\pi$ miles for each lap. Four laps will be $4 \cdot \frac{1}{4}\pi = \pi$ miles, or about 3.14 miles per workout.

2. **D.** The area of the entire lawn is 250 square meters, but she is only considering 80 percent. $250(.8) = 200$ square meters that needs grass seed. If each square meter gets 1,000 seeds and she has to plant 200 square meters, then she will need 1,000 x 200 total seeds, or 200,000.

3. **B.** This problem is best visualized by drawing a picture. Take any size rectangle and draw a diagonal line from one corner to the opposite one. This splits the rectangle into two equally sized triangles.

4. **E.** The formula relating circumference of a circle to diameter is C = πd. Divide the circumference by π and you will be left with the diameter, 15in.

5. **D.** The entire circumference is 360 degrees. Three-quarters of the distance around represents $(\frac{3}{4})360° = 270°$.

6. **C.** No matter how large a circle becomes, it always has 360 degrees.

7. **B.** Each corner of the square is 90 degrees. When Line Segment AC is drawn it bisects a angle DAB, the result is two 45 degree angles. Angle CAD is one of these angles.

8. **B.**

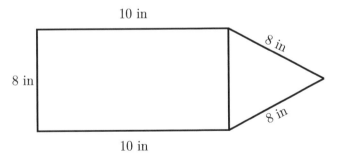

Figure 14.9

Begin by drawing Figure 14.9 (shown above). The perimeter, or distance around the object, is 8in. + 10in. + 10in. + 8in. + 8in. = 44in.

9. **E.** The diameter must be longer than any other chord in the circle. Choice E is the only possible length of the diameter.

10. **A.** If the side lengths are integers, the area must be a perfect square (e.g. 3^2, 4^2, 5^2, etc.) Choice A, 20in^2, is the only non-perfect square.

11. **D.** The length, or longer side, of the rectangle extends across the diameter of the circle. The width, or shorter side, spans from the middle of the circle to its edge, which is equal to the circle's radius. The radius is one half the diameter, in this case 5cm. From this information we can say that the dimensions of the rectangle are 10 cm by 5cm, and the area is lw, 10cm $\times$ 5cm $= 50\text{cm}^2$.

12. **B.** Pizza A has an area of $\pi r^2 = \pi(10\text{in})^2 = 100\pi\text{in}^2$, which, if $\pi = 3.14$, is approximately 314 square inches. Pizza B has an area of $lw = 20\text{in} \times 17\text{in} = 340 \text{ in}^2$. Since pizza B is only slightly larger than pizza A, but is twice as expensive, pizza A is a better deal.

13. **A.** Line segments EB and BF are each 4 inches because they are half of the sides of the square ABDC. Rotate triangle EBF so BF becomes the base and EB the height. The formula for area of a triangle is $\frac{1}{2}bh = \frac{1}{2}(4 \text{ in})(4 \text{ in}) = 8\text{in}^2$.

Chapter 15

Area, Perimeter and Volume

Perimeter

Perimeter is the measure around a figure. Imagine running the bases around a baseball diamond. The distance you run is the perimeter of the diamond. Perimeter can be measured with a ruler or tape measure; it is a one-dimensional, or 1-D, measurement. Possible units for perimeter are inches, feet, centimeters, meters, kilometers, etc.

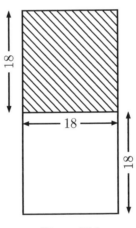

Figure 15.1

Example 1 Two adjacent squares share one side that measures 18 centimeters. What is the perimeter of Figure 15.1?

A. 36 cm   B. 72 cm   C. 108 cm   D. 144 cm   E. 324 cm

ANSWER: C. Begin by drawing a picture of the figure, as shown above. The side length of 18 cm applies to every side, since all the sides of a square are equivalent. Six segments compose the perimeter of this figure, $6 \times 18 = 108$.

Example 2   Which of the following expressions is not true:

I. The perimeter of a parallelogram is *base* × *height*.

II. The perimeter of a rectangle can be expressed by $2l + 2w$, where l is length and w is width.

III. The perimeter of a square is four times the length of one side.

  A. I only

  B. II only

  C. I and II only

  D. II and III only

  E. I,II, and III

ANSWER: A. Statements II and III are both accurate expressions of perimeter. Statement I represents the formula for area of a parallelogram, and therefore, is not true.

Area

In math, area refers to the amount of two-dimensional space taken up by a plane figure. Imagine coloring in a rectangle. The space you would color in is the area of that rectangle. Relevant area formulas are listed below:

Area of a triangle $= \frac{1}{2}b \times h$, where b is the base and h is the height

Area of a rectangle $= l \times w$, where l is the length and w is the width

Area of a square $= s^2$, where s is the length of one side

Area of a circle $= \pi \times r^2$, where r is the radius of the circle

Three dimensional solids have measurements called surface area. This is simply the sum of the area of each face of the figure. Cubes and rectangular solids have six faces. To find their surface area find the total area of all six faces.

Example 3   Which of the following statements is necessarily true?

A. The area of a square with side x is greater than the area of a circle with diameter x.
B. The area of a square with side x is greater than the area of a rectangle with sides x and y.
C. Increasing the circumference of a circle will decrease its area.
D. The area of a rectangle will increase if the width becomes smaller and the length stays the same.

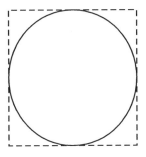

Figure 15.2

ANSWER: A. Draw a square, like the one in Figure 15.2 of any side length and then draw a circle inside of that square. In the picture, the diameter of the circle is equal to the square's side length. Since the circle fits inside of the square (with extra space at the corners), we can deduce that the area of the square is larger.

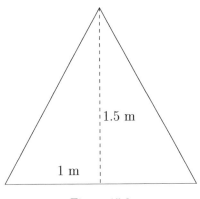

1.5 m

1 m

Figure 15.3

Example 4   Calculate one-half of the area of the triangle pictured in Figure 15.3.

A. 0.75m²   B. 0.375m²   C. 1.5m²   D. 3m²   E. 0.25m²

ANSWER: A. To calculate the area of the triangle, use the formula $A = \frac{1}{2}b \times h$ to get $\frac{1}{2} \times 2$ m $\times$ 1.5 m = 1.5m². One-half of that area is 0.75 m².

Volume

We have seen that perimeter is a one-dimensional measurement and area is a two-dimensional measurement. Volume occupies three-dimensions. It is physical space like dice (cube), a cereal box (rectangular solid), a basketball (sphere), a traffic cone (cone), or a soup can (cylinder). Units for this measurement are raised to the third power: mm^3, cm^3, in^3, ft^3, etc.

Here are some important formulas for calculating volumes of certain solid figures:

Volume of a Sphere $= \frac{4}{3}\pi r^3$; $r =$ radius of the sphere

Volume of a Cube $= s^3$; $s =$ length of a side

Volume of a Rectangular Solid $= lwh$; $l =$ length, $w =$ width, and $h =$ height of the figure

Volume of a Cylinder $= \pi r^2 h$; $h =$ height of the cylinder, $r =$ radius of the circular base

Example 5 A soup can has a height of 12 cm and a diameter of 5 cm. How many milliliters (ml) does the soup can contain? (1 $cm^3 = 1$ mL)

    A. 30π mL
    B. 45π mL
    C. 60π mL
    D. 75π mL
    E. 90π mL

ANSWER: D. Use the formula for volume of a cylinder, the geometric shape of a soup can, $\pi r^2 h$. In this problem, the radius is 2.5 cm, half of the diameter, and the height is 12 cm. Plug into the formula, $(2.5)^2$ $cm^2 \pi \times 12$ cm to get a total volume of 75π cm^3. The unit cm^3 is equal to mL, so the answer is D.

Example 6 Bill has to fill up his spherical fish tank to 75 percent of its capacity. If the fish tank has a radius of 7 inches, how many cubic inches of water will he need?

    A. 135π in^3
    B. 155π in^3
    C. 257π in^3
    D. 343π in^3
    E. 457π in^3

ANSWER: D. Capacity of a 3-D figure is related to its volume. First find the volume of the spherical fish tank, $\frac{4}{3}\pi r^3 = \frac{4}{3}\pi(7 \text{ in.})^3$. 75 percent $\left(\frac{3}{4}\right)$ of the volume is: $\frac{3}{4} \times \frac{4}{3} \times \pi \times 7^3 = 343\pi$ in^3.

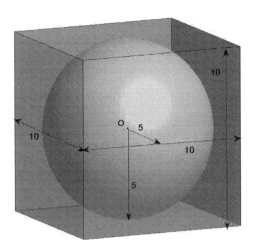

Figure 15.4

Example 7   Figure 15.4 shows a sphere inside of a cube. The length of one side of the cube is 10 cm. If the sphere touches the cube on the inside of all 6 faces, approximately how much volume remains unfilled in the box? (Use $\pi = 3.14$)

   A. 239 cm^3 B. 247 cm^3 C. 289 cm^3 D. 343 cm^3 E. 477 cm^3

ANSWER: E. The unfilled volume equals the difference between the volume of the box and the volume of the sphere. The formula to solve this is $s^3 - \frac{4}{3}\pi r^3$. The radius of the sphere, $r = 5$ cm. Substitute the measurements into the formula to get $(10 \text{ cm})^3 - \frac{4}{3}\pi(5 \text{ cm})^3$ which simplifies to $1000 \text{ cm}^3 - 523 \text{ cm}^3 = 477 \text{ cm}^3$.

Example 8   Which of the following expressions relates Area of a square to Volume of a cube correctly?

   A. $A = \dfrac{V}{s}$ B. $\dfrac{A}{h} = V$ C. $A = \dfrac{V}{hl}$ D. $A^2 = V$ E. $A \times P = V$

ANSWER: A. The area formula states that $A = s^2$, and the volume formula describes that $V = s^3$. Substitute A into the right side of the Volume equation for (s^2). The expression becomes $V = (A)s$ which can be solved for area, $A = \frac{V}{s}$.

Example 9   Complete the analogy, Volume is to 3-Dimensions as Length is to?

   A. Area

   B. 4-Dimensions

   C. 1-Dimension

   D. Perimeter

   E. 2-Dimensions

ANSWER: C. Volume is a 3-Dimensional measurement, and length is a 1-Dimensional measurement.

Practice Problems

1. A rectangle has an area of 64 m². What is the smallest possible perimeter of this rectangle?

    A. 16 m
    B. 24 m
    C. 32 m
    D. 38 m
    E. 40 m

2. A triangle has a base of 9 in and a height of 7 in. A rectangle has a length of 9 in and a height of 7 in. What is the ratio of the area of the triangle to the area of the rectangle?

    A. 1:4
    B. 1:2
    C. 1:1
    D. 3:2
    E. 2:1

3. How many 2cm x 2cm x 2cm cubes will fit inside a rectangular solid that measures 4cm x 8cm x 4cm?

    A. 8 cubes
    B. 10 cubes
    C. 12 cubes
    D. 14 cubes
    E. 16 cubes

4. Shelly wants to tile her bathroom floor in a black and white checkerboard pattern. Each tile measures 1 square foot. If her bathroom measures 8 feet by 9 feet, how many white tiles will she need? (Assume that there are an equal number of black and white tiles.)

    A. 16 white tiles
    B. 18 white tiles
    C. 24 white tiles
    D. 32 white tiles
    E. 36 white tiles

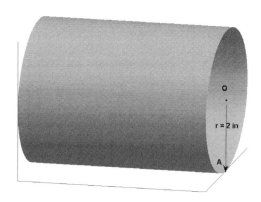

Figure 15.5

5. How far would the cylinder pictured in Figure 15.5 roll in 2 complete revolutions?

   A. 5π in
   B. 6π in
   C. 8π in
   D. 9.5π in
   E. 11π in

6. A cylinder holding 50 cm^3 of water is poured into a cube with side length of 4cm. What percent of the cube is filled?

   A. 70%
   B. 78%
   C. 85%
   D. 88%
   E. 93%

7. What is the volume of a cube whose face has an area of 64 cm^2?

   A. 268 cm^3
   B 320 cm^3
   C. 512 cm^3
   D. 640 cm^3
   E. 1,024 cm^3

8. How many cubes of 2in^3 will fit into a rectangular box that measures 4 ft. by 4 ft. by 4 ft.?

   A. 4 blocks
   B. 8 blocks
   C. 12 blocks
   D. 16 blocks
   E. 20 blocks

9. What is the area in centimeters of a 1 m by 1 m square?

   A. 10 cm^2
   B. 100 cm^2
   C. $1,000 \text{ cm}^2$
   D. $10,000 \text{ cm}^2$
   E. $100,000 \text{ cm}^2$

10. A painter has been hired to paint a large wall, but the wall contains 3 windows. If the wall measures 30 ft. by 12 ft. and each window measures 7 ft. by 6 ft., how much wall, in ft.^{2}, does he have to paint?

   A. 42 ft^2
   B. 120 ft^2
   C. 234 ft^2
   D. 318 ft^2
   E. 360 ft^2

11. Which of the following units can be used to measure volume?

   A. cm^3
   B. in^2
   C. m^2
   D. feet
   E. mm

12. What is the perimeter of a square with its corners at the following coordinate points: $(-4, 2)$, $(0, 2)$, $(-4, -2)$ and $(0, -2)$?

   A. 6 units   B. 8 units   C. 12 units   D. 15 units   E. 16 units

Solutions to Practice Problems

1. **C.** The factors of the area are length and width, which make up the perimeter. To solve this problem we need to find the lowest sum of the factors that will yield an area of 64 cm². The factors are 64 and 1, 32 and 2, 16 and 4, and 8 and 8. The lowest sum is 16, $8 + 8$, so the perimeter of this rectangle is $2l + 2w = 2(8 \text{ cm}) + 2(8 \text{ cm}) = 32$ cm. There is a geometric rule stating that a square has the smallest perimeter for a given rectangular area. (Remember that squares are rectangles!)

2. **B.** Without solving for the area of the two figures, we know this ratio. The triangle's base and height are equal to the rectangle's length and width, and we have seen that two triangles make up a rectangle. The ratio of the triangle's area to the rectangle's will be 1:2.

3. **E.** Since this question requires splitting up a larger volume into equally sized smaller units, we are dealing with division. Draw a rectangular cube. Two of the faces will have a dimension of 8 cm by 4. An 8cm × 4cm × 2cm cube will hold $4 \times 2 = 8$ cubes. But we have twice that spaces, enough for 16 cubes.

4. **E.** In a checkerboard pattern, one-half of the squares are one color and the other half another color. This problem asks for the area of white tiles, which will be one-half the area of the entire floor. The area of the floor, $l \times w$, is 72 square feet. Half of this area is 36 feet and since each tile is 1 square foot, there will be 36 white tiles.

5. **C.** As the cylinder rolls, it will travel a distance equal to the circumference of the circular base with each revolution. Calculate the circumference of the circle, $C = 2\pi r = 2(2\text{in})\pi = 4\pi$ in. In two revolutions it will travel 8π in.

6. **B.** The total volume of the cubic tank will equal $s^3 = 64\text{cm}^3$, so the 50 cm³ from the beaker will fill up only a percentage of the tank. To find any percentage, divide the part by the whole and multiply by 100 percent, $\frac{part}{whole} \cdot 100$ percent. $\frac{50 \text{ cm}^3}{64 \text{ cm}^3} \cdot 100 = 78$ percent.

7. **C.** If the area of one face is 64 cm² then the edge of the cube measures 8 cm, because if $s^2 = 64$ cm², then $s = 8$. Then, to find the volume cube the side length, $(8 \text{ cm})^3 = 512cm^3$.

8. **B.** We have two rows of $2cm \times 2cm \times 2cm$ cubes. Each row can hold 4 cubes. So we have $2 \times 4 = 8$ cubes.

9. **D.** Each side of the square is 1m, which is equal to 100cm. The area of the square in cm is $100cm \times 100cm = 10,000cm^2$.

10. **C.** The entire wall measures 360ft², but he does not have to paint the 3 windows that each measure $42ft^2$. The total window area is $3 \times 42ft^2 = 126ft^2$. Subtracting out the window area, we are left with $360\text{ft}^2 - 126\text{ft}^2 = 234\text{ft}^2$.

11. **A.** Units must be cubed (x^3) to measure volume.

12. **E.** Draw a sketch of the square on a coordinate plane and count the perimeter, or distance around the figure. It is 16 units.

Section VI: Graphs

Chapter 16

Coordinate Geometry

Coordinate Plane

When you think of the Coordinate Plane (Cartesian Plane), think "location." You have probably used the Coordinate Plane outside of math class and didn't even realize it. The popular game BattleShip uses coordinates (a number and a letter) to sink ships. A given location is indicated by an *ordered pair*, in the form (x, y) where x and y are numbers that specify the exact location on the horizontal and vertical axes respectively. The location of points in the coordinate plane is based on one central point called the *origin*. The origin is where the two axes intersect and has the coordinates $(0, 0)$.

Figure 16.1 displays a coordinate plane that shows that the vertical axis is termed the y-axis, and the horizontal axis is termed the x-axis. Note that the values on the y-axis increase when moving upwards and decrease when moving downwards, while the x-values increase when moving right and decrease when moving left. The x-and y-axes divide the coordinate plane into four quadrants denoted as I, II, III, and IV, as seen in Figure 16.1. Also, in Figure 16.1, point A has coordinates of $(3, 1)$, point B has coordinates of $(-3, 1)$, point C has coordinates of $(-3, -1)$, and point D has coordinates of $(3, -1)$. The first number in the ordered pair indicates the location of a point in the x direction (left or right), while the second number in the ordered pair indicates the location of the same point in the y direction (up or down).

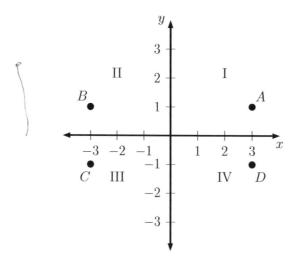

Figure 16.1

Example 1   Plot the following points on Figure 16.2.

1. $A(3, 2)$

2. $B(2, 3)$

3. $C(2, 0)$

4. $D(0, 3)$

5. $E(-2, 2)$

6. $F(-2, -1)$

7. $G(-2, 0)$

8. $H(2, -3)$

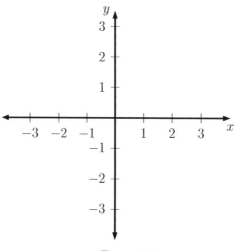

Figure 16.2

To plot each ordered pair, start at the origin $(0, 0)$ and remember "x before y" in the alphabet, therefore move along the x-axis first, then the y-axis. For example, $A(3, 2)$ tells us to move 3 units right along the x-axis and 2 units up the y-axis (See Figure 16 3 below).

214

ANSWER:

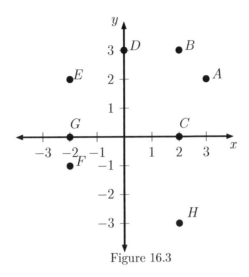

Figure 16.3

Example 2   In Figure 16.4 below, which point has the coordinates $(-4, -1)$?

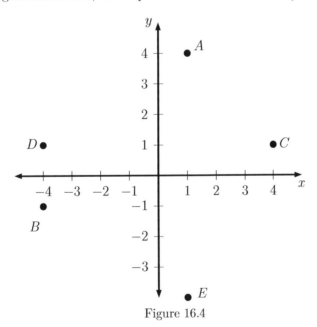

Figure 16.4

ANSWER: B. The ordered pair $(-4, -1)$ tells us that we are moving 4 units left of the origin and 1 unit down from the origin. The only point to the left, *and* below, the origin is point B.

Example 3 Which choice represents the coordinates of point Z in Figure 16.5?

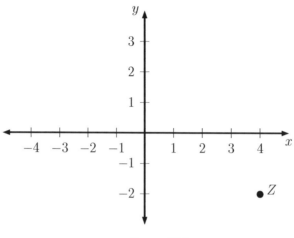

Figure 16.5

A. $(4, -2)$ B. $(-2, 4)$ C. $(-4, -2)$ D. $(-2, -4)$ E. $(4, 2)$

ANSWER: A. Point Z is to the right and below the origin. The x-coordinate will be positive, and the y-coordinate will be negative. The only answer choice that satisfies these conditions is A.

When plotting points on the coordinate plane, there are four types of transformations that we can do to move the points to different locations. These transformations are translations, reflections, rotations, and dilations. In this book, we will refer to only translations and reflections. When thinking of translations, think of sliding the figure from one place to another without changing the size, or rotating the figure.

Translation

Translation is the movement of a point or geometric figure from one location to another on the coordinate plane, with the condition that each point of the figure is moved in exactly the same direction and moved exactly the same distance. A translation will always produce a new figure that is identical in size, shape, and orientation to the original figure.

When translating a geometric figure (not a single point), find the new position of each individual point of the figure, and connect the points together to form the translated image.

Example 4 Use Figure 16.6 to translate segment AB one unit to the left and two units down.

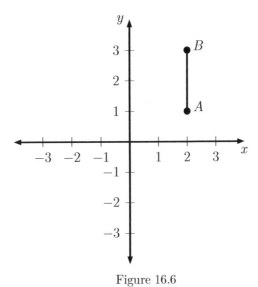

Figure 16.6

The translated segment is $A'B'$, shown in Figure 16.7, below. Point A, which has coordinates $(2, 1)$, will be moved one to the left (which will give a new x-coordinate of $2 - 1 = \mathbf{1}$), and two units downward which will give a new y-coordinate of $1 - 2 = -\mathbf{1}$). Follow the same procedure with point B.

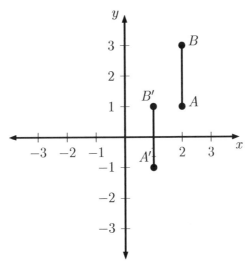

Figure 16.7

217

Example 5 To translate the triangle in Figure 16.8 one unit to the left and two units up, translate points A, B and C of the triangle (according to the dashed lines in this example) before forming the new image. Points A', B' and C' are the translated points, of the original points A, B and C respectively.

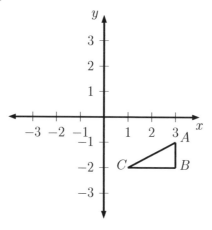

Figure 16.8

ANSWER: Start with point A and move the point 1 unit left and 2 units up. The new coordinate is $A'(2, 1)$. Both points B and C are moved in the same fashion and give new points $B'(2, 0)$ and $C'(0, 0)$. The graph is shown in Figure 16.9.

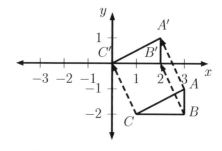

Figure 16.9

Example 6 Describe the transformation of figure ABC in Figure 16.10 below.

A. Up 1, left 2.

B. Up 2, left 1

C. Down 2, up 1

D. Down 2, down 1

E. Down 1, right 2

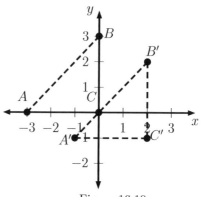

Figure 16.10

ANSWER: E. You can choose any point to start with. If we start at A, we see that A' is 2 units right and 1 unit down.

Reflection

Reflection of a point in the coordinate plane is comparable to reflecting an object in a mirror. To reflect a point, note the line (or point) of reflection, and find the shortest distance from the original point to the specified line (or point) of reflection. Once the distance from the point to the line (or point) of reflection is found, move the same distance past the line (or point) of reflection to find the position of the new point. An example is shown in Figure 16.11 (below), where the original point, F, which has coordinates of $(3, 2)$, is reflected across the y-axis. Point F is three units from the line of reflection (the y-axis), so the new point, F', will be exactly three units past the line of reflection, on the opposite side.

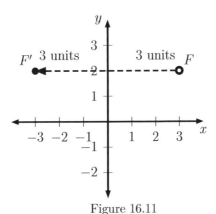

Figure 16.11

Example 7 Use Figure 16.12 to plot the reflection of segment $\overline{AB}$ over the y-axis.

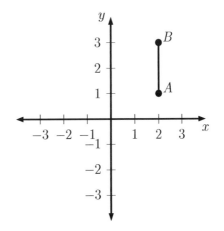

Figure 16.12

219

ANSWER: The answer is segment $A'B'$, below. The line of reflection, which is the y-axis, is two units to the left of point A. Continue an additional two units in the same direction to find A'. Point B' is found in the same manner. Once the location of the two points are found, connect A' and B' to plot the segment.

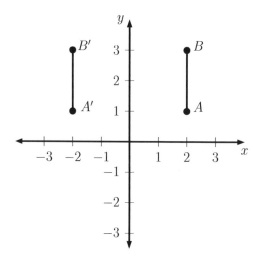

Figure 16.13

Slope

The slope of the line is the steepness of the line. A line that increases from left to right has positive slope, whereas a line that decreases from left to right has negative slope. A horizontal line has zero slope and a vertical line has undefined slope. The slope is measured by taking any two points on the line, and measuring the horizontal and vertical distance between them. The slope is the change in y-values divided by the change in x-values. For example, if one point on a line is at $(3, 4)$ and the other is at $(5, 8)$, then the change in y-values is $8 - 4 = 4$, whereas the change in x-values is $5 - 3 = 2$. Therefore the slope is the change in y, 4, divided by the change in x, 2. This is calculated as: $\frac{4}{2} = 2$.

Example 8 In Figure 16.14 (pictured right), which line has a slope of zero?

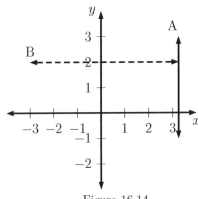

Figure 16.14

Answer: Line B We know that *horizontal lines* have a slope of zero. Therefore line B is the solution because the line doesn't slant upward or downward. Line A, a vertical line, has infinite slope.

Example 9 What is the slope of the line in the Figure 16.15?

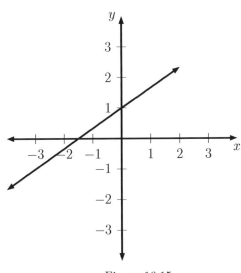

Figure 16.15

ANSWER: slope $= \frac{2}{3}$. To find the slope, we can use rise (the change in y values) over run (the change in x values). We begin with any point on the line. We see that $(-3, -1)$ and $(0, 1)$ are points on the line (see below). We need to move vertically two positive units, and right 3 units. Therefore our slope, m is $\frac{2}{3}$ (See Figure 16.16).

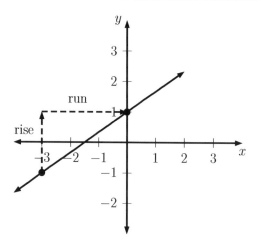

Figure 16.16

Lines in the coordinate plane

The slope-intercept form of a line is the equation $y = mx + b$. There is a simple way to identify the properties of a line in the coordinate plane, where m represents the slope, ("steepness" of a line; the *rise over run*) and b represents the y-intercept (where the line intersects the y-axis). This point can be represented with the ordered pair $(0, b)$, where b is the value of the y-intercept.

Example 10 What is the y-intercept of the line shown in Figure 16.17? Is the slope positive or negative?

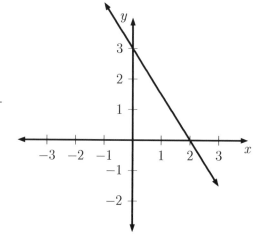

Figure 16.17

ANSWER: 3, negative. To find the y-intercept, we are looking at where the graph (line) crosses the y-axis (vertical axis). We see that the y-intercept of this graph is 3. Since the line slants downwards from left to right we know that the slope is negative.

Practice Problems

1. Plot the following points on a coordinate plane in Figure 16.18:

   (a) $A(-2, 3)$ (c) $C(-2, 0)$ (e) $E(-1, 3)$ (g) $G(2, 4)$

   (b) $B(0, -3)$ (d) $D(0, 2)$ (f) $F(-2, -3)$ (h) $H(-3, 2)$

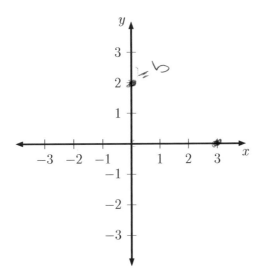

Figure 16.18

2. What is the equation of the line shown in Figure 16.19 below?

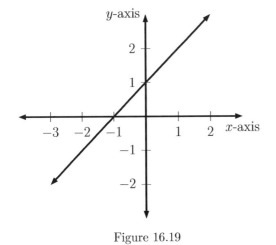

A. $y = -2x + 1$
B. $y = -x - 1$
C. $y = 2x - 1$
D. $y = x + 1$
E. $y = -x + 1$

Figure 16.19

223

3. Point A lies on an x, y-coordinate plane at $(3, -2)$. If this point is reflected about the x-axis, what would be the coordinates of the new point?

    A. $(2, 3)$
    B. $(-2, 3)$
    C. $(3, 2)$
    D. $(-3, 2)$
    E. $(-3, -2)$

4. In Figure 16.20 (below), ABC is reflected across the x-axis. Find the coordinates of the image of point B.

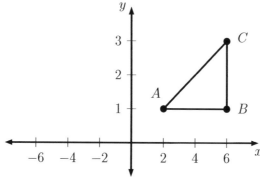

Figure 16.20

5. Find the slope of a line passing through points $A(0, -2)$ and $B(3, -3)$.

    A. $-\dfrac{1}{4}$ B. $-\dfrac{1}{3}$ C. 0 D. $\dfrac{1}{4}$ E. $\dfrac{1}{3}$

6. Which statement best represents the graph in Figure 16.21?

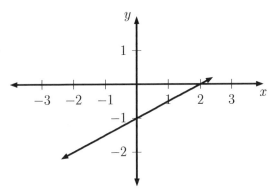

Figure 16.21

A. As x increases, y increases
B. As x increases, y remains the same
C. As x increases, y decreases
D. As x decreases, y remains constant
E. As x decreases, y increases

7. What is the slope of the line in Figure 16.22?

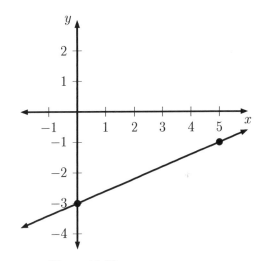

Figure 16.22

A. $\dfrac{4}{9}$ B. $\dfrac{2}{7}$ C. $\dfrac{3}{5}$ D. $\dfrac{3}{8}$ E. $\dfrac{2}{5}$

8. Given Figure 16.23 (below), draw the figure translated one unit up and 3 units to the left.

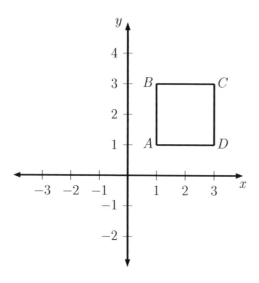

Figure 16.23

9. In which quadrant does point D lie in Figure 16.24?

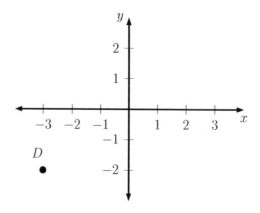

Figure 16.24

10. Write the coordinates of each of the points shown in Figure 16.25.

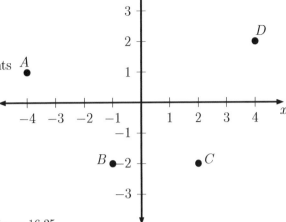

Figure 16.25

11. What is the y-intercept of the line shown in Figure 16.26?

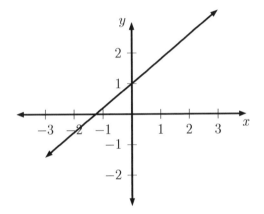

Figure 16.26

A. -1.25
B. -.5
C. 0
D. 1
E. 2

Solutions to Practice Problems

1.

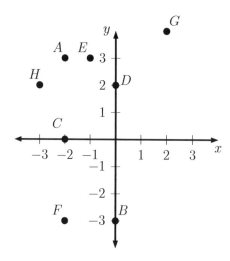

2. **D.** When looking at the specified line, notice the y-intercept and slope of that line and remember the slope-intercept equation of a line: $y = mx + b$. The y-intercept, the point at which the line intersects the y-axis, is $(0, 1)$, and the slope of the line is also positive, as the line increases from right to left. The only answer choice with a y-intercept of 1 and a positive slope is D.

3. **C.** Since we are reflecting over the x-axis, the y-coordinate will change to the opposite sign, while the x-coordinate stays the same. Therefore $A'(3, 2)$. The reflection is shown in Figure 16.27.

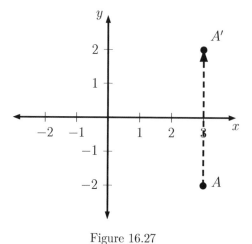

Figure 16.27

4. **(6,-1).** The x-coordinate stays the same and the y-coordinate changes to the opposite sign, therefore, $B'(6, -1)$ is our solution.

5. **B.** One approach to finding the slope of a line is to identify two points on the line and find the ratio $\dfrac{\text{rise}}{\text{run}}$, from one of these points to the other. Run is always left to right, while rise is always bottom to top. In this question, for example, from point A to point B, would require moving down 1 unit (rise=-1), and moving to the right 3 units (run=3), yielding a slope $= \dfrac{\text{rise}}{\text{run}} = -\dfrac{1}{3}$.

6. **A.** The slope of this graph is positive, because the graph is moving "up" as we move from left to right. Since the slope is positive, it tells us that both x and y are increasing as we move left to right. Note that answer choices C and E are equivalent.

7. **E.** Begin by locating two points on the graph (see Figure 16.28). We see that $(0, -3)$ and $(5, -1)$ are points on the graph. Starting at $(0, -3)$ move up 2 units and move right 5 units to get $(5, -1)$. Therefore the slope, m is $\frac{2}{5}$.

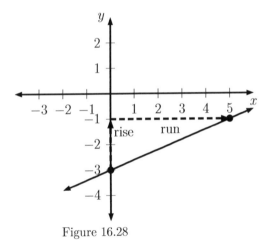

Figure 16.28

8. Each x-coordinate moves left 3 units, while each y-coordinate moves 1 unit up. The solution is sketched in Figure 16.29

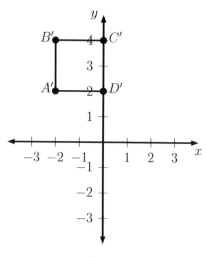

Figure 16.29

9. **Quadrant III.**

10. The coordinates of each point are written below. We move horizontally first, then vertically to find each point.

$$A(-4, 1), B(-1, -2), C(2, -2), D(4, 2)$$

11. **D.** The y-intercept is the point where our line crosses the y-axis (vertical axis). Therefore, we see that in this case the graph crosses the y-axis at 1, therefore, our y-intercept is 1.

Chapter 17

Interpretation of Graphs

The Praxis exam is sure to include at least a few questions on some type of graph. (You may be more comfortable thinking of these items as charts rather than graphs, but the words are essentially interchangeable). These graph questions nearly always involve one of three types of graphs: bar graphs, line graphs or circle graphs. This chapter explains each type and how to interpret them quickly and accurately to solve problems.

Bar Graphs:

Like traditional Cartesian coordinate graphs (x vs. y) that you might be used to, bar graphs also have two axis lines.

Here's an example of a graph:

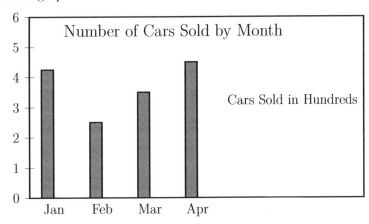

A few details to notice on this graph that you may encounter on the test are as follows. The numbers on the y-axis are in single digit units. But note that to the right of the graph, it is written "in hundreds," meaning that each tic mark on the *y*-axis represents 100 instead of 1.

Whenever you encounter a bar graph, use a simple three step approach:

1) Read the labels
2) Analyze the data
3) Use the data to solve what the question is asking.

For example, a common question regarding the above graph might be: About how many fewer cars were sold in February than in January? Following the 3-step process above, we quickly find the labels for January and February. Then we analyze that data. Be aware that this step requires us to estimate. While it is clear that 250 cars were sold in February, 350 in March and 450 in April, the bar for January is between the lines. As it is closer to the bar above than the one below, 430 is a fairly good estimate. So $430 - 250 = 180$ fewer cars sold in February. A common variant of a bar graph is the double bar graph, which compares more than one type of data. For example, the same chart above might appear as:

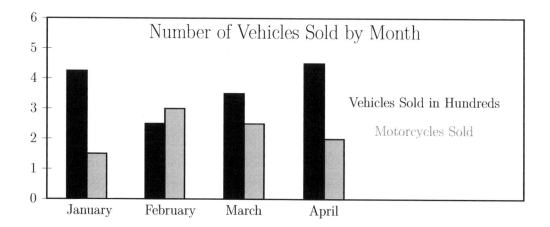

Line Graphs:

Bar graphs often show discrete or set intervals of time (such as months or years), or they can represent categories. Line graphs however are useful for showing changes over time. The slope of a line at any particular point determines whether something is increasing, decreasing or remaining the same.

Similar to a bar graph, a line graph has two axis lines. One is marked with a scale; and the other is usually marked in regular time intervals.

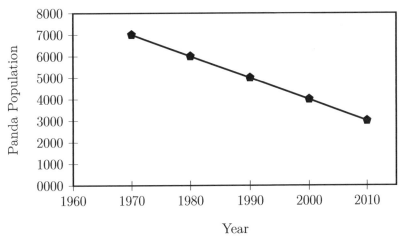

A common question here may ask a test-taker to estimate the number between the marked intervals. Such a question could read: About how many pandas were there in 1978? Moving a little before 1980 on the graph we are able to estimate about 6,200.

Circle Graphs:

A circle graph, also known as a pie chart, shows a series of fractions that make up a whole. Circle graphs consist of a single circle with different size slices that usually have labels and percentages. Sometimes they will have fractions instead of percentages. The size of each slice also corresponds to the fraction of the whole circle that the section represents. For example, a section labeled 50 percent will be half the circle, a section labeled 25 percent will be one fourth of the circle.

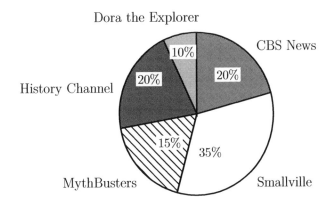

Note in the figure above that the larger percentages correspond to larger slices of the circle. For these types of graphs, a common type of question might be: Lilly only watches Smallville. Her father only watches the History Channel. If the total TV viewed in a week at the Parker household is 20 hours, how many more hours did Lilly watch in a week than her father?

If the total number of hours watched in the Parker household is twenty hours a week, that means that 1 hour = 5 percent. (because $\frac{1}{20} = .05 = 5\%$). So Lilly's 35 percent equals 7 hours. Her father's 20 percent equals 4 hours. 7 - 4 = 3. Lilly watches three more hours of TV than her father does.

Percent and Percent Change:

Before you read this chapter, makes sure you understand percentages well. Read the chapter on percentage if you haven't already. A common question using graphs will ask a test taker to change from a fraction to a percent or vice versa. Remember that 'percent' means 'out of a hundred'. The basic method is to divide the change in a number or the subset by the beginning total, and then divide by 100:

Percent change: $\dfrac{\text{end value - original value}}{\text{original}} \times 100\%$. The reasoning is that you are finding the change in value compared to what you started out with. We must convert that result to percentage by multiplying by 100 if the question is asking us to find the answer in percent form.

First, let's look at an example involving a ratio converted to a percent: If a graph shows that 320 action figures were sold and you are told that 80 of these are Ninja Turtle Action figures, you may well be asked what percentage of the total action figures sold are Ninja Turtle Action Figures.

To determine this you would divide 80 by 320 which yields a quotient of .25. We multiply this by 100 to get an answer of 25%.

Sample Questions:

Examples 1 and 2 refer to the chart at the right.

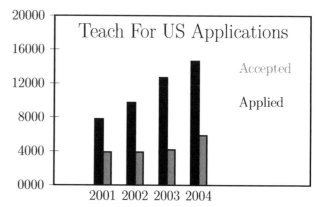

234

Example 1 In which year is the percentage of applicants accepted the greatest?

A. 2001
B. 2002
C. 2003
D. 2004

ANSWER: A. In 2001, there are about half as many acceptances as there are applicants. The rate of applications goes up dramatically every year, but the rate of acceptances goes up much slower. Therefore, the highest proportion of applicants accepted occurs in the first year. In 2001 there are 8,000 applicants and 4,000 acceptances so the acceptance rate was 50%.

Example 2 In what year was there the greatest percentage increase in applicants as compared to the previous year?

A. 2002
B. 2003
C. 2004
D. The percentage increase was the same each year.

ANSWER: B. This requires us to estimate the number of applicants from each year based upon the graph. There are 8,000 applicants in 2001, 10,000 in 2002, 13,000 in 2003, and 15,000 in 2004. This means that the biggest percentage increase in applicants was between 2002 and 2003 (30 percent). Between 2001 and 2002 there was a 25% increase. The percent increase is calculated as: $\dfrac{\text{end value - beginning value}}{\text{beginning value}} \times 100\%$ The end value is 10,000 and the beginning value is 8000.

$$\frac{10,000 - 8,000}{8,000} \times 100\% = 25\%$$

Between 2003 and 2004:

$$\frac{15,000 - 13,000}{13,000} \times 100\% = 15.4\%$$

Note that we can eliminate answer choice A because we have not been given data for 2001.

Example 3 In the sample line graph shown earlier in this chapter, which decade showed the greatest percentage decrease in the population of pandas?

    A. 1970-1980

    B. 1980-1990

    C. 1990-2000

    D. 2000-2010

    E. They are all the same.

ANSWER: D Although the overall decrease in numbers of pandas is the same each decade, this question asks for the percentage decrease. This is a bit tricky. It looks like since it is a line, the percent change is the same along the line. But that is deceiving. We can look at the first line segment and the last line segment. Between 1970 and 1980 there is a drop of 14.3%. This is calculated as follows:

$$\frac{6,000 - 7,000}{7,000} \times 100\% = 14.3\%$$

In 2010, we have:

$$\frac{3,000 - 4,000}{4,000} \times 100\% = 25\%$$

We can see that even though the slope of the line segments are the same from year to year, the percent change drops from the first year to the last. Therefore we do not have to calculate the other years.

Examples 4 and 5 refer to the chart below. The chart shows the percentage of a 24-hour day Amanda is engaged in a particular activity.

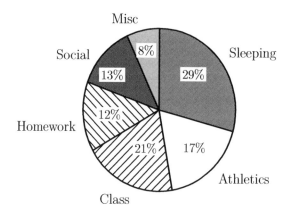

Example 4 For about how many hours a day is Amanda either in class or doing homework?

  A. 6 hours
  B. 7 hours
  C. 8 hours
  D. 9 hours
  E. 10 hours

ANSWER: C. The circle graph shows that the percentage of time spent in class is 21 percent and that the percentage of time spent doing homework is 12%. Adding these together give us 33%. That is about one third of a 24 hour day, or 8 hours.

Example 5 Amanda's mother asks if she is getting at least 8 hours of sleep a night. Is she?

ANSWER: No. 8 hours of sleep would be equivalent to 33.3% of the day. Amanda only spends 29% of her time sleeping, so she does not quite get 8 hours, but she is pretty close.

Examples 6, 7 and 8 refer to the chart below.

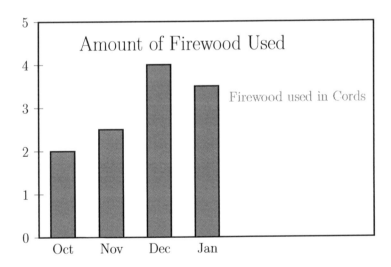

Example 6 This chart shows the amount of firewood used by a household from October 2009 through January 2010. What is the total number of cords that were used by the household during the last three months of 2009?

ANSWER: 8.5 cords. The graph shows that 4 cords were consumed in December, 2.5 cords in November and 2 in October. These are the last three months in the year, and if you add these three amounts together you get 8.5 cords.

Example 7 What percent of the total amount of wood used during the four months shown is used during December?

    A. 15%
    B. 20%
    C. 25%
    D. 33%
    E. 40%

ANSWER: D Adding up the total number of cords for the four months gives us 12 ($2 + 2.5 + 4 + 3.5 = 12$). Since 4 cords are burned in December, $\frac{4}{12} \times 100\% = 33\%$.

Example 8 Did the Coopers burn more wood in December 2009 than in November and October of 2009 combined?

ANSWER: No. Here we just sum the amounts from October and November. $2 + 2.5 = 4.5$ which is greater than the 4 cords burned during December.

Examples 9 and 10 refer to the chart below.

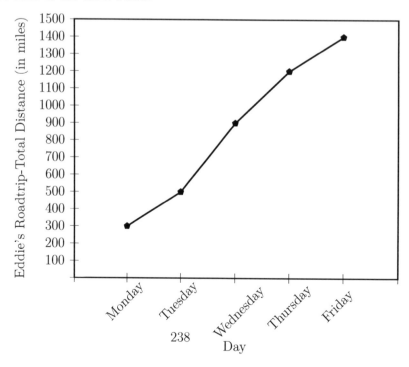

Eddie is going on a road trip through the American Southwest for the beginning of the summer. The tic marks show the total distance he has travelled at the end of the day.

Example 9 What is the average daily distance that Eddie has travelled over the course of the five days?

ANSWER: 280 miles per day To calculate this we simply take the final distance at day's end on Friday (1,400 miles) and divide that by the total number of days (5 days). Note that we do NOT add the figures for the days because the graph shows the running total from one day to the next. In other words, the figures are already added up for us in the graph.

Example 10 During which day did Eddie cover the most distance?

   A. Monday
   B. Tuesday
   C. Wednesday
   D. Thursday
   E. Friday

ANSWER: C By looking at the line, the greatest difference between the values of the distance at day's end occurs between Tuesday and Wednesday. This is because the slope of the line is greatest between those days. Therefore, he covered the most distance on Wednesday.

Practice Problems

Questions 1, 2 and 3 refer to the chart below.

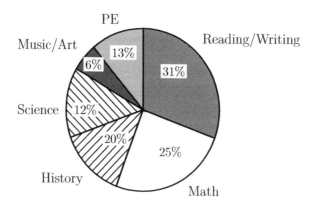

Colin, who has a fifth grade classroom, teaches all subjects to his students.

1. If Colin spends two hours teaching math, how many hours long is the entire school day?

   A. 2 hours
   B. 6 hours
   C. 7 hours
   D. 8 hours
   E. 24 hours

2. Does Colin spend more time teaching reading and writing combined or math and science combined?

3. In an eight hour day, how much more time is spent on math than is spent on Music/Art?

Questions 4, 5 and 6 refer to the chart below.

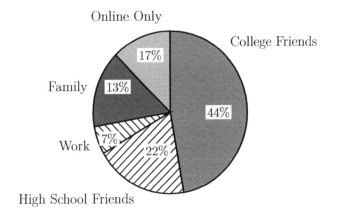

4. If Jen is connected to 150 people total, how many of her friends are college friends?

5. If Jen has 200 friends total, how many of them are high school friends?

   A. 20 friends
   B. 22 friends
   C. 33 friends
   D. 44 friends
   E. 50 friends

6. If Jen has a total of 300 friends on her favorite social networking site, how many more of her friends has she met in person than has she met only online?

   Questions 7, 8 and 9 refer to the chart below.

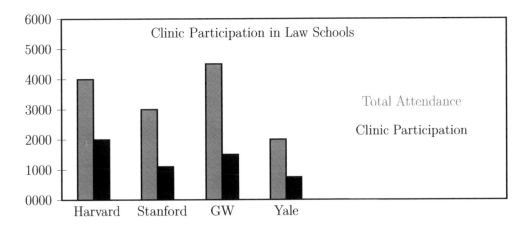

7. Which law school has the highest percentage of its total student body participating in a clinical education program?

   A. GW
   B. Harvard
   C. Yale
   D. Stanford

8. Among the four law schools, what is the average percentage of students who took part in a clinical education program?

   A. 24%
   B. 29%
   C. 35%
   D. 42%

9. Which law school had a higher percentage of its student body enhance their legal education with a clinical experience: Stanford or Harvard?

   Questions 10, 11 and 12 refer to the chart below.

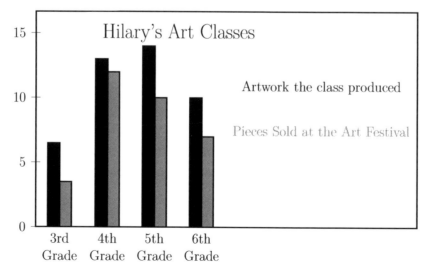

Hilary teaches art classes to 4 different grade levels at Santa Fe Middle School. The black columns represent the total number of artwork pieces that the class produced, and the grey columns represent the number of pieces that were sold at the art festival at the end of the year.

10. What percentage (%) of the art pieces produced by the 6th grade class were sold?

11. Which class had the smallest percentage of their pieces sold?

    A. 3rd Grade
    B. 4th Grade
    C. 5th Grade
    D. 6th Grade

12. What was the average percentage of pieces sold among all four classes?

    Questions 13, 14 and 15 refer to the chart below.

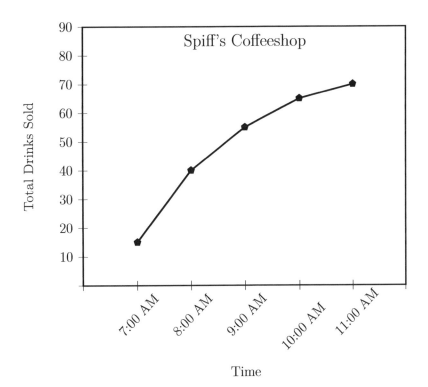

The top coffee shop in Gurneville California keeps records that indicate the total amount of coffee sold during an average Tuesday morning by noting the total count of drinks sold at the end of each hour that they are open.

13. During what hour do they sell the most drinks?

    A. Between 6 and 7.
    B. Between 7 and 8.
    C. Between 8 and 9.
    D. Between 9 and 10.

14. How many fewer drinks were sold between the hours of 9:00 - 11:00 than were sold during the hours between 7:00 - 9:00?

15. What is the average number of drinks sold per hour between 6:00 am and 11:00 am?

Solutions to Practice Problems

1. **D.** We see from the circle graph that math instruction takes up 25 percent, or one fourth, of the day. If this percentage is equivalent to 2 hours of time, then the whole days is 4 times 2 hours, or a total of 8 hours.

2. **Math and science combined**. The Reading/Writing portion of the graph is 31 percent. The Math section is 25% and the Science is 13% so Math and Science combined is 38%.

3. **1.5 hours more.** This problem requires us to convert from percentages to hours. The difference between the subjects is 25% - 6% = 19%. Therefore we need to calculate 19% of 8 hours. We make the following calculation: $\frac{19}{100} \cdot 8 = \frac{152}{100} = 1.52$ or about 1.5 hours.

4. **66 friends.** 44% of 150 is 66.

5. **D.** 22% of 200 is 44%.

6. **198 friends.** Online only is 17 percent so the remaining percentage (83%) are the ones she has met in person. The difference between these two figures is 83% - 17% = 66%. 66% of 300 is 198.

7. **B.** Harvard has a total attendance of 4,000 students and clinical participation of 2,000. This means the percentage of clinic participation is 50%. This is significantly higher than the other schools.

8. **D.** This question requires us to add the total participation in clinics across all four schools as well as the total attendance. Attendance = 4,000 + 3,000 + 4,500 + 2,000 = 13,500. Clinic Participation = 2,000 + 1,000 + 1,500 + 500 = 5,000. So we have 5,000 divided by 12,000, which produces a quotient of 41.666 percent which rounds to 42%.

9. **Harvard.** The percentage of students that take part in Stanford is 33% (1,000 out of 3,000). The percentage at Harvard is about 50% (2,000 out of 4,000).

10. **70%.** In the 6th grade, 10 pieces were produced. The column representing the pieces sold is 7. 70% of 10 is 7.

11. **3rd Grade.** In 3rd grade there were 7 pieces produced and 4 sold. This is a sales percentage of 57%, which is considerably lower than the other three grades represented.

12. **75%.** There were 44 total pieces produced. The total number sold was 33. 33 is 75% of 44.

13. **B.** The graph is steepest between 7:00 and 8:00. 25 drinks were sold during this hour which is greater than the amount sold during any other one hour time period.

14. **25 drinks.** Between 7 and 9, $55 - 15 = 40$ drinks were sold, while between 9 and 11, $70 - 55 = 15$ drinks were sold. The difference between 40 and 15 is 25.

15. **14 drinks per hour.** 70 drinks total divided by 5 hours equals 14 drinks per hour.

Section VII: Statistics

Chapter 18

Statistics

Probability is defined as "The extent to which an event is likely to occur, expressed as the ratio of the actual cases to the total number of possible cases." In short, it is the likelihood of something happening. The probability of an event is equal to:

$$\text{Probability} = \frac{\text{Number of favorable outcomes possible}}{\text{total number of possible outcomes}}$$

Example 1 As an example, three marbles are in a hat – one red, one blue, and one yellow. What is the probability of picking a yellow marble at random out of the hat?

ANSWER: $\frac{1}{3}$. The number of favorable outcomes in this case (picking a yellow marble) is 1, while the total number of possible outcomes is 3. So there is a one in three chance of picking a yellow marble.

Example 2 An independent event means that the event does not depend on another event. For example, a woman who gives birth, has a fifty-fifty chance of delivering a male. After she delivered a male, two years later she gives birth again. What is the probability of her delivering another male?

ANSWER: $\frac{1}{2}$. The reason the probability is one in two is because the second birth does not depend on the first birth. The two events are independent.

When two independent events, A and B, occur, the probability of A occurring and then B occurring, is the probability of $A \times B$ occurring. Similarly, the probability of A occurring followed by B occurring, followed by C occurring, is $A \times B \times C$, and so forth.

Example 3   A woman gives birth to three babies in her lifetime. What is the probability that all three babies are male?

ANSWER: The probability of a baby boy is one in two, or $\frac{1}{2}$. The probability of the next baby being male is also $\frac{1}{2}$. The probability of the next baby being male is, again, $\frac{1}{2}$. So the probability of 3 baby boys is $\frac{1}{2} \times \frac{1}{2} \times \frac{1}{2} = \frac{1}{8}$.

Why is this true? Lets call a baby boy, B, and a baby girl, G. What are the possible outcomes?

B,B,B means a boy, followed by a boy, followed by a third boy. B,G,G, is a boy, followed by a girl, followed by another girl. To summarize the eight possibilities, we get:

B,B,B
B,B,G
B,G,B
B,G,G
G,G,G
G,B,G
G,B,B
G,G,B

Those are the only eight possibilities, as we calculated above.

Example 4   There are 10 marbles in a hat – 3 blue, 2 red, 4 green, and 1 yellow. What is the probability of picking a blue marble, without putting the marble back into the hat, (without replacement) followed by a green marble (again, without replacement), followed by a yellow marble (without replacement)?

ANSWER: $\frac{1}{60}$. The probability of picking a blue marble is 3 in 10, or $\frac{3}{10}$. Now there are 9 marbles left in the hat: 2 blue, 2 red, 4 green, and one yellow. The probability of picking a green marble is four in nine or $\frac{4}{9}$. Now there are 8 marbles left in the hat. The probability of picking a yellow marble is one in eight $\frac{1}{8}$. According to our argument above, the probability of those three events happening as described in the problem, since they are independent events, is $\frac{3}{10} \times \frac{4}{9} \times \frac{1}{8} = \frac{3 \times 4 \times 1}{10 \times 9 \times 8} = \frac{12}{720} = \frac{1}{60}$.

Example 5   In the same hat as in the above question, with the same distribution of marbles, what is the probability of picking a blue marble, then a green marble, then a yellow marble, with replacement (meaning that you return each marble back into the hat after you take it out)?

ANSWER: $\frac{3}{250}$. The probability will be $\frac{3}{10} \times \frac{4}{10} \times \frac{1}{10} = \frac{12}{1000} = \frac{3}{250}$.

Mean, Median, and Mode

There are three terms in statistics you need to know: Mean, Median, and Mode. The **mean** of a set of data is what you know as "average." To find the mean (or otherwise known as arithmetic mean) of a set of data, you add up all the numbers in the data set, and then divide by the number of data points you added up. **Median** is the number exactly in the middle of all data points, when the data points are arranged from lowest to highest. If there is an even number of data points, the median is the mean of the two middle most numbers. The **mode** is the most frequent number that occurs in the data. It is possible to have more than one mode, or none if there are no repeats.

Example 6   Given the following data set, find the mean, median, and mode:

$$\{1, 3, 5, 9, 12, 20, 21, 23, 23\}$$

ANSWER: Mean=13, Median=12,Mode=23. To find the mean, we add up all the numbers to obtain 117, and then divide by the number of numbers in this set, 9, to obtain: $\frac{117}{9} = 13$. The median is the middle number, in this case 12, since there are 4 numbers to the left of 12 and 4 numbers to the right of 12. The mode is 23, because there are two 23's, which is the most frequently occurring number.

Example 7   Given the following data set, find the mean, median, and mode:

$$\{13, 2, 4, 15, 16, 14, 13\}$$

First place the numbers in order from lowest to highest:

$$\{2, 4, 13, 13, 14, 15, 16\}$$

ANSWER: Mean: 11, Median: 13, Mode: 13. To find the mean, we add up the numbers to obtain 77, and then divide by 7 (the number of numbers in the set), to obtain 11. The median is 13. The mode is also 13.

Example 8   The arithmetic mean of 11 numbers is 13. What is the sum of those numbers?

ANSWER: 143 Let's call the sum of the numbers, x. That means that the mean of the numbers is: $\frac{x}{11} = 13$. Multiplying both sides of the equation by 11, we obtain, $x = 13 \times 11 = 143$.

Example 9   What is the average of $\frac{5}{6}$ and $\frac{3}{4}$?

A. $\dfrac{19}{24}$

B. $\dfrac{23}{24}$

C. $\dfrac{25}{27}$

D. $\dfrac{29}{27}$

E. $\dfrac{31}{27}$

ANSWER: A. We add the two fractions, and divide by two: $\frac{\frac{5}{6}+\frac{3}{4}}{2} = \frac{\frac{19}{12}}{2} = \frac{19}{24}$.

Example 10   What is the sum of the mean, median, and mode of the following set of numbers:

$$\{1, 4, 7, 13, 15, 16, 16, 16\}$$

A. 32

B. 35

C. 37

D. 41

E. 43

ANSWER: D. The mean of the 8 numbers is $\frac{88}{8} = 11$. The median is $\frac{13+15}{2} = 14$, and the mode is 16. The sum of the mean, median, and mode is $11 + 14 + 16 = 41$.

Practice Problems

1. A woman gives birth to four babies in her lifetime. What is the probability that of her having 3 boys and one girl?

    A. $\dfrac{1}{4}$

    B. $\dfrac{1}{8}$

    C. $\dfrac{1}{12}$

    D. $\dfrac{1}{16}$

    E. $\dfrac{1}{24}$

2. A spinner contains 16 numbers from 1 to 16. What is the probability that the needle will land on an odd number divisible by 3?

    A. $\dfrac{1}{3}$

    B. $\dfrac{1}{16}$

    C. $\dfrac{3}{16}$

    D. $\dfrac{5}{16}$

    E. $\dfrac{8}{16}$

3. A hat holds twenty four balloons: 1 red, 11 blue, 3 yellow, 4 green, 1 purple, and 4 orange. What is the probability of picking a non-blue balloon out of the hat?

    A. $\dfrac{9}{24}$ B. $\dfrac{11}{24}$ C. $\dfrac{13}{24}$ D. $\dfrac{15}{24}$ E. $\dfrac{17}{24}$

4. A hat holds pieces of paper containing one number each, from 1 through 40. What is the probability of picking a prime number?

    A. $\dfrac{3}{20}$

    B. $\dfrac{2}{5}$

    C. $\dfrac{13}{40}$

    D. $\dfrac{3}{10}$

    E. $\dfrac{14}{41}$

5. A jar holds 10 marbles: 2 blue, 5 yellow, and 3 red. What is the probability of picking a red marble, then a blue marble, if the red marble is not replaced?

    A. $\dfrac{1}{15}$

    B. $\dfrac{1}{18}$

    C. $\dfrac{1}{30}$

    D. $\dfrac{3}{38}$

    E. $\dfrac{7}{90}$

6. A jar holds 15 marbles: 10 red, 3 blue, and 2 green. What is the probability of picking 2 green marbles in a row, if the first marble is not replaced in the jar?

    A. $\dfrac{1}{105}$

    B. $\dfrac{2}{103}$

    C. $\dfrac{1}{225}$

    D. $\dfrac{2}{225}$

    E. $\dfrac{1}{75}$

7. Given the following data set, what is the sum of the mean, median, and mode?

$$\{1, 4, 7, 7, 8, 9, 12, 17, 19, 19, 19, 22\}$$

    A. 36.25
    B. 38.50
    C. 41.50
    D. 42.75
    E. 43.00

8. Given the following data set, find the median:

$$\{5, 17, 5, 9, 18, 22, 25, 3\}$$

    A. 16.5
    B. 13.0
    C. 18.6
    D. 18.8
    E. 19.2

9. What is the difference between the mode and median in the following data set:

$$\{3, 4, 5, 8, 15, 4, 8, 2, 8, 6, 3\}$$

    A. 1
    B. 1.50
    C. 2.50
    D. 3
    E. 4.20

10. What is the average of $\frac{3}{7}$ and $\frac{3}{14}$?

    A. $\dfrac{3}{28}$

    B. $\dfrac{5}{28}$

    C. $\dfrac{9}{28}$

    D. $\dfrac{3}{42}$

    E. $\dfrac{9}{42}$

Solutions to Practice Problems

1. **A.** The probability of having either sex is one in two. Since we are working with such a small amount of children, we can list the possible cases: GBBB, BGBB, BBGB, BBBG. There are four ways to have girl, so $\frac{4}{16}$ or $\frac{1}{4}$.

2. **C.** These are the numbers between 1 and 16 that are odd and divisible by 3: 3,9,15. Therefore the probability of the needle landing on any one of those numbers is 3 in 16.

3. **C.** There are 24 balloons, including 11 blue ones. If there are 11 blue ones, that means there are 24-11 = 13 non-blue balloons. The probability of picking a non-blue balloon is $\frac{13}{24}$.

4. **D.** A prime number is divisible only by itself *and* one. Many non-mathematicians erroneously believe that 1 is a prime number. It is not. 2 is the first prime number. The other prime numbers that follow through the number 40 are 3,5,7,11,13,17,19,23,29,31,37. So there are 12 prime numbers, out of 40 numbers, or 12 out of 40, or 3 out of 10.

5. **A.** The probability of picking a red marble is 3 in 10, or $\frac{3}{10}$. Now there are 9 marbles left. The probability of picking a blue marble is 2 in 9, or $\frac{2}{9}$. The probability of picking a red, then a blue marble if the red marble is not returned to the hat (not replaced), is $\frac{3}{10} \times \frac{2}{9} = \frac{6}{90} = \frac{1}{15}$.

6. **A.** The probability of picking a green marble is $\frac{2}{15}$. After this, the jar contains only 14 marbles, one of which is green, so the probability of picking a green marble this time is $\frac{1}{14}$. The two events, when combined, have a probability of $\frac{2}{15} \times \frac{1}{14} = \frac{1}{105}$

7. **C.** The mean is calculated as follows: $\frac{1+4+7+7+8+9+12+17+19+19+19+22}{12} = 12$. The median is the number exactly in the middle of the data set. In this case we have an even number of data, so the middle two numbers are 9 and 12, and the mean of those numbers is 10.5, so the median is 10.5. The mode is the most frequent number in the data set, or 19. Together, we have 12 + 10.5 + 19 = 41.5.

8. **B.** First place the numbers in order from lowest to highest: 3,5,5,9,17,18,22,25. Since there are an even number of numbers in this data set, the median number is the average between the two numbers in the middle of the data set. In this case, they are 9 and 17. The average is $\frac{9+17}{2} = 13$.

9. **D.** First, arrange the numbers in order from smallest to largest: 2,3,3,4,4,5,6,8,8,8,15. The median is the middle number, in this case, 5. The mode is 8. The difference is the mode minus the median = 8 − 5 = 3.

10. **C.** We calculate the average as: $\frac{\frac{3}{7}+\frac{3}{14}}{2} = \frac{\frac{6}{14}+\frac{3}{14}}{2} = \frac{\frac{9}{14}}{2} = \frac{9}{28}$.

Section VIII: Miscellaneous Topics

Chapter 19

Scientific Notation

Scientific notation is used to format numbers, but not change their values. Although it can be used to represent any number, it is most often used for very large and very small numbers, such as ones that would not fit on a calculator screen. Earth's circumference or the mass of an electron are measurements that are typically represented in scientific notation. Please review the chapter on exponents before reading this chapter.

Review of Exponents

Before we understand scientific notation, we must understand exponents. If we wanted to express $10 \times 10 \times 10 \times 10 \times 10 \times 10$ using exponents, we count the number of times 10 appears, which is 6 in this case, and simply write: 1,000,000. But what if you are an astrophysicist and want to represent the number 1,000,000,000,000,000,000? It is inconvenient to count zeros. Instead we can represent the number more simply in scientific notation as 1.0×10^{18}. The exponent, 18, is the number of zeros after the decimal point.

What if we wanted to express instead of a huge number, a tiny number, such as the weight of a proton? The mass of the proton is $1.67262171 \times 10^{-27}$ kilograms. The negative exponent indicates that the absolute value of the number is less than 1. In fact it is: 0.00000000000000000000000000167262171 kilograms. Now you know why we need exponents!

Examples of exponents of 10:

$$10^3 = 10 \times 10 \times 10 = 1000$$
$$10^2 = 10 \times 10 = 100$$
$$10^1 = 10$$
$$10^0 = 1$$
$$10^{-1} = \frac{1}{10} = 0.1$$
$$10^{-2} = \frac{1}{10^2} = \frac{1}{10 \times 10} = \frac{1}{100} = 0.01$$

Format of Scientific Notation

The form of scientific notation is $a \times 10^n$, where a is the coefficient and $1 \leq a < 10$ or $-10 < a \leq -1$, and n is the exponent, any integer.

Examples:

0.00456 is written as 4.56×10^{-3} in scientific notation. Here a is 4.56 and n is -3.

$-910,000$ is written as -9.1×10^5 in scientific notation. Here a is -9.1 and n is 5.

To change a number to scientific notation, move the decimal point so that it is after the first non-zero digit. Take the number 13.4. We want to change it so that it is in scientific notation. 1.34 would be in scientific notation. But changing 13.4 to 1.34 moves the decimal point to the left once. Therefore, we need to multiply by 10 raised to the first power to obtain 1.34×10^1. Here the exponent above the 10 is positive one. It's positive because we moved the decimal to the left, and one because we moved the decimal once. Now take the number .0134. Again, we want to change it so that the number is 1.34. We move the decimal place two units to the right this time. Therefore, we multiply by 10 raised to the negative two power, to get 1.34×10^{-2}. It's negative because we moved the decimal to the right, and two because we moved the decimal two places.

To sum up, when we take a number that is not in scientific notation, and we change it into scientific notation, if we move the decimal place to the right, the exponent, n, will be negative. Similarly, if we move the decimal place to the left, the exponent, n, will be positive, as in the case with the number 13.4.

We can form four rules:

Rule 1: In going from scientific notation to standard decimal form, a positive exponent moves the decimal point to the right.

Rule 2: In going from scientific notation to standard decimal form, a negative exponent moves the decimal point to the left.

Rule 3: In going from a number to scientific notation, if you move the decimal to the left, the exponent will be positive.

Rule 4: In going from a number to scientific notation, if you move the decimal to the right, the exponent will be negative.

Example 1   Write 3200 in scientific notation.

ANSWER: 3.2×10^3. We have a beginning number greater than 1. Therefore we have to move the decimal point to the left which will make the exponent n positive (see Rule 3) . In order to have an a value $1 \le a < 10$ we move the decimal 3 places to the left (Remember if the decimal is not seen, it is always at the far right 3200.). Therefore, $3200 = 3.2 \times 10^3$.

Example 2   Write $-910,000$ in scientific notation.

ANSWER: -9.1×10^5. Even though the number is negative, we will still move the decimal point to the left. Therefore, n will be positive (Rule 3). In order to have an a value between $-10 < a \le -1$ we must move the decimal place 5 places to the left. Thus, $-910,000 = -9.1 \times 10^5$.

Example 3   Express .345 in scientific notation.

ANSWER: 3.45×10^{-1}. Since our number is less than 1, we know that we have to move the decimal point to the right in order for $1 \le a < 10$. Since we are moving the decimal point right, the exponent n will be negative (Rule 4). Thus, $.345 = 3.45 \times 10^{-1}$

To go from scientific number to a number in standard form, we simply do the opposite. For the next two examples, follow Rules 1 and 2.

Example 4   Write 4.56×10^{-3} in standard form.

ANSWER: .00456. Since the exponent n is negative, we have to move the decimal point 3 to the left (Rule 2). Therefore, $4.56 \times 10^{-3} = .00456$

Every number can be expressed in scientific notation. Here are a few more examples:

$$10 = 1 \times 10^1$$
$$67890.12 = 6.789012 \times 10^4$$
$$-100,0000,000.012345 = -1.00000000012345 \times 10^8$$

If the decimal does not need to be moved (the absolute value of the original number is greater than or equal to 1 and less than 10), then i is 0.

$$1 = 1 \times 10^0$$
$$8.345 = 8.345 \times 10^0$$

Remember: The decimal point for an integer is after the number. For example, 980 and 980. are the same number. The decimal is not required after integers, but can be helpful when manipulating numbers into scientific notation.

Example 5 Write 9876543.21098 in scientific notation.

ANSWER: 9.87654321098 × 10⁶. Since the number is larger than one, move the decimal point to the left, making the exponent positive (Rule 3).

Example 6 Write −0.0081 in scientific notation.

ANSWER: −8.1 × 10⁻³. Move the decimal so that it is after the 8. Because it had to be moved 3 places to the right, the exponent must be −3.

Example 7 0.048042 can be written as 4.8042×10^x. What is the value of x?

   A. -4
   B. -2
   C. 1
   D. 2
   E. 4

ANSWER: B. The decimal point is moved 2 places to the right, so the exponent must be -2.

Example 8 Write 8.2 in scientific notation.

ANSWER: 8.2 × 10⁰. The decimal point does not need to be moved, so the exponent is zero. Also, recall that $x^0 = 1$ so $8.2 \times 10^0 = 8.2 \times 1 = 8.2$.

Example 9 Convert 3.334×10^5 to decimal form.

ANSWER: 333,400 Move the decimal point 5 places to the right since the exponent is positive 5.

Example 10 $(4 \times 10^3) \times (2 \times 10^3)$ can also be written in which way?

    A. 6×10^6
    B. 6×10^3
    C. 8×10^3
    D. 8×10^6
    E. 96×10^1

ANSWER: D. The Associative Property of Multiplication allows us to change the order of multiplication. Then multiply $10^3 \times 10^3$ to get 10^6 by adding the exponents when the bases are the same. So we have: $(4 \times 2) \times (10^3 \times 10^3) = (8) \times (10^6)$.

Example 11 2.5×10^0 is greater than which number?

    A. 0.25×10^2
    B. 2.5×10^{-2}
    C. 2.5×10^1
    D. 2.5×10^5
    E. 2500×10^{-1}

ANSWER: B. The numbers can be written in decimal form to be compared to $2.5 \times 10^0 = 2.5$.

Example 12 Compute $(5 \times 10^6) + (2 \times 10^8)$.

    A. 2.05×10^8
    B. 7×10^2
    C. 7×10^{14}
    D. 7×10^{48}
    E. 10×10^{14}

ANSWER: A. The coefficients can only be added if they have the same base and exponent. Change the numbers so that they have the same power of 10. $5 \times 10^6 = 0.05 \times 10^8$. Use the Distributive Property to add the coefficients and keep the same power of 10. $(0.05 \times 10^8) + (2 \times 10^8) = (0.05 + 2) \times 10^8 = 2.05 \times 10^8$.

Example 13   81550 can also be represented by:

 A. 0.08155×10^{-2}
 B. 8.1550×10^3
 C. 8.155000×10^4
 D. 8155.000×10^2
 E. 8155.0×10^3

ANSWER: C. Change each answer choice to decimal form to see which one is equal.

$0.08155 \times 10^{-2} = 0.0008155$ $8.1550 \times 10^3 = 8155.0$ $\mathbf{8.155000 \times 10^4 = 81550.00}$ $8155.000 \times 10^2 = 815500.0$ $8155.0 \times 10^3 = 8,155,000$

Example 14 19.0753×10^{-3} can be written in scientific notation as

 A. 0.190753
 B. 1.90753×10^{-4}
 C. 1.90753×10^{-2}
 D. 19075.3
 E. 19075.3×10^0

ANSWER: C. $19.0753 \times 10^{-3} = 0.0190753$ in decimal form since the exponent of -3 indicates that the decimal should be moved 3 places to the left. To put 0.0190753 in scientific notation, the decimal must be moved to between the 1 and to 9, which is 2 places. This gives us 1.90753×10^{-2}.

Practice Problems

1. Write 802,000,000 in scientific notation.

2. Write 0.00091 in scientific notation.

3. Convert $-34,000,100.01$ to scientific notation.

4. Write 9.0630×10^{-3} in decimal form.

5. 500,900,700 can be written as 5.009007×10^c. What is the value of c?

   A. -8
   B. -6
   C. 3
   D. 6
   E. 8

6. Which choice represents 5×300 in scientific notation?

   A. 1.5×10^2
   B. 1.5×10^3
   C. 15.0×10^{-2}
   D. 15.0×10^2
   E. 1500

7. Which of the following numbers is equal to 580,000 and expressed in scientific notation?

   A. 0.580000×10^4
   B. 0.58×10^6
   C. 5.8×10^5
   E. 58×10^4
   E. 58.0000×10^4

8. How is 6 represented in scientific notation?

    A. 6
    B. 6.0
    C. 6×10^0
    D. 6×10^1
    E. 6.00×10^2

9. Express 0.01071977 in scientific notation.

    A. 0.1071977×10^{-1}
    B. 1.071977×10^{-2}
    C. 1.071977×10^2
    D. 10.71977×10^{-3}
    E. 10.71977×10^3

10. $\frac{5}{100000}$ is equal to which number?

    A. 0.000005
    B. 0.5×10000
    C. 5×10^{-5}
    D. 5×10^{-4}
    E. 5×10^4

11. 8.9898×10^3 has the same value as which of the following?

    I. 8989.8
    II. 89.898×10^2
    III. 89898×10^{-1}

    A. I only
    B. II only
    C. III only
    D. I and II only
    E. I, II and III

12. $\frac{12 \times 10^8}{3 \times 10^2}$ is equal to:

    A. 4×10^4 B. 4×10^6 C. 9×10^6 D. 15×10^{10} E. 36×10^{10}

13. Which statements are true?

    I. $5.8 \times 10^3 < 5.8 \times 10^4$
    II. $5.8 \times 10^{-3} < 5.8 \times 10^{-4}$
    III. $5.8 \times 10^{-4} < 5.8 \times 10^{-3}$

    A. I only
    B. II only
    C. III only
    D. I, III only
    E. I, II, III

14. 9.82×10^{-5} is less than which of following numbers?

    A. -9.82×10^{-4}
    B. -9.82×10^5
    C. 9.82×10^{-6}
    D. 9.82×10^0
    E. 982×10^{-8}

15. Which number is NOT equivalent to 2.468×10^8?

    A. 0.2468×10^9
    B. 2.468×10^{-8}
    C. 24.68×10^7
    D. $246,800,000$
    E. $246,800,000 \times 10^0$

Solutions to Practice Problems

1. **8.02×10^8**. Since we have to move left, the exponent will be positive. We have to move the decimal place 8 spots left for a to be between 1 and 10. Therefore, we get 8.02×10^8.

2. **9.1×10^{-4}**. Move the decimal to the right 4 places so that it is after the first non-zero digit, 9. Because you moved the decimal 4 places to the right, the exponent will be -4.

3. **-3.400010001×10^7**. Move the decimal to the left 7 places, so that it is after the first non-zero digit. Since you moved the decimal 7 places to the left, the exponent is positive 7.

4. **0.009063**. Since the exponent is -3, move the decimal 3 places to the left.

5. **E.** The decimal must be moved from the end of the number 8 places to the left. The exponent is positive since we moved the decimal to the left.

6. **B.** First compute $5 \times 300 = 1500$. Then move the decimal from the end of the number to the left so that it is after the 1. Because this required a movement of three places, and $1500 > 10$, the exponent is positive 3.

7. **C.** Move the decimal so that it is placed after the first non-zero digit, 5. The decimal had to be moved 5 places to the left. This makes the exponent positive 5.

8. **C.** The decimal is after the 6 in the original number and does not move anywhere, so the exponent is 0.

9. **B.** Place the decimal after the first 1. To get it there, it must be moved 2 places to the right. Since we moved the decimal to the right, the exponent must be negative.

10. **C.** $\frac{5}{10000} = \frac{5}{10^5} = 5 \times 10^{-5}$. Note that when we divide by 10,000, that is the same as moving the decimal to the left 5 spaces.

11. **E.** 8.9898×10^3 can be rewritten as 8989.8 in decimal form. The second choice, 89.898×10^2, can be written as 8989.8, because the decimal is moved to the right two places. The third choice, 89898×10^{-1}, can also be written as 8989.8 because the decimal is moved one place to the left. All three choices are equal.

12. **B.** $\frac{12 \times 10^8}{3 \times 10^2} = \frac{12}{3} \times \frac{10^8}{10^2} = 4 \times 10^6$ Why is it 10^6? Because $10^8 = 100,000,000$ and $10^6 = 1,000,000$. Six zeros cancel, and we're left with 100 or 10^2

13. **D.** Statement I can be written as $5,800 < 58,000$, which is true. Statement II can be written as $0.0058 < 0.00058$, which is false. Statement III can be written as $0.00058 < 0.0058$, which is true.

14. **D.** $9.82 \times 10^{-5} = 0.0000982$. This is less than $9.82 \times 10^0 = 9.82 \times 1 = 9.82$.

15. **B.** Rewrite 2.468×10^8 as $246,800,000$ by moving the decimal 8 places to the right. Rewrite each of the answers to see that $2.468 \times 10^{-8} = 0.00000002468$. Clearly these are not equal.

Chapter 20

Measurements

There are two major systems of measurement: the English System of Measurement and the Metric System of Measurement. These two systems are made up of units that are used to describe some amount of time or an object's length, width, weight, or volume.

The English (Standard) System of Measurement

Length	
1 foot (ft) =	12 inches (in.)
1 yard (yd) =	3 feet (ft)

Weight	
1 pound (lb.) =	16 ounces (oz.)
1 ton (t) =	2,000 pounds (lb.)

Liquid Volume	
1 cup (c) =	8 fluid ounces (fl. oz.)
1 pint (pt) =	2 cups (c)
1 quart (qt) =	2 pints (pt)
1 gallon (gal) =	4 quarts (qt)
1 gallon (gal) =	8 pints (pt)
1 gallon (gal) =	16 cups (c)

Time	
1 minute (min) =	60 seconds (sec)
1 hour (hr) =	60 minutes (min)
1 day =	24 hours (hr)
1 week =	7 days
1 year (yr) =	12 months (mo)
1 year (yr) =	365 days

The Metric System of Measurement

The meter (m) - Measures length

kilo- (km)	hecto- (hm)	deka- (dam)	meter (m)	deci- (dm)	centi (cm)	milli- (mm)
1,000m	100m	10m	1m	0.1m	0.01m	0.001m

The gram (g) - Measures mass

kilo-	deka-	gram	milli-
(kg)	(dag)	(g)	(mg)
1,000g	10g	1g	0.001g

The liter (l) - Measures volume

liter	milli-
(L)	(mL)
1L	0.001L

Most **PRAXIS I** problems involving measurement will ask you to turn a larger unit of measurement into a smaller unit or vice versa. As a result, the ability to convert between units is an essential skill to master.

Example 1   A book weighs 80 ounces. How many pounds does the book weigh?

A. 1.2 lb.
B. 2.7 lb.
C. 5 lb.
D. 7.1 lb.
E. 8.3 lb.

ANSWER: C. This problem requires a knowledge of The English System of Measurement, specifically the units pound (lb.) and ounce (oz.). In order to complete the problem we must convert the book's weight in ounces to pounds. To accomplish this we take the weight of the book in ounces, 80 ounces, and divide that number by the total number of ounces in one pound. Notice that in the calculation below, the units for ounces have been omitted as early as the third step. When a term is found to be in both the numerator and the denominator of a fraction, it can be canceled. The following illustrates this:

$$80\text{oz.} \times \frac{1\text{lb.}}{16\text{oz.}} = \frac{(80\text{oz.})(1\text{lb.})}{16\text{oz.}} = 5(1\text{lb.}) = 5\text{lb.}$$

Example 2   John travels 3,600 m to school each day. How many kilometers does John travel?

A. 2.1 km   B. 3.0 km   C. 3.2 km   D. 3.6 km   E. 4.2 km

ANSWER: D. This problem requires a knowledge of The Metric System of Measurement, specifically the unit meters and the prefix kilo. First, it is important to know that there are 1,000 meters in a single kilometer. Thus, in order to solve the problem we must take the total number of meters, in this case 3,600, and divide by 1,000 in order to get the total number of kilometers. Notice, that in the calculation below, the units for meters have been omitted at the second step. When a term is found to be in both the numerator and the denominator of a fraction, it can be canceled. The following illustrates this:

$$3,600\text{m} \times \frac{1\text{km}}{1,000\text{m}} = \frac{(3,600)(1\text{km})}{(1,000)} = 3.6\text{km}$$

Example 3 Thomas has 7 pieces of rope, each piece measuring 144 in. What is the total length of all 7 pieces of rope in feet?

A. 79 ft
B. 84 ft
C. 87 ft
D. 109 ft
E. 129 ft

ANSWER: B. In order to solve this problem, two operations must be completed. First, we must calculate the total length of each piece of rope when combined. If each piece of rope is 144 inches long, and there are 7 pieces of rope, the total length in rope can be determined through the expression, 7 pieces × 144 inches, which equals 1,008 inches total. This number must then be divided by the number of inches in a single foot in order to determine the length of rope in feet. Notice that in the calculation below, the units for pieces have been omitted as early as the second step. When a term is found to be in both the numerator and the denominator of a fraction, it can be canceled. The following illustrates this:

$$7\text{pieces} \times \frac{144\text{in}}{1\text{piece}} = \frac{(7)(144\text{in})}{1} = \frac{1,008\text{in}}{1} \times \frac{1\text{ft}}{12} = \frac{(1,008)(1\text{ft})}{12} = 84\text{ft}$$

Example 4 A swimming pool hold 9,000 liters of water. How many milliliters of water are in the pool?

A. 9,000 mL
B. 90,000 mL
C. 900,000 mL
D. 9,000,000 mL
E. 90,000,000 mL

ANSWER: D. In order to solve this problem it is important to understand the relationship between liters and milliliters. The prefix milli- tells us that there are 1,000 milliliters in 1 liter.

Thus, solving this problem requires the multiplication of 9,000 liters by 1,000 since there are 1,000 milliliters in a liter. Notice that in the calculation below, the units for liters have been omitted as early as the second step. When a term is found to be in both the numerator and the denominator of a fraction, it can be canceled. The following illustrates this:

$$9,000L \times \frac{1,000mL}{1L} = \frac{(9,000)(1,000mL)}{(1)} = 9,000,000mL$$

Example 5 Vincent ran a 10,000 meter dash on Sunday. How many centimeters did Vincent run?

A. 100,000 cm
B. 1,000,000 cm
C. 10,000,000 cm
D. 100,000,000 cm
E. 10,000,000,000 cm

ANSWER: B. This problem requires a knowledge of The Metric System of Measurement, specifically the relationship between meters and centimeters. As previously mentioned in this chapter, there are 100 centimeters in one meter. Thus, to complete this problem, we must multiply the number of meters by 100 in order to determine the number of centimeters. The following illustrates this calculation:

$$10,000m \times \frac{100cm}{1m} = \frac{(10,000)(100cm)}{(1)} = 1,000,000cm$$

Example 6 Which of the following represents 7.2 feet in inches?

A. 0.864 in.
B. 8.64 in.
C. 86.4 in.
D. 864 in.
E. 8640 in.

ANSWER: C. This problem requires a knowledge of the Standard System of Measurement, specifically the relationship between feet and inches. There are 12 inches in one foot. Therefore, in order to solve this problem, you must multiply the number of feet represented in the problem by the number of inches in one foot. The following illustrates this calculation:

$$7.2feet \times \frac{12inches}{1foot} = 86.4inches$$

Example 7   Which of the following represents 11 km in millimeters?

   A. 110,000 mm
   B. 1,100,000 mm
   C. 11,000,000 mm
   D. 110,000,000 mm
   E. 1,110,000,000 mm

ANSWER: C. This problem requires the completion of two conversions. Both of these conversions require a knowledge of the Metric System of Measurement. To complete the problem you must first convert kilometers to meters. It is important to remember that there are 1,000 meters in one kilometer. Next, you must convert meters to millimeters, and there are 1,000 millimeters in one meter. The following illustrates this calculation:

$$11\text{km} \times \frac{1,000\text{m}}{1\text{km}} \times \frac{1,000\text{mm}}{1\text{m}} = 11,000,000\text{mm}$$

Example 8   Which of the following represents 7.5 yards in inches?

   A. 27 in.
   B. 270 in.
   C. 2,700 in.
   D. 27,000 in.
   E. 270,000 in.

ANSWER: B. This problem requires the completion of two conversions. Both of these conversions require a knowledge of the Standard System of Measurement. First, you have to convert 7.5 yards to feet. Once your have completed this conversion, you then have to convert feet to inches. The following illustrates this calculation:

$$7.5\text{yards} \times \frac{3\text{feet}}{1\text{yard}} \times \frac{12\text{inches}}{1\text{foot}} = 270 \text{ in.}$$

Example 9 Which of the following represents 2 gallons in pints?

A. 16 pints
B. 160 pints
C. 1,600 pints
D. 16,000 pints
E. 160,000 pints

ANSWER: A. This problem requires the completion of two conversions. Both of these conversions require a knowledge of the Standard System of Measurement. First, you must convert from gallons to quarts, and then from quarts to pints. The following represents this calculation:

$$2 \text{ gallons} \times \frac{4 \text{ quarts}}{1 \text{ gallon}} \times \frac{2 \text{ pints}}{1 \text{quart}} = 16 \text{ pints}$$

Example 10 Vince weighs 175 lbs. How many ounces does Vince weigh?

A. 28 oz.
B. 280 oz.
C. 2,800 oz.
D. 28,000 oz.
E. 280,000 oz.

ANSWER: C. This problem requires a knowledge of the Standard System of Measurement. In order to arrive at a solution you must convert between pounds and ounces. The following represents this conversion:

$$175 \text{ lbs} \times \frac{16 \text{oz}}{1 \text{lb}} = 2,800 \text{ oz.}$$

Practice Problems

1. John runs for 3.5 hours. Which of the following represents John's run in minutes?

   A. 2.10 min
   B. 21.0 min
   C. 210 min
   D. 2,100 min
   E. 21,000 min

2. A golf ball has a mass of 0.045 kg. How many grams is the golf ball?

   A. 45 g
   B. 450 g
   C. 4,500 g
   D. 45,000 g
   E. 450,000 g

3. Tyler walked 7.2 km. How many meters (m) did Tyler walk?

   A. 7.2 m
   B. 72 m
   C. 720 m
   D. 7,200 m
   E. 72,000 m

4. A length of rope measures 15.7 feet. How many inches long is the same piece of rope?

   A. 188.4 in
   B. 1,884 in
   C. 18,840 in
   D. 188,400 in
   E. 1,884,000 in

5. John purchases 3L of orange juice at the grocery store. How many mL of juice did John purchase?

   A. 30 mL
   B. 300 mL
   C. 3,000 mL
   D. 30,000 mL
   E. 300,000 mL

6. Raul drives a car across the United States in 40 days. How many hours does it take Raul to drive across the United States?

   A. 9.6 hours
   B. 96 hours
   C. 960 hours
   D. 9,600 hours
   E. 96,000 hours

7. Jessie needs 13 ounces of vanilla extract to bake a cake. How many cups of vanilla extract does Jessie need?

   A. 1.625 cups
   B. 16.26 cups
   C. 0.1625 cups
   D. 0.01625 cups
   E. 0.001625 cups

8. Shelby traveled 10 km to visit her grandmother. How many meters did Shelby travel?

   A. 10 meters
   B. 100 meters
   C. 1,000 meters
   D. 10,000 meters
   E. 100,000 meters

9. A large truck weighs 3 tons. How many ounces does the truck weigh?

   A. 6,000 oz
   B. 6,600 oz
   C. 60,000 oz
   D. 96,000 oz
   E. 960,000 oz

10. How many seconds are in one day?

   A. 14 sec
   B. 140 sec
   C. 1,440 sec
   D. 10,440 sec
   E. 86,400 sec

11. Kevin needs 100 ounces of water to make a large batch of oatmeal. How many quarts of water does Kevin require?

    A. 1.125 quarts
    B. 1.725 quarts
    C. 2.125 quarts
    D. 2.725 quarts
    E. 3.125 quarts

12. Alison walks 2.5 kilometers (km) to school each day. How many meters does Alison walk each day?

    A. 2,500 meters
    B. 3,000 meters
    C. 3,500 meters
    D. 4,000 meters
    E. 4,500 meters

13. A moving truck can carry 3.5 tons of furniture. How many pounds of furniture can the truck carry?

    A. 5000 lbs
    B. 5,500 lbs
    C. 6,000 lbs
    D. 7,000 lbs
    E. 7,500 lbs

14. How many seconds are in one week?

    A. 30,288 seconds
    B. 363,288 seconds
    C. 382,288 seconds
    D. 456,288 seconds
    E. 604,800 seconds

15. Taylor drove a car approximately 400,000 meters (m). How many kilometers (km) did Taylor drive?

    A. 250 km   B. 400 km   C. 420 km   D. 440 km   E. 480 km

Solutions to Practice Problems

1. **C.** This problem requires a knowledge of the Standard System of Measurement. To solve this problem you must convert between hours and minutes. The following represents this calculation:

$$\frac{3.5\text{hrs}}{1} \times \frac{60\text{mins}}{1\text{hr}} = 210 \text{ minutes}$$

2. **A.** This problem requires a knowledge of the Metric System of Measurement. In order to solve this problem you must remember that there are 1,000 grams in one kilogram. The following represents the calculation required:

$$\frac{0.045\text{kg}}{1} \times \frac{1,000\text{g}}{1\text{kg}} = 45\text{g}$$

3. **D.** This problem requires a knowledge of the Metric System of Measurement, specifically the meter. In order to complete the problem you must convert between kilometers and meters. Thus, it is important to remember that there are 1,000 meters in one kilometer. The following represents the necessary calculation:

$$\frac{7.2\text{km}}{1} \times \frac{1,000\text{m}}{1\text{km}} = 7,200\text{m}$$

4. **A.** This problem requires a knowledge of the Standard System of Measurement, specifically the foot and inch. In order to solve the problem, you must convert between feet and inches. Thus, it is important to remember that there are 12 inches in one foot. The following represents the necessary calculation:

$$\frac{15.7\text{ft}}{1} \times \frac{12\text{in}}{1\text{ft}} = 188.4 \text{ inches}$$

5. **C.** This problem requires a knowledge of the Metric System of Measurement, specifically the liter and milliliter. In order to solve the problem you must convert between liters and milliliters. Thus, it is important to remember that there are 1,000 milliliters in one liter. The following represents the necessary calculation:

$$\frac{3L}{1} \times \frac{1,000mL}{1L} = 3,000mL$$

6. **C.** In order to solve this problem you must have a working knowledge of the Standard System of Measurement, specifically the day and the hour. Therefore, it is important to remember that there are 24 hours in one day. Using this information, it is possible to convert days to hours. The following represents this calculation:

$$\frac{40 \text{ days}}{1} \times \frac{24 \text{hrs}}{1 \text{ day}} = 960 \text{ hours}$$

7. **A.** In order to solve this problem you must have a working knowledge of the Standard System of Measurement, specifically the ounce and the cup. Therefore, it is important to remember that there are 8 fluid ounces in one cup. The following represents the necessary calculation:

$$\frac{13oz}{1} \times \frac{1 \text{ cup}}{8oz} = 1.625 \text{ cups}$$

8. **D.** This problem requires a working knowledge of the Metric System of Measurement, specifically the meter and kilometer. In order to solve the problem it is important to remember that the prefix, kilo-, means 1,000. Therefore, there are 1,000 meters in one kilometer. The following represents the required calculation:

$$\frac{10km}{1} \times \frac{1,000m}{1km} = 10,000 \text{ meters}$$

9. **D.** In order to solve this problem you must have a knowledge of the Standard System of Measurement, specifically the ton, pound, and ounce. Further, the problem requires a two-step conversion. First, you must convert from tons to pounds, and then pounds to ounces. To accomplish these conversions it is important to remember there there are 2,000 pounds in one ton, and 16 ounces in one pound. The following represents this conversion:

$$\frac{3 \text{ tons}}{1} \times \frac{2,000lbs}{1 \text{ ton}} \times \frac{16oz}{1lb} = 96,000 \text{ ounces}$$

10. **E.** In order to solve this problem you must have a working knowledge of the Standard System of Measurement, specifically the hour and the minute. Remember, there are 60 minutes in an hour. The following represents the required calculation:

$$\frac{24 \text{ hours}}{1} \times \frac{60 \text{ mins}}{1hr} \times \frac{60 \text{ secs}}{1 \text{ min}} = 86,400 \text{ seconds}$$

11. **E.** This problem requires a knowledge of the Standard System of Measurement. To solve this problem you must convert between ounces, cups, pints, and quarts. The following represents this calculation:

$$100oz \times \frac{1c}{8oz} \times \frac{1pt}{2c} \times \frac{1qt}{2pt} = 3.125 \text{ quarts}$$

12. **A.** This problem requires a knowledge of the Metric System of Measurement. To solve this problem you must convert between kilometers and meters. The following represents this calculation:

$$2.5km \times \frac{1,000m}{1km} = 2,500 \text{ meters}$$

13. **D.** This problem requires a knowledge of the Standard System of Measurement. To solve this problem you must convert between tons and pounds. The following represents this calculation:

$$3.5 \text{ tons} \times \frac{2,000 \text{ lbs}}{1 \text{ ton}} = 7,000 \text{ lbs}$$

14. **E.** This problem requires a knowledge of the Standard System of Measurement. To solve this problem you must convert between weeks, days, hours, minutes, and seconds. The following represents this calculation:

$$1 \text{ week} \times \frac{7 \text{ days}}{1 \text{ week}} \times \frac{24 \text{ hrs}}{1 \text{ day}} \times \frac{60 \text{ min}}{1 \text{ hr}} \times \frac{60 \text{ secs}}{1 \text{min}} = 604,800 \text{ secs}$$

15. **B.** This problem requires a knowledge of the Metric System of Measurement. To solve this problem you must convert between kilometers and meters. The following represents this calculation:

$$400,000 \text{ m} \times \frac{1 \text{ km}}{1,000 \text{ m}} = 400 \text{ km}$$

Chapter 21

Patterns and Functions

Some math teachers will teach their students that mathematics is all about patterns. If you get familiar at seeing and describing patterns, you can do anything. Indeed, patterns in some form or another appear throughout mathematical studies, whether you are learning your times tables, graphing an algebraic function, or solving an equation in Calculus. A *pattern* is a series of numbers whose sequence is determined by a particular rule. You can figure out what rule has been used by studying the terms you are given. Think to yourself: What operation or sequence of operations will always result in the next term in the series? Once you determine the rule, you can continue the pattern. Consider the example below:

Example 1   Find the sixth term in this sequence: 3, 9, 27, 81,

    A. 6
    B. 243
    C. 486
    D. 729
    E. 2187

ANSWER: D. First we want to determine the rule. Looking at the first two numbers suggests a few possible ways of going from 3 to 9. Perhaps we are adding 6 to each term in the sequence. Perhaps we are multiplying by three. Perhaps each term is being squared in order to generate the next term. If the first possibility was the case, we would expect the third term to be 15. If the second possibility, it would be 27. If the third possibility, it would be 81. The third term IS 27, so this suggests the rule is that we multiply each term by three to generate the next term. Testing this rule to move from the third to the fourth term works. We have been given the first four terms and been asked to find the sixth. We continue the pattern by employing the rule we have found to generate each term from the previous term. Multiplying 81 x 3 gives us the fifth term: 243. Multiplying that number by 3 gives us the sixth term: 243 x 3 = 729.

A pattern can also be described by a function. A function is an algebraic rule that shows how the terms in one sequence of numbers are related to the terms in another sequence. For instance, in the example above, if we are trying to find the nth term, we can say that:

$$S_n = 3 \cdot S_{n-1}$$

The $S_{(n-1)}$ means "the term that comes before S_n." If we are looking for the fifth term, n would be equal to 5 and $(n\text{-}1)$ would be equal to 4. Therefore, the value of the fifth term would be three times the value of the fourth term. This is called a *recursive function* because it is a sequence where each subsequent term is generated by doing the same operation to the previous term.

An even better way of describing this pattern would be: nth term = 3 to the power of n. This is a better way for two reasons: 1) It is shorter, and 2) It does not require knowledge of the previous term.

Example 2 Imagine a souvenir shop that charges $12.50 for tee-shirts. The chart below shows how much it would cost to buy one to six tee-shirts. What would be a function that would show the price of buying n shirts?

ANSWER : **P = n(12.50)**. Quick explanation: Here, we could say that the amount a tourist will pay is a function of (or depends on) the number of shirts a customer orders. This function could be written as: Price = number of shirts (12.50) or $P = n(12.50)$. If you know the function, and are given a value for n (number of shirts purchased), you can solve for the total price paid.

Using Functions and Patterns to Solve Word Problems:

Functions are useful in a variety of day-to-day activities. They are especially useful for business applications and can be used to rapidly calculate profit, cost, employee wages, and taxes.

Example 3 Panda Printing Press offers poster production services. They charge $150 to lay out the design and print the first poster. They then charge $5 for each additional poster printed. In advertising their prices, they tell clients that the costs for printing posters can be given by the function $C = 150 + 5(n-1)$ where C is the cost in dollars of the job, and n is the number of posters produced. If a client, Emu Energy Inc., wants to print 20 posters for an upcoming conference, how much will this cost them?

ANSWER: C = $245 Use the Function to solve the problem

$$C = 150 + 5(n - 1)$$
$$= 150 + 5(20 - 1)$$
$$= 150 + 5(19)$$
$$= 150 + 95$$
$$= 245$$

Example 4   Kia just got his pilot's license and loves flying. It costs $350 per hour to rent a plane, and 50 dollars per hour for the fuel costs. He can also buy a small plane for $8,000. This plane gets slightly worse fuel millage and costs $60 per hour for the fuel costs. He expects that he will clock 25 hours of flight time this year. Will it be cheaper to rent a plane or buy a plane to get all his flying done this year?

ANSWER: Buy a Plane.   Whether he buys or rents, the price (P) that Kia will pay is a function of the number of hours (h) he flies. If he buys: $P = 8000 + 60h$ If he rents: $P = (350 + 50)h$. To determine what is the better deal for 25 hours of flying, we would first calculate the costs if he buys:

$$P = 8000 + 60h$$
$$= 8000 + 60(25)$$
$$= 8000 + 1500$$
$$= 9500$$

Then we use the second function to calculate the cost if he rents:

$$P = (350 + 50)h$$
$$= 400(25)$$
$$= 10,000$$

From the results, we can conclude that for 25 hours of flight, it is less expensive if he buys the plane.

A more difficult version of this problem may ask: "What is the maximum number of hours that Kia could fly for less money by renting than by buying?"

We see, in the example above, that 25 hours produces prices that are fairly close. We could approach this problem by trying each of the integers less than 25. When we plug in 24 for h, we get 9440 dollars to buy and 9600 dollars to rent, so it is still cheaper to buy. However, when we plug in 23 for h, we get 9380 dollars to buy and 9200 dollars to rent, so it is cheaper to rent.

Therefore, for any number of hours equal to or less than 23, it is cheaper to rent.

Example 5 Using the function $y = 5x - 7$, what is the value of y when $x = -6$?

ANSWER: -37. By substitution,

$$y = 5(-6) - 7$$
$$y = -30 - 7$$
$$y = -37$$

Example 6 Using the function $p = 45 + 3\,(2+m)$, what is the value of p when $m = 7$?

A. 126
B. 72
C. 458
D. 84
E. 7

ANSWER: B. We have:

$$p = 45 + 3(2 + 7)$$
$$p = 45 + 3(9)$$
$$p = 45 + 27$$
$$p = 72$$

Example 7 A bike shop rents bikes for a base rate of $40 for the first two hours, and then $12 for each additional hour. Choose the function that represents this situation for any rental longer than two hours.

A. $40 + 2h + 12$
B. $40h + 12$
C. $40h + 12(h - 2)$
D. $40 + 12(h - 2)$
E. $12(h - 2) - 40$

ANSWER: D. It is important to note that this question only asks for the equation that describes any rental longer than two hours. This makes the solution simpler. We know that it is $40 for the first two hours, and $12 for the next hour. So we are looking for an equation that will produce 40 when h = 2 and 52 when h = 3. The only equation that works for this is D, therefore the correct answer choice is D. We can test this equation. Begin by plugging 2 into h. We get $40 + 12(2 - 2) = 40 + 0 = 40$. That works. With $h = 3$, we have $40 + 12(3 - 2) = 40 + 12 = 52$.

Example 8 The Peppermint Pipers are looking for a studio where they can record their new CD. Acme studio charges an initial fee of $250 for any group to use their studio, plus 50 dollars per hour. Buttered Stuff studio charges an initial fee of $130 for use of their studio plus 80 dollars per hour. How many hours would the Pipers have to record for Acme Studios to be the less expensive option?

ANSWER: Greater than 4 hours. The equation for Acme is: $p = 250 + 50h$ where p is the price in dollars and h is the number of hours. The equation for Buttered Stuff studio is $p = 130 + 80h$. An easy way to think of this is to look at the difference between the initial prices. Buttered stuff studio is $120 cheaper initially. However, it costs $30 more for each hour. 120 divided by 30 is 4, therefore if the Pipers record for anything more than 4 hours, it will be cheaper for them to use Acme Studios.

An alternate solution would be to set the equation representing each studio to be equal to the other.

$$250 + 50h = 130 + 80h$$
$$120 = 30h$$
$$4 = h$$

This shows that 4 hours is the point where the Pipers would break even.

Example 9 Amy wants to become more informed about world events during this school year. She is trying to decide whether to start reading the Economist or another publication called Stratfor. A subscription to the Economist is $4 per week. Stratfor is an online publication. It costs a $90 subscription fee to sign up, but is only $1.50 for each week after that. There are 38 weeks in Amy's school year. Is it a better deal for her to subscribe to the Economist or Stratfor?

ANSWER: Stratfor. This can be solved with a strategy similar to the problem above. There is a $90 difference in the original price and a $2.50 difference in the cost of a weekly issue. 90 divided by 2.50 = 36. Therefore, for any length of time over 36 weeks, Stratfor would be the more affordable option. Another way to solve it would just be to plug Amy's time value (38) into the equation for each magazine and see which produces the smaller result. For Stratfor, we have:

$$P = 90 + 1.50(38)$$
$$= 90 + 57$$
$$= 147$$

For the Economist, we have:

$$P = 4.00(38)$$
$$= 152$$

Therefore, Amy saves a total of $5 by investing in Stratfor during her school year.

Example 10   Find the fifth term in the sequence: 5, 15, 35, 65,

ANSWER: 105. Looking at the difference between the numbers, we see that the first increase was by 10, the next by 20, and the third by 30. This is enough to conclude that the next increase will be by 40, so the fifth term will be 105.

Practice Problems:

1. Find the 50th term in this pattern: 7, 13, 19, 25, 31...

2. Find the 25th term in the pattern: 20, 17, 14, 11, 8...

3. Joe can clean a fish in 5 minutes, and Rich can clean a fish in 4 minutes. Working together, how many fish could they clean in an hour?

4. Nina enrolled in Ivy League Tutoring Connection for help with her ACT test prep. Before she began, her score was 27. After each study session, she takes another practice exam (Nina is a very diligent student). The table below shows her results with her total number of tutoring hours:

   1 hour : score of 27
   2 hour : score of 28
   3 hour : score of 28
   4 hour : score of 29
   5 hour : score of 29
   6 hour : score of 30

   If this pattern continues in exactly the same way, how many tutoring hours total will she need to hit her target score of 34?

5. What is the next number in this pattern?

$$2, 5, 10, 17, 26, 37, 50...$$

   A. 67
   B. 63
   C. 64
   D. 65
   E. 66

6. $y = 55 - 6(x - 3)$, what is the value of y when $x = 5$?

7. What is the next number in this pattern?

$$\frac{1}{2}, \frac{3}{4}, \frac{7}{8}, \frac{15}{16}...$$

8. Dave can iron 5 shirts in an hour. How long will it take him to iron all 17 shirts that he owns?

    A. 17 mins

    B. 75 mins

    C. 135 mins

    D. 204 mins

    E. 300 mins

9. Sahtiya is looking to get lab supplies for a classroom project for her students. Supply company Alpha sells lab kits for a flat rate of \$6.50 a student. Supply company Beta charges a base rate of \$140 to set up the central equipment. However, after that they only charge \$3 for each student set. What is the minimum number of students that would result in Sahtiya getting a better deal if she goes with company Beta?

    A. 25

    B. 41

    C. 61

    D. 81

    E. 140

10. Using the function $y = -\frac{x}{5} + 4$, what is the value of y when $x = -14$?

    A. -1.2

    B. - 6.8

    C. 1.2

    D. 3.8

    E. 6.8

11. What is the 7th term in this sequence?

$$9, 16, 30, 58, 114...$$

12. What is the next number in this pattern?

$$1600, -400, 100, -25, ...$$

13. What is the 55th term in the sequence?

$$14, 17, 21, 24, 28, 31, 35...$$

14. $y = -3 - 6(x - 3)$, what is the value of y when $x = 5$?

15. Charlie's Chocolate Factory runs a catering service where they will bring chocolate fountains (which can cover any food with chocolate) and chocolate bars to children's birthday parties. They charge $200 for delivering each chocolate fountain and the chocolate they put in the fountain costs about $20 per pound. The premium chocolate bars are $4.50 a piece. Deborah expects 40 guests to attend her daughter's birthday party. She estimates that they would each eat about 2 chocolate bars. If she rented the chocolate fountain instead, how many pounds of chocolate could she get for the same price?

Solutions to Practice Problems:

1. **301.** This is increasing by 6 each time. Obviously, it will take quite a while to write out fifty terms. Therefore, a better tactic is to create a function that describes the pattern. We know that the 1st term is 7 and each additional term increases by 6 so an appropriate equation would be: nth term $= 7 + 6(n-1)$. Plugging in 50 for n gives us an answer of 301.

2. **-52.** Same idea, except this time we are decreasing by increments of 3. The appropriate equation is: nth term $= 20 - 3(n-1)$. Plugging in 25 gives us:
   25th term = 20 - 3(24)
   25th term = 20 - 72
   25th term = -52

3. **27 fish.** There are a couple ways you could solve this. One method that uses functions would be to set up an equation that gives each of their rates per minute, so for Joe:

$$f = .2m$$

   where f is the number of fish cleaned and m is the number of minutes. For Rich, the equation is:

$$f = .25m$$

   If they are working together, we can combine the right sides of the equations and get

$$f = .2m + .25m$$
$$= .45m$$

   Plugging in 60 to this equation gives us: f $= .45\,(60) = 27$ so the final answer is 27 fish.

4. **14 hours.** The pattern shows that every even hour (2, 4, 6) the score increases by 1. Following this pattern produces:
   8 hours : 31
   10 hours : 32
   12 hours : 33
   14 hours : 34
   So the total number of hours needed to reach a score of 34 is 14.

5. **D.** This is a more difficult pattern than some. The answer is not immediately apparent from looking at the numbers. A good idea to try in a situation such as this is to create a secondary sequence of numbers generated by the difference between each successive term. Doing that in this sequence produces: Up 3, Up 5, Up 7, Up 9, Up 11, Up 13. So obviously the next one is Up 15. Now we add 15 to the last number (50) to get $50 + 15 = 65$. To generalize, now we can see that the series is much more obvious. It is increasing by the next higher odd number for each term.

6. **43.** Plugging 5 in for x on the right side of the equation produces

$$y = 55 - 6(5 - 3)$$
$$y = 55 - 6(2)$$
$$y = 55 - 12$$
$$y = 43$$

7. $\frac{31}{32}$. In this pattern, the denominator is doubling in each term. The numerator is simply 1 less than the denominator. If we double 16, we get 32 for the denominator. The numerator is 1 less so the next term will be $\frac{31}{32}$. Or you can see that adding the numerator and the denominator of each fraction gives you the following numerator.

8. **D.** Dividing the 60 minutes in an hour by the five shirts gives us an average time of 12 minutes per shirt. This produces the simple rate of one shirt every 12 minutes. Multiplying 12 by 17 produces 204 mins. So the Answer is D.

9. **B.** This is another problem where we have to compare costs between two different price plans. The approach with these types of problems is to set up a function for each option that expresses the total price (p) in terms of the number of students (n.) The appropriate equation for company Alpha is $p = 6.5n$. The appropriate price function for company Beta would be $p = 3n + 140$. The question asks how many students would result in 'a better deal,' and this indicates that we must first find the point at which the price under the different plans would be equal and then increase by one. We set the two equations equal to each other and solve for n:

$$6.5n = 3n + 140$$
$$3.5n = 140$$
$$n = 40$$

Thus the answer is one greater than this number, or 41.

10. **E.** Plugging -14 into the equation in place of x produces:

$$y = -\frac{(-14)}{5} + 4$$
$$y = \frac{14}{5} + 4$$
$$y = 2.8 + 4$$
$$y = 6.8$$

The correct answer is E.

11. **450.** This is a somewhat difficult pattern. Upon an initial glance, the first two terms suggest a possible sequence of squares, but it is clear from subsequent terms that this is not the case. Looking at the differences between the numbers provides a secondary sequence of 7, 14, 28, 56. This sequence is doubling with each subsequent term, so we can use that method to find the next two terms. Twice 56 is 112 so we add 112 to the last term in the original sequence to generate the next term. $114 + 112 = 226$ as the sixth term in the original sequence. Adding 224 to this produces the 7th term: 450.

12. **6.25.** The terms alternate between positive and negative so we know that the next term is positive. It is also clear that each term is being generated by dividing the preceding term by -4. So we divide -25 by -4 and that produces 6.25.

13. **203.** This one is a little complicated. The sequence is clearly increasing, and looking at the differences between the terms clearly shows that the pattern of increase is: 3, 4, 3, 4, 3... This is simple enough, but it asks for the 55th term, and we want to make sure we don't waste time writing out all those numbers. Therefore, we want to find a function. This is easier if we try to write a function that just produces the odd number of terms. (We choose odd rather than even because the term it wants us to find is the 55th and is odd). Each odd term is 7 greater than the last term with the first term being 14. So a function that produces the nth odd term is: $14 + \frac{7(n-1)}{2}$. Plugging 55 into this gives us:

$$= 14 + 7\left[\frac{(55-1)}{2}\right]$$
$$= 14 + 7\left[\frac{(54)}{2}\right]$$
$$= 14 + 7[27]$$
$$= 14 + 189$$
$$= 203$$

14. **-15.** $y = -3 - 6(5-3) = -3 - 6(2) = -3 - 12 = -15$

15. **8 pounds.** 40 guests x 2 chocolate bars = 80 chocolate bars consumed. 80 bars x $4.50 per bar = $360.00 spent on the bars. If that amount was spent on the fountain, we would subtract the $200 for the initial rental and divide the $160 left over by 20. This gives us the answer of 8 pounds of chocolate.

Chapter 22

Estimation

Although not as precise as exact calculation, estimation can be a valuable tool for solving problems. This is true for three reasons: 1) It can be used to generate a preliminary result which you can later use to check a final answer. 2) It can be used to eliminate distractors (incorrect answer choices), and 3) Some of the questions on the test may ask for an estimation rather than an exact value. Some individuals consider estimation to be a frustration rather than a time saver. Regardless, the third reason is unavoidable. There may be questions on the Praxis exam that include estimation, so it is best to be comfortable using it. Fortunately, estimation is relatively easy and straightforward. A technical definition of 'estimation' is that it is the calculated approximation of a result which is usable even if input data may be incomplete or uncertain. Put more simply, an estimate is made when you round numbers before performing a calculation.

The examples below provide some estimation techniques to consider and practice:

Example 1   The hit new band, 'Beatbeat Whisper', puts on a series of three shows. Approximately how many people attended the 3-concert series if attendance was 3,028 at the first performance, 1,919 at the second, and 3,110 at the third?

ANSWER: 8000. The problem asks *approximately* how many people; thus we can use estimation. Sometimes there is uncertainty about whether we should estimate by rounding to the nearest 10, 100, or 1000, etc. (This uncertainty is why many people are frustrated with estimation.) In this case, we notice that all the numbers are fairly close to either 2,000 or 3,000 so it is sensible to round them to the nearest thousand. Then we calculate the total by adding them all together. This gives us $3,000 + 2,000 + 3,000 = 8,000$.

Example 2   Imagine that a company wants to be able to purchase 2,369 worth of rock climbing equipment in one year's time. Approximately, how much should he buy per month?

ANSWER: $200. Again, this problem asks us *approximately* how much; therefore we know that we can estimate. We will have to divide to figure out how many equal parts of the total goal need to be saved. There are twelve months in a year, so the numbers we need to solve the problem are 12 and 2,369.

Round one or both of the numbers so that they are easy to divide. Round 2,369 to 2,400, and then divide. $\frac{2400}{12} = 200$.

As we mentioned at the start of this chapter, estimation can also be used to help you narrow down answer choices in multiple choice problems or to check your calculation. In the problem below, we demonstrate both of those strategies.

Example 3 What is the best estimate of $77 + 22$?

ANSWER: 100. The numbers given are double digit, so it makes sense to round them to the nearest ten. This produces $80 + 20$. So the correct answer is 100. Notice that an exact calculation produces the sum of 99, which is very close to our estimated answer.

Example 4 Suzanne, Thomas and Chris are selling arts and crafts at three booths. Their sales are $379, $405, and $286 respectively. What is the total amount of sales?
  A. $665
  B. $784
  C. $1170
  D. $1070
  E. $1280

ANSWER: D. Strategy 1: You can estimate an answer by rounding values to the nearest hundred. This eliminates options (A), (B) and (C), because $400 + $400 + $300 = $1100 and only choices (D) and (E) are close to this.

Strategy 2: You can calculate an answer and then check it against an estimate to see if your answer makes sense. The solution is $379 + 405 + 286 = $1070. This answer is close to our earlier estimation of $1,100.

The answer you get when you use estimation on a problem depends on what place value you round to. Sometimes the determination of what place value to round to is very simple. In other cases, it is more ambiguous what place value you should round to. In these cases, we should be able to isolate the correct answer simply by making a reasonable choice.

Example 5 What is the best estimate of 4965 + 3899 ?

A. 8870
B. 8000
C. 8780
D. 8970
E. none of these

ANSWER: A. In this case, it is initially unclear how we should round the given numbers. If there were no answer choices provided, it may be appropriate to round the given numbers to the nearest 100 or even 1000. However, looking over the answer choices shows that they are exact to the nearest ten. Therefore we should round both the numbers we are given to the nearest 10. 4,970 + 3,900 = 8,870.

Note: If we had rounded to the nearest 100, it would have resulted in the answer 8,900. However, that answer does not appear on the answer choices so we can safely assume that we should not round to the nearest 100. The same holds true with respect to the absence of 9,000 among the answer choices, excluding the possibility that we could round to the nearest 1,000.

Example 6 Ron and Amanda collected 497 buttons, but they used 177 of them while fixing some jackets. About how many buttons do they have now? Choose the best estimate.

A. 500
B. 400
C. 300
D. 200
E. 100

ANSWER: C. It is important to recognize that all the answer choices are multiples of 100, so it is implicit that we should round to the nearest 100. This produces: 500 - 200 = 300.

Example 7 Cynthia and her father made 514 mini-cupcakes for the bake sale. 266 sold in two days. About how many cupcakes are left?

A. 230
B. 240
C. 250
D. 780
E. 790

ANSWER: C. All the answer choices are multiples of ten, so round to the nearest 10. Two of the distractors are results that could be generated by adding, but the word problem clearly signifies subtraction. After rounding to the nearest 10, the problem becomes 510 - 260. The answer is 250.

Example 8 287 of Lizzy's 609 screws got lost in the garage. About how many screws does she have now? Use the best estimate.

ANSWER: 300. In the absence of answer choices, it is unclear whether we should round to the nearest 10 or 100. However, the numbers given are both close to the nearest 100, so that seems probable. The problem becomes: 600 - 300 which results in an answer of 300.

Example 9 Darragh flew 4,196 miles to get to the UN conference meeting. The flight was 7 hours, 5 minutes long. Approximately how fast was the average plane speed during the flight?

  A. 500 mph
  B. 550 mph
  C. 600 mph
  D. 650 mph
  E. 700 mph

ANSWER: C. Here the answers appear in increments of fifty, so a test-taker might be initially uncertain whether they should round to the nearest 10 or to the nearest 100. In this case, it doesn't matter which we pick because the answer will be the same. The problem will round to: 4,200 / 7 hours = 600 mph.

Example 10 At their first concert, Beatbeat Whisper sold 207 CDs for a price of $8.97 each. About how much money did they make on CD sales?

  A. 1700
  B. 1800
  C. 1950
  D. 2000
  E. 2100

ANSWER: B. This problem calls for a bit of a judgement call. Do we round to 200 or 210? Do we round to 9 dollars or 10 dollars? The most appropriate choice would be to round to 200 and 9 dollars. The reason is that 200 is slightly less than 210, but 9 is slightly more than 8.97. This yields a simpler problem of 200 x $9 = $1,800. The exact value is $1856.79.

Practice Problems

1. The owners of Solid Gold sold 393 adult concert tickets for $14.97 and 204 children's tickets for $9.97 How much did the owners make on ticket sales?

    A. $1900
    B. $2000
    C. $7000
    D. $8000
    E. $9100

2. What is the best estimate of 287 + 408?

    A. 680
    B. 690
    C. 708
    D. 700
    E. 710

3. Remington wants to study 90 hours for his law school finals over the next four weeks. About how many hours a day must he study to reach that goal?

    A. 2 hours
    B. 2.5 hours
    C. 3 hours
    D. 3.5 hours
    E. 4 hours

4. Adventure Rents is a business that rents out kayaks. During a three day weekend, they made $ 653 on Saturday, $721 on Sunday and $415 on Monday. Approximately how much did they make over the three day weekend?

    A. 1700
    B. 1800
    C. 1850
    D. 1900
    E. 1950

5. Sarah the Cyclist spends a week biking from Portland to San Francisco along the coast. The total distance is 719 miles. As an estimate, what was the average distance she covered each day?

6. A 3-day series at a local soccer stadium had 3,451 people attend the first day, 3,689 people attend the second day and 3,380 people attend the third day. Approximately how many people in total attended the series?

7. George wants to estimate how many comics he and his friends have. He has 875, Josh has 772 and Tommy has 472. About how many do they have? (ten's place.)

    A. 2,100
    B. 2,120
    C. 2,140
    D. 2,200
    E. 2,300

8. Chris wants to estimate how many stamps he and his friends have. He has 640, Warren has 272 and Sandy has 280. About how many do they have? (hundred's place.)

9. Allyson wants to estimate how many baseball cards she and her friends have. She has 2,162, Nancy has 962 and Brian has 1,680. About how many do they have? (thousand's place.)

    A. 4,800
    B. 4,900
    C. 5,000
    D. 6,000
    E. 7,000

10. Hus and Carly want to buy a house two years from now. They need to make an initial down-payment of $35,750. Approximately how much will they have to save each month?

11. Chris gets charged $4.99 a minute for each minute he goes over his allotted monthly minutes on his cell phone bill. He goes 31 minutes over. Approximately how much does he have to pay in overcharges?

12. Box Office Video charges $1.98 for each video it rents out. Last year, they rented Godfather I 33 times, Godfather II 18 times and Godfather III 21 times. Approximately how much money did they make from renting out the Godfather trilogy last year?

    A. $ 66   B. $80   C. $ 102   D. $ 140   E. $ 160

Questions 13-15 relate to the statement below.

Pam Revere goes on a on a week-long motorcycle ride. She goes 389 miles on Monday, 491 miles on Tuesday, 618 miles on Wednesday, 503 miles on Thursday, 179 miles on Friday, 414 miles on Saturday and 224 miles on Sunday.

13. What is the approximate total distance (rounded to the nearest hundred that she travels.

14. In the question above, what is the average daily distance (rounded to the nearest 100) that Pam covers?

15. If Pam rode for 7 hours on Tuesday, what was her approximate average speed on that day?

16. 458 + 765 - 372 (in tens) =

17. 5,239 + 1,271 + 451 (in thousands) =

18. 7,641 - 418 + 1091 (in hundreds)=

19. Percy the Congressional Page measures that it is exactly .91 miles between his Congresswoman's office and the House Floor. If he runs back and forth 4 times during the day, what is the approximate distance he runs?

20. Anna has a bucket with 1,195 nails in it. She uses 312 nails to make a platform on her treehouse. Estimate in order to calculate how many more platforms she could make that are the same size.

21. Lenny has 643 baseball cards. Benny secretly goes through them and takes the 78 Yankee cards. Estimate to the nearest 10 to calculate how many cards remain in Lenny's possession.

22. 59,239 + 1,271 + 43,851 (in thousands) =

23. 41,876 + 121,528 + 47,591 (in Ten-thousands) =

Solutions to Practice Problems

1. **D.** Rounding produces: $400(15.00) + 200 (10.00) = \$8,000$.

2. **D.** Round this to the nearest 100, which gives us: $300 + 400 = 700$.

3. **C.** We can round four weeks to 30 days. This makes the problem 90 divided by 30. Remington should study for about 3 hours a day.

4. **B.** By approximating each of these figures to the nearest hundred, we have $600, $700, and $400. Adding those figures together produces $1,700.

5. **100 miles.** We round the total distance to 700, and divide by the number of days in a week (7) to get an average daily distance of 100 miles.

6. **10,500.** All three of these figures are close to 3,500. Therefore we can get a fairly good approximation by multiplying 3,500 by 3. $3,500 \times 3 = 10,500$.

7. **B.** $880 + 770 + 470 = 2,120$

8. **1,200.** $600 + 300 + 300 = 1,200$

9. **C.** $2000 + 1000 + 2000 = 5000$

10. **$1,500.** Rounding the downpayment amount to the nearest $1,000 gives us a figure of $36,000. Dividing this by 24 (the number of months in two years) gives us a monthly savings goal of $1,500. Rounding to 36,000 is helpful because we know there are 12 months in a year and 36 is divisible by 12.

11. **$150.** Rounding these figures gives us a simple multiplication problem of $5 times 30. This results in an additional fee of $150.

12. **D.** The price of a video rental is rounded to $2. If we round the number of each movie rental to the nearest 10, we get $30 + 20 + 20 = 70$. Multiplying that by $2 equals $140.

13. **2,800.** Rounding each daily mileage to the nearest 100 produces $400 + 500 + 600 + 500 + 200 + 400 + 200$. The sum of these seven figures is 2,800.

14. **400 mi/day.** Dividing 2,800 by 7 produces a quotient of 400 miles a day.

15. **70 mph.** If we round Pam's mileage on Tuesday to the nearest tenth, it is 490. Dividing this number by 7 gives us an average speed of 70 miles per hour.

16. **860.** $460 + 770 - 370 = 860$

17. **6000.** $5,000 + 1,000 + 0 = 6,000$. Note: This problem illustrates the problem with estimation if it is done too loosely. Here, the solution shows the calculation done correctly according to the approximation parameters in the problem. However, the actual answer is much closer to 7,000.

18. **8,300.** (Hundreds) $7,600 - 400 + 1,100 = 8,300$

19. **7 miles.** Remember to use common sense when interpreting problems. Here Percy walks back and forth 4 times, which means that he covered the distance 8 times. Multiply 8 by .9 produces a product of 7.2 or about 7 miles.

20. **3 platforms.** Rounding to the nearest hundreds gives us $1,200 - 300 = 900$. She has enough nails to make about three similar platforms on her treehouse.

21. **560.** $640-80=560$.

22. **104,000.** $59,000 + 1,000 + 44,000 = 104,000$

23. **210,000.** $40,000 + 120,000 + 50,000 = 210,000$

Section IX: Final Test

Chapter 23

Final Test

1. Simplify the following expression completely: $\dfrac{12p}{6} - \dfrac{10p}{2}$

   A. $2p - 5$

   B. 0

   C. $\dfrac{2p}{1} - \dfrac{5p}{1}$

   D. $7p$

   E. $-3p$

2. Simplify the following expression completely: $3x - 8 + 4(2x + 1)$

   A. $3x - 8 + 4(2x + 1)$
   B. $11x - 4$
   C. $7x - 7$
   D. 0
   E. $3x - 8 + 8x + 4$

3. Which of the following sets of terms contains all like terms?
   A. $8, 2x, 3x^2, -x$
   B. $2x, 3x^2, 5x^3$
   C. $-8x^2, -3x, -4$
   D. $8x^3, 2x^3, -6x^3$
   E. $2x, 4x^3, 2y$

4. Which fraction is already in simplest form?

   A. $\dfrac{7x^2}{-3y}$

   B. $\dfrac{12x}{4x^2}$

   C. $\dfrac{a^3}{4a^7}$

   D. $\dfrac{2j}{4j}$

   E. $\dfrac{9y^3}{6y^4}$

5. What is the sum of $5\dfrac{2}{3} + 4\dfrac{5}{6}$?

6. Simplify $\dfrac{5}{8} - \dfrac{2}{5}$

7. Evaluate the expression, $\dfrac{36}{[4(5-2)+6]} =$

   A. 2
   B. 12
   C. 18
   D. 36
   E. 43

8. Evaluate the expression, $20^2 - 4 \times 2 + 3 =$

   A. 380
   B. 395
   C. 400
   D. 425
   E. 795

9. Which of the following is the <u>least</u>?

   A. 4^{-2}
   B. 4^{-1}
   C. 4^0
   D. 4^1
   E. 4^2

10. In the ice cream cone pictured at the right, the cone obscures half of the bottom scoop. If the radii of the scoops equals 2 cm, what is the total volume of visible ice cream? (Volume of a sphere $= \frac{4}{3}\pi r^3$)

   A. $\dfrac{16}{3}\pi$ cm^3

   B. $\dfrac{32}{3}\pi$ cm^3

   C. 16π cm^3

   D. $\dfrac{64}{3}\pi$ cm^3

   E. 33π cm^3

11. If $x \geq 5$ and $x \neq 8$ and $x < 12$, which of the following are ALL possible values of x?

   A. 4, 5, 7, 9, 10
   B. 5, 6, 8, 9, 10, 11
   C. 5, 6, 8.5, 9, 11, 12
   D. 6, 8, 9, 10, 11
   E. 5, 6, 7, 9, 10, 11

12. Solve for x: $-x + 12 < 15$

   A. $x > -3$ B. $x < 3$ C. $x < 27$ D. $x > 27$ E. None of the above

13. What is the fraction equivalent of 68%?

    A. $\dfrac{1}{3}$

    B. $\dfrac{12}{25}$

    C. $\dfrac{33}{50}$

    D. $\dfrac{17}{25}$

    E. $\dfrac{2}{3}$

14. An item at a store is priced at \$36. With sales tax, the item is \$39. What is the approximate sales tax rate on the item?

    A. 7.7%
    B. 8.3%
    C. 9.1%
    D. 10.0%
    E. 12.3%

15. The following theorems can be used to prove that two triangles are congruent:

    A. AAA, SSS
    B. SSS, ASA
    C. AAA, ASA
    D. AAA, SAS
    E. All of the above

16. Plot the following points on a coordinate plane shown in Figure 23.1:

    a. $A(-4, 3)$ c. $C(1, -3)$ e. $E(2, 3)$ g. $G(-2, -4)$

    b. $B(3, -3)$ d. $D(-4, 1)$ f. $F(-2, -3)$ h. $H(-4, -2)$

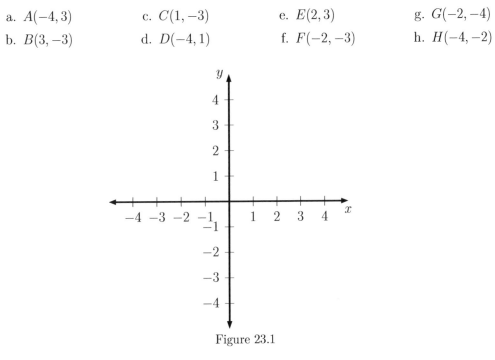

Figure 23.1

17. What is the slope of the line shown in Figure 23.2?

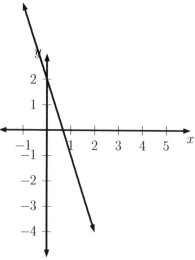

Figure 23.2

A. $-\dfrac{1}{3}$

B. $\dfrac{1}{3}$

C. -3

D. 3

E. None of the above

18. Point A lies in an x, y-coordinate plane at $(3, -2)$. If this point is reflected in the y-axis, what would be the coordinates of the new point?

A. $(2, 3)$
B. $(-2, 3)$
C. $(3, 2)$
D. $(-3, 2)$
E. $(-3, -2)$

19. A hat contains 4 red rubber bands, 3 blue rubber bands, and 3 green rubber bands. What is the probability of picking two red rubber bands, then a green rubber band if the rubber bands are returned to the hat after each time they are picked?

   A. $\dfrac{2}{63}$

   B. $\dfrac{2}{77}$

   C. $\dfrac{3}{46}$

   D. $\dfrac{3}{82}$

   E. $\dfrac{6}{125}$

20. In the following data set, which number is greatest?

$$\{1, 2, 3, 4, 5, 6, 7, 7, 8, 9, 14\}$$

   A. The average of the mode and median
   B. The mean
   C. The mode
   D. The median
   E. The average of the mean and median

21. Write $45,654 \times 10^{-5}$ in scientific notation.

   A. 4.5654×10^{-12}
   B. 4.5654×10^{-1}
   C. 4.5654×10^{12}
   D. 456.54
   E. 456.54×10^{0}

22. Using the function $a = -\frac{(b)}{7} - 3$, what is the value of a when $b = -14$?

23. The up-and-coming rapper Joe-E performs at a local Hip Hop venue. He needs to pay $60 to rent the equipment he needs for the show, but receives 75 cents for each guest that enters the club that night. What is the equation for a function that would represent the amount of money he gained (or lost) that evening? How many people have to show up before he begins to earn money? Assume the variable g represents the number of guests that come to the club and the variable m stands for the money gained or lost.

24. What is the 36th term in the sequence?

$$200, 192, 184, 176, 168, 160...$$

A. 240
B. 280
C. 80
D. -80
E. -40

25. Using the equation $f(x) = -5\sqrt{x} + 12$, what is the value of y when $x = 144$?

26. If Dennis reads a fourth of a book on Tuesday and one fifth of the book on Tuesday, what is the ratio of the part of the book he read to the part he did not read?

A. 2:3
B. 3:4
C. 4:5
D. 9:11
E. 12:7

27. Evaluate the expression, $100 - 10(2 + 3^2) + 4^2 =$

A. 0
B. 6
C. 43
D. 110
E. 123

28. Evaluate the expression, $2 \times 9 - 3(6 - 1) + 1 =$

A. 4
B. 8
C. 24
D. 64
E. 72

29. Which measurement is most useful to a cyclist who is mapping out a new route?

    A. Area
    B. Perimeter
    C. Volume
    D. Speed
    E. Acceleration

Questions 30 and 31 refer to the chart below.

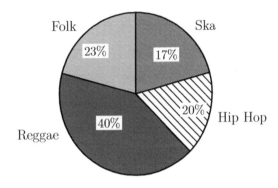

30. The most popular type of music played at the Harmony festival is Reggae. In the figure above, what other two genres can be combined to create a larger percentage of the musical lineup than reggae by itself?

31. If there are 60 hours of music played at the entire conference, how many more hours of Reggae is there than hours of Hip Hop?

32. Luis rides a bike for 7.5 hours. Which of the following represents Luis' bike ride in seconds?

    A. 18,000 sec
    B. 20,000 sec
    C. 27,000 sec
    D. 29,000 sec
    E. 33,000 sec

33. Write 0.00045654×10^5 in scientific notation.

    A. 4.5654×10^1
    B. 4.5654×10^{-4}
    C. 4.5654×10^9
    D. 45.654
    E. 45.654×10^0

34. Samantha's Shala Yoga class does a series of 12 poses in a forty-five minute session. Every one of her classes includes a 10 minute warm-up exercise period at the beginning of the class and a five minute cool down period at the end. Each pose takes approximately the same amount of time. If the studio were to have a session with 30 poses, how long would we expect that session to take? Come up with a function that represents this situation and solve for the time.

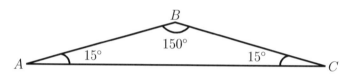

Figure 23.3

35. What is the name of the triangle in Figure 23.3?

    A. Obtuse isosceles
    B. Obtuse equilateral
    C. Right isosceles
    D. Acute isosceles
    E. None of the above

36. In Figure 23.4 below, chord AB measures 5.5 cm. What is one possible measurement of the diameter of Circle O.

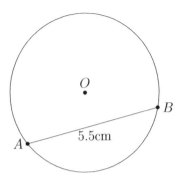

Figure 23.4

A. 4 cm
B. 4.5 cm
C. 5 cm
D. 5.5 cm
E. 6 cm

37. The pie chart below shows the distribution of causes of crime in the United States in percentage terms. According to the chart, which of the following is true?

A. The majority of crime in the United States is committed because of mental illness
B. More crime is committed by mental illness than by income disparity, stress, and job loss combined.
C. The smallest cause of crime is stress
D. Mental illness and job loss combined cause most of the crime in the United States
E. None of the above

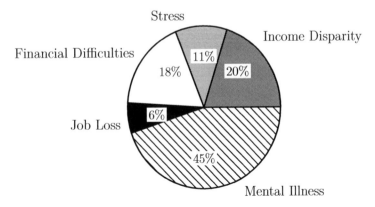

Questions 38-39 pertain to the graph below.

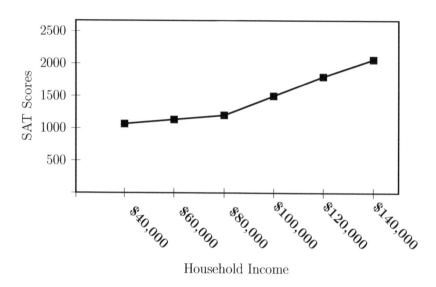

38. Which one of the following conclusions is valid based on the data shown in the graph below:

    A. SAT scores are independent of Household income
    B. Household income depends on SAT scores
    C. SAT scores depend on Household income
    D. The higher the household income, the lower the SAT scores
    E. The data in this graph is inaccurate as SAT scores have no relationship with household income.

39. According to the graph, what is the average SAT score of test takers?

    A. 1100
    B. 1300
    C. 1500
    D. 1800
    E. Cannot be determined from the information given

40. The graph below shows box office sales for the opening night of several movies during a summer.

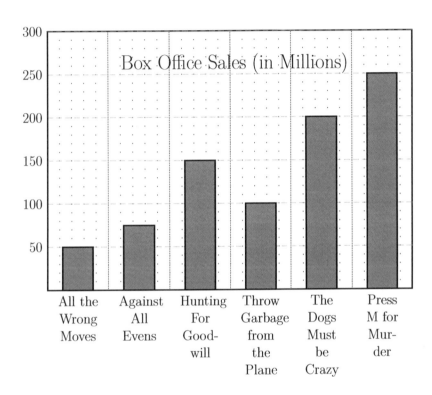

Which of the following is true:

A. More people liked "Press 'M' for Murder" than the other movies shown on the graph

B. Ticket sales of "All the Wrong Moves" was disappointing

C. "The Dogs Must be Crazy" a story about a dyslexic Bushman, sold more tickets than the average of "Against All Evens" and "Throw Garbage from the Plane"

D. "All the Wrong Moves" was the least successful movie of the weekend

E. The average box office sales for "Against All Evens" and "All the Wrong Moves" combined was greater than "The Dogs Must be Crazy"

Solutions to Final Exam

1. **E.** The first fraction simplifies to $2p$ and the second fraction to $5p$. This leaves $2p - 5p = -3p$. Answer choice C is mathematically equivalent but not simplified completely.

2. **B.** First apply the distributive property to get rid of the parentheses, which will yield $3x - 8 + 8x + 4$. This can be simplified by combining like terms to $11x - 4$.

3. **D.** Only in D are all the variables and exponents the same (all contain x, and all are raised to the 3rd power).

4. **A.** In A, nothing in the denominator is a factor of anything in the numerator: -3 does not divide into 7, and y does not divide into x^2.

5. $10\dfrac{1}{2}$.

$$
\begin{aligned}
5\frac{2}{3} + 4\frac{5}{6} &= \frac{17}{3} + \frac{29}{6} \\
&= \frac{17 \cdot 2}{3 \cdot 2} + \frac{29}{6} \\
&= \frac{34}{6} + \frac{29}{6} \\
&= \frac{63}{6} \\
&= 10\frac{3}{6} \\
&= 10\frac{1}{2}
\end{aligned}
$$

6. $\dfrac{9}{40}$.

$$
\begin{aligned}
\frac{5}{8} - \frac{2}{5} &= \frac{5 \cdot 5}{8 \cdot 5} - \frac{2 \cdot 8}{5 \cdot 8} \\
&= \frac{25}{40} - \frac{16}{40} \\
&= \frac{9}{40}
\end{aligned}
$$

7. **A.**

First, perform all operations inside parentheses in the denominator. $\dfrac{36}{[4(3)+6]} =$

Now, multiply inside the brackets in the denominator. $\dfrac{36}{[12+6]} =$

Next, add inside the brackets in the denominator. $\dfrac{36}{18} =$

Finally, divide 32 by 18. 2

8. **B.** Evaluate the expression, $20^2 - 4 \times 2 + 3 =$

First, simplify all exponents. $400 - 4 \times 2 + 3 =$

Now, perform all multiplication operations. $400 - 8 + 3 =$

Finally, add from left to right accordingly. 395

9. **A.**

A. $4^{-2} = \frac{1}{4^2} = \frac{1}{16}$
B. $4^{-1} = \frac{1}{4}$
C. $4^0 = 1$
D. $4^1 = 4$
E. $4^2 = 16$

10. **C.** One and a half scoops of ice cream are visible. This is the volume that needs to be calculated. For one scoop, the volume is $\frac{4}{3}\pi r^3 = \frac{4}{3}\pi(2cm)^3 = \frac{32}{3}\pi$ cm^3. Multiply this volume by 1.5 for the volume of one and a half scoops: $\frac{32}{3}\pi \times 1.5 = \frac{32}{2}\pi = 16\pi$

11. **E.** In this problem, x must be greater than or equal to 5 and less than 12, and additionally cannot be 8. Thus x could be 5, or any number between 5 and 12, but can be neither 8 nor 12.

12. **A.** Subtract 12 from both sides to get $-x < 3$; then multiply (or divide) both sides by -1, meaning the comparison symbol must be flipped, to get $x > -3$.

13. **D.** Percent means "out of one-hundred." So to convert 68% to a fraction, simply reduce from 68 out of one-hundred:

$$\frac{68}{100} = \frac{34}{50} = \frac{17}{25}$$

14. **B.** This problem is like a percent increase problem. The final price of the item after sales tax is $39, the original price is $36. The sales tax is the difference, $3. The percent change, which is equivalent to the sales tax rate, is $3 divided by the original price of $36:

$$\frac{3}{36} = \frac{1}{12} = 8.3\%$$

15. **B.** AAA cannot be used to prove that two triangles are equal as in the case in Figure 23.5 (below):

Figure 23.5

16.

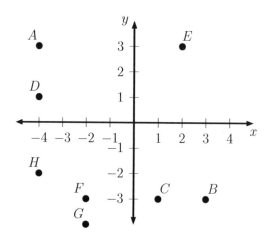

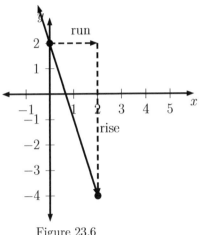

Figure 23.6

17. **C.** Choose two points that are on the line. Two points are $(0, 2)$ and $(2, -4)$. Since the line is moving downward from left to right, the slope is negative. We see that we move 2 units right from $(0, 2)$ to $(2, -4)$ and 6 units down for the y coordinate, therefore, the slope m is -3. This is calculated as $\frac{-6}{2} = -3$. See Figure 23.6.

18. **E.** When reflecting over the y-axis the x-coordinate changes to the opposite sign, while the y-coordinate stays the same. Therefore, both coordinates are negative and we would get $(-3, -2)$.

19. **E.** There are ten rubber bands in all. The probability of picking a red rubber band is $\frac{4}{10}$. If the red rubber band is placed back in the hat, then there are still 10 rubber bands, and the probability of picking a red rubber band is again $\frac{4}{10}$. After the red rubber band is returned to the hat, the probability of picking a green rubber band is $\frac{3}{10}$. Together, the probability of the three events occurring is: $\frac{4}{10} \times \frac{4}{10} \times \frac{3}{10} = \frac{48}{1000} = \frac{6}{125}$

20. **C.** The mean is $\frac{1+2+3+4+5+6+7+7+8+9+14}{11} = \frac{66}{11} = 6$. The mode is 7 and the median is 6. Let's take a look at each answer choice and compare them. From choice A, the average of the mode and median is $\frac{7+6}{2} = 6.5$. From choice E, the average of the mean and median is $\frac{6+6}{2} = 6$. Of the five answer choices, the mode, 7, is the greatest number.

317

21. **B.** Change $45,654$ into scientific notation by moving the decimal 4 places to the left to get 4.5654×10^4.
Multiply $4.5654 \times 10^4 \times 10^{-5}$ to get 4.5654×10^{-1}.

22. We have been given the value for b, therefore by substitution and simplifying, we get

$$
\begin{aligned}
a &= -\frac{(-14)}{7} - 3 \\
&= -(-2) - 3 \\
&= 2 - 3 \\
&= -1.
\end{aligned}
$$

23. **80.** Regardless of whether or not people show up, Joe-E is out $60 to rent the equipment. So if no one shows up, he will have just lost $60. This means that when g = 0, m = -60. The positive term is going to relate the number of people who show up (g) to the money he gets from each person (75 cents). Thus, the function will be m = -60 + .75g. We can figure out the number of people needed to break even by setting m equal to 0 and solving for g. This produces an answer of g = 80.

24. **D.** The pattern here is fairly clear; it begins at 200 and decreases by 8 for each term. The function would simply be $x = 200 - 8(n - 1)$, where x is the given value and n is the term number. Plugging $n = 36$ into the equation produces

$$
\begin{aligned}
x &= 200 - 8(35) \\
x &= 200 - 280 \\
x &= -80
\end{aligned}
$$

25. **-48.** $y = -5\sqrt{144} + 12 = -5(12) + 12 = -60 + 12 = -48.$

26. **D.** To determine how much of the book Dennis has read, we add $\frac{1}{4} + \frac{1}{5} = \frac{9}{20}$. This means that we still have $\frac{11}{20}$ to go. Therefore, the ratio of the part of the book he read (9) to the part he did not read (11) is $9 : 11$.

27. **B.**

First, simplify the exponents inside the parentheses.	$100 - 10(2 + 9) + 4^2 =$
Now, simplify the exponents outside of the parentheses.	$100 - 10(2 + 9) + 16 =$
Next, add the numbers inside of the parentheses.	$100 - 10(11) + 16 =$
Then, multiply.	$100 - 110 + 16 =$
Finally, add from left to right.	6

28. **A.** First, subtract the numbers inside of the parentheses, $2 \times 9 - 3(5) + 1$. Now, multiply from left to right accordingly, $18 - 15 + 1$. Finally, add and subtract from left to right accordingly, to arrive at 4.

29. **B.** Cyclists need to know the total distance of their routes when they are planning. Perimeter is the measurement most closely related to distance.

30. **Folk and Hip Hop.** 23% (Folk) and 20% (Hip Hop) add up to 43% which is greater than the 40% of Reggae.

31. **12 hours.** If there are 60 hours total, then 20% = 12 hours and 40% = 24 hours.

32. **C.** This problem requires a knowledge of the Standard System of Measurement. To solve this problem you must convert between hours, minutes, and seconds. The following represents this calculation:

$$7.5 \text{ hrs} \times \frac{60 \text{ mins}}{1 \text{hr}} \times \frac{60 \text{ secs}}{1 \text{ min}} = 27,000 \text{ secs}$$

33. **A.** Rewrite 0.00045654×10^5 in decimal form, which is 45.654. In scientific notation, that's equal to 4.5654×10^1.

34. **90 minutes.** The problem tells us that each session includes 15 minutes without any set poses, so we subtract 15 from 45 to get the time spent on poses. We can find the average time per pose through division. Dividing 30 by 12 gives 2.5 minutes per pose. So the appropriate function would be:

$T = 15 + 2.5p$, where T is the total time and p is the number of poses.

We can plug $p = 30$ into this equation to get a solution:

$$T = 15 + 2.5(30)$$
$$T = 15 + 75$$
$$T = 90$$

35. **A.** It is obtuse since one of its angles is greater than $90°$ and $\angle B = \angle C$, which means side AB = Side AC.

36. **E.** The diameter, which must pass through the center of a circle, is the longest line segment connecting two points on a circle.

37. **B** 45% of the crime in the United States is caused by mental illness, while income disparity (20%)+ stress(11%)+job loss (6%)=37%. A. is incorrect because "majority" means greater than 50%, while, D. is also wrong because mental illness and job loss combined is 51% which is <u>not</u> considered "most."

38. **C.** The independent variable is always shown on the x-axis, while the dependent variable is always shown on the y-axis. That is, the data shown on the y-axis depend upon the data on the x-axis. Therefore, according to the graph, SAT scores depend on household income, because as household income increase, it can be seen that SAT scores also increase. Choice E is incorrect because the question does not ask for an opinion, rather it is based upon data, assumed to be valid.

39. **E.** We cannot determine from the graph what the average SAT score is because data is only given for six income levels, and not all income levels. If this were a bar graph we could determine the average, but this is a line graph that connect all data points, which are not all shown.

40. **D.** Choice A is wrong because box office sales do not necessarily reflect how the audience liked or disliked the film. Choice B is wrong because no data is given about the expectations of movie sales. C is wrong because the data gives the total box office sales in dollars, not in number of tickets, which could be different because of the varying prices of tickets across the country and times of showings. E, the average of the first two movies was $50 million and $75 million, which is $67.5 million, versus $200 million for the "The Dogs Must be Crazy."

To contact the author, please email info@thetutorpro.com. You can also visit our book's website at www.praxis1mathmyprivatetutor.com.

Made in the USA
Charleston, SC
17 August 2012